Other Books by Patrick Nachtigall...

Passport of Faith: A Christian's Encounter with World Religions
(Warner Press 2006)

Faith in the Future: Christianity's Interface with Globalization
(Warner Press 2008)

Mosaic: A Journey Across the Church of God
(Warner Press 2010)

In God We Trust?: A Challenge to American Evangelicals
(Warner Press 2015)

Facing Islam Without Fear: A Christian's Guide to Engaging the Muslim World
(Warner Press 2015)

Keine Angst Vor Dem Islam: Die Meistgefürchtete Weltreligion besser Vertstehen und Muslimen offen begegnen
(GerthMedien 2016)

About the Author

Patrick is originally from Costa Rica and received his B.A. from Anderson University and his M.A.R. from Yale University where he studied religion and modern Chinese history. He is the author of five books that deal with the nexus between globalization and religion, has lived and worked on six continents and has traveled to more than 80 countries. He has written articles on a wide variety of subjects in various publications and is a popular speaker. He can be found flying his chocolate spaceship on his podcast Get Your World On (www.getyourworldon.com).

Dedication

For my son, Marco. I'm so proud to be your father. Keep searching, asking difficult questions, doubting, believing, using your intellect, opening your heart and serving others. Your journey belongs to you alone. You are free.

This book is also dedicated to the Tigard High School Class of 1988. Go Tigers!

Author's Note

As this book was heading off to print, the Global Covid-19 Pandemic of 2020 broke out around the world. I considered suspending the publication of the book. Since the book deals with issues of life and death, but also includes quite a lot of humor, I wondered if it would be better to postpone the release. In the end, I decided that the pandemic was a reminder that the issues this book deals with are always with us and always will be. I decided to go forward with the publication. I hope that was the right choice. *This book is also dedicated to the medical workers around the world, quite a few that are friends of mine, risking their lives for others.*

The Pandemic of 2020 is a reminder of both the fragility of life and the beauty of life. It is also a moment that demonstrates that our ancestors were right in believing that there is a need to respect the powers beyond our control as well as the unseen.

Autobiography is only to be trusted when it reveals something disgraceful. A man who gives a good account of himself is probably lying, since any life when viewed from the inside is simply a series of defeats.

—George Orwell

Contents

The End: An Introduction

I am dead, and I am laying in my coffin. Friends from every decade of my life are passing by me, wiping away tears, staring at my lifeless body, and touching the mahogany wood of my casket.

I died 36 hours ago, and most people are still in shock. I feel especially bad for my beloved wife Jamie, and my beautiful son Marco. They are heartbroken. Their faces are profiles in pain. It is an anguishing situation. I seemed to be fine a day and a half ago. Healthy, walking around, making jokes, laughing, and spending time with friends and family. And now I am gone; and the suddenness of it all is almost more than my wonderful family can take.

It is the saddest day of their lives.

And amidst this scene of mourning, sobbing, and terrible loss, there is something even more anguishing: I am in the coffin wearing a dark blue suit. Why is this bad? It disturbs me because this is not what I requested in my will and funeral instructions. I specifically requested to be buried in the same outfit that Simon Le Bon wore in the 1982 Duran Duran video for the song "Rio." It's the *Miami Vice* '80s pastel look that I have always preferred. It's a crème-colored suit with a deep blue shirt beneath and a white tie. Somebody must have nixed that request. But who? My wife Jamie? The uptight pastor doing the eulogy who doesn't even really know me? Duran Duran's management? Who did this to me in my final moment on life's stage? I also requested to be buried with a can of Nestle's chocolate Quick and Roxy Music's 1982 album *Avalon*, but these things are not in my coffin with me either. But it gets even worse! I wanted to be buried with my collection of die-cast metal airplanes, and a British Airways 747-400 toy plane attached to my lapel. Once again, that request has been completely ignored at my own funeral. The worst day of my life somehow managed to get worse!

As people walk by, I hear a variety of comments. "He looks so handsome," which, while emphatically true when I was alive, is a ridiculous comment now that I am filled with embalming fluid and look like a poorly made mannequin in a Costa Rican JC Penney window.

My Latin American friends and family recite every religious cliché in the book as they walk by, "*El esta en las manos del senor.*" A few people sob, some sniffle, and a couple are so over-the-top in their crying, it's like I'm a North Korean dictator that has died.

An American walks by my casket and says, "He did so much good in his life." That's a nice comment, but a bit cliché. Well, 'thanks' to that person, whoever they are, for at least focusing on the positive. I did some good things, and I did plenty of bad things too. I have a ton of regrets and things I would have done differently. But I'm glad nobody is going to be talking about those bad things as they walk past the coffin. Things like:

"He stiffed me with the bill at Red Lobster! Twice!"

"He never forgave me after our last disagreement," and

"He murdered three of my family members and was acquitted on all charges!" These are all things people could easily have said about me at my funeral, and they would have all been true, but people were gracious and forgiving enough to not bring up any of those stains on my life during the open sharing time. People tend to let bygones be bygones at a funeral. You could steal a US election with the help of the Russians, dismantle the justice system, make fun of the disabled and sleep with porn stars behind your pregnant wife's back and they will still say something nice about you when you die:

"He was a lovely color of orange."

"Oh, yes, he was."

"The finest orange person ever."

Now someone passes by my coffin who looks like they are thrilled that I am gone. There is a gleam in their eye, and they are having the temporary last laugh. "That jerk died before I did," they say to themselves. "Serves him right! Not such hot stuff now, eh Patrick?" No. I'm not hot stuff. Actually, I'm ice cold and frozen stiff. It's a triumphant moment for them, and to be honest, I'll bet they are not alone in being happy that I'm gone. And to be honest, I'm hoping not to have to see that guy ever again either. If he ends up in Heaven and I end up in Heaven, then that would automatically make it Hell! Life after death is so confusing.

There are no angels, no clouds, and the music sucks. Someone is playing an organ. An organ?? Do they know who I am?? Why are they not playing "One Nation Under a Groove" by Funkadelic, or Chic's "Good Times", or at least Duran Duran's "Save a Prayer," if we need a more somber tone for emotional closure. "Another One Bites the Dust" by Queen would have been totally fine by me, but "Draw me Nearer to Thee" on an organ? Are you frickin' kidding me??

Well, overall, it was a good life. It started religious, then became spiritual, and then turned into something mystical and undefinable. That's a common trajectory for many people as they age. Life gets more mysterious and puzzling as we get older. We are so much more full of certainty when we are young, before life shoves reality and complexity right up that place where the sun don't shine—and I'm not talking about Ireland! I was never going to end up as holy as I wanted to be. I really wanted to be a deeply good, consistent person who made a positive difference in the world and who never had a bad moment. Well, that clearly didn't happen. But I don't think I ended up as bad as I feared. I never led a Germanic nation to humiliation and defeat in a world war, so that's good! I never became a serial killer who kept dead people in my fridge. And I never raped and pillaged my way across Asia and Europe with a Mongol horde. The cost financially, morally and psychologically would have been astronomical, so I opted against it. Yes, my moral behavior really could have been worse. But it sure could have been better.

It was a life of searching, loving, and hurting. Just like every other life. And now we will see what comes next for eternity. Whether there is damnation, forgiveness, angels, demons and whether there is a good buffet with free refills at that final destination; wherever it is I go.

Really Patrick? A Memoir? What the Holy Hell!

Why am I writing my memoirs considering I am still relatively young and haven't accomplished much? Is it an act of vanity? Am I having a mid-life crisis? Is it an attempt to prove to my teenage son that Dad wasn't always a total bore? Of course, it's all the above!

As I begin writing my memoirs today, I can assure you that I plan to leave out my most embarrassing, lame moments, so I guess we can put a check in the vanity column. But I'm also not interested in sharing parts of my life that make me look noble, strong, and superior. That would be boring, dishonest and for me, if not for you, physically nauseating. Other than the fact that I have tremendous legs for someone my age, I do not intend to heap praise upon myself in this book—at least not in this *non*-illustrated memoir of my life. The pop-up book version, on the other hand, will be tremendous.

Why Do We Have to Talk About Religion?

I have always been a person of faith, having been raised in a religious home. But like so many in today's day and age, I am uneasy with religion, religious institutions, and the way dogma and belief have historically been used to manipulate people and hurt them. As I sit down to write this, a number of different news stories are breaking about horrific religious abuse around the world. The Rohingya Muslims are being hunted and killed by Buddhists. Yes, Buddhists kill people and sometimes Muslims are the victims. In India, Hindu nationalists are planning the eradication of Christianity and Christians. Christian nationalism is rising in a number of countries throughout the world in Latin America, Europe and the United States. ISIS continues to capture women and enslave them in the name of Islam. And in the paper today there is a story that particularly catches my attention like no other: It is a story of priests in a Roman Catholic Church in Pennsylvania that not only formed a secret club to sexually molest boys, but they had the boys pose in their underwear as if they were on a cross. They gave the children special crucifixes to wear to help other priests identify which kids were okay to molest. This is repulsive and evil. The Christian symbol of God's love and salvation was literally used to single out which children could be sexually abused by "God's representatives on Earth," so that they could get away with it. I've long understood that religion can indeed be incredibly dangerous and easy to manipulate for very nefarious purposes, but this is truly sick. It's disingenuous for any religious person to not admit that.

These horrific crimes don't just happen in Catholic churches. This year has been filled with scandals in evangelical churches including in the most famous one of all: Willow Creek. Abuses of other human beings and fellow believers happen in Buddhist temples, Hindu ashrams, and Islamic mosques. The late, ferociously anti-theistic critic Christopher Hitchens wrote a book entitled *Religion Poisons Everything*. I was a fan of his writings, but that title is a bit of a generalization. Religion does *not* poison everything.

Nevertheless, people of faith have not always been honest about the amount of damage that religious people, religious groups, and religious institutions can do to human beings. It always surprises people to hear that religious violence is actually much lower today than in any other period in history. And contrary to popular belief, only 7% of wars throughout history were about religion (they are almost always about land and resources).[1] But we still live in a world where religion often provides the fuel for conflict and hatred. These dark incidents are enough to turn one off from religion entirely—and that is increasingly what is happening around the world. Secularism is growing, even in areas like the Middle East and Africa where people have always been highly religious.

Yet religion is not going away anytime soon. By 2050, the world's 20 most populous countries will overwhelmingly be *very* religious societies, even factoring in growing secularization. Scientists and doctors continue to find that not only do religious people live longer and happier lives, but it seems our brain is hardwired to become re-energized, less stressed, and emotionally healthy when we have religious belief and when we practice meditation or prayer. Science, and now neuroscience is increasingly revealing how healthy religious belief and the practice of spiritual disciplines can be good for the brain and body.

There is also the lingering fact that nobody has been able to successfully prove what happens to us when we die; and fear of death and what comes after continues to make religion relevant. Religions tend to give answers regarding the ultimate questions of human existence. For instance, religion addresses the very concrete human fear of death. What happens when we die? Do we disappear forever? Do we

---

[1] The Historian Charles Philips calculated this in his *Encyclopedia of Wars* after examining 1763 wars throughout history.

face eternal torment? Or do we all end up like those three people at the end of *Superman 2*—stuck in some mirror spinning through space for eternity? (Personally, I think it's the latter).

When I was 31 in 2002, I wrote my first book *Passport of Faith* in which I argued that religion was an important part of human society and morality, but that we were entering a time of dangerous political and cultural upheaval in which religion would be the dangerous fuel for many of those cultural and historical grievances.[2] Sadly, that has come to pass in spades. Despite that bleak prediction, I wrote that religion overall was a positive force for good. That first book took the reader across the world to examine the major religions of the world to show how religion mostly helps the world. I stand by that first book, but I also feel the need to examine the danger of religion, and why it is still a part of the world. The complicated truth is that both ideas are true, and it has been said that being a grown-up means being able to hold two competing ideas together at the same time. The world overall and individuals have both benefitted greatly by religion and religious experience, and many in the world have been hurt significantly by religion. This book will explore how and why that happens and what it means for us in the fast-changing 21st century. And I'll reluctantly share some stories of my own spiritual quest, not because I really want to (to be honest), but in the hopes that it might help someone—whether they are religious or not.

While I chose a life of faith, it has not come without doubt, disillusionment, and serious questions about whether it is all

---

[2] It is in *Passport of Faith* that I examine the core beliefs of the world's major religious faiths and contrast them to Christianity. This book does not aim to do that, but rather wants to discuss the role of religion overall. I highly recommend that you buy that book after this one, buy my other books, and offer to take me to Red Lobster.

worth it. I have tremendous compassion and understanding for my atheist and agnostic friends who think poorly of religion. They have seen that religion can be used to manipulate people, divide societies, build greedy self-serving institutions, and create neurotic self-hatred. It's a true fact that the occupation of pastor is in the top 10 careers that narcissists choose (lawyers are number one). Many Theravada Buddhist monks in Asia are in it for the money and have no spirituality whatsoever. Some Hindu nationalists plan acts of terrorism and, despite believing in 30 million gods, can be incredibly intolerant if you choose one not included in that list of 30 million. And ISIS is primarily interested in trafficking sex-slaves and engaging in other black-market crime, instead of spreading its version of "authentic Islam." It would be easy for me to write an uplifting book about how great religion, particularly Christianity, is. Filled with feel good stories that omit or gloss over the dark side. But that would be disingenuous, and it is not where I am at, or where much of the world is at right now. Like those poor victims of abuse in Pennsylvania, we know all too well that religion can go horribly wrong.

So, I want to write a memoir to share my struggle in faith as well as my observations about religion as a bit of a scholar, as a believer, as a Duran Duran fan, and as a failed saint. Unlike my previous books, this one is not meant to be academic, but to reflect on some lessons I've learned as I've studied, practiced, and observed religion. I grew up in the traditional Latin American evangelical church in Central America before attending an African American church in the 'hood of Oakland, California. I worked in the underground, non-western churches in China, and in post-religious societies in Europe. The rapidly changing spiritual atmosphere of the globalized world has been home to me for all my life. As a lifelong traveler and student of religion, I think we are living in a period of history where spirituality and faith will be more important than ever, but in which religious institutions will be more challenged than ever before. Spirituality will flourish, religion will struggle. And maybe it should.

To Believe or Not to Believe: That is the Question

My closest, most trusted friends have always consisted mostly of non-believers and my favorite songs, musicians, books, and films have always been non-religious. Never have I felt particularly "holy" or "good" amidst my spiritual pilgrimage. Quite the contrary, I've spent most of my life either believing I'm going to hell or deserve to go to hell even if I squeak by on a technicality. Faith has always been a struggle for me, and the secular world has always been a place of great joy and freedom. Nevertheless, faith is not going away in my life in the same way that it is not going to go away on Planet Earth. Even if we choose to live a life outside of religion, we will *all* have to engage with faith, religion, and spirituality one way or another. You may be a self-proclaimed atheist, but your inner caveman with its lizard brain has a soft spot for spirituality, even if you won't admit to it. It probably also has a soft spot for *The Jerry Springer Show*. We're weird creatures.

I have chosen a life of faith with all the complexities, contradictions, and downsides that this choice entails, but it has also offered freedom, hope, purpose, and even intellectual stimulation. My purpose is not to write a book to glorify my life. If anything, I hope you are just amused and laugh occasionally, because laughing, like meditating, is good for your body, mind and soul. That alone will make this worth it to you. I'm your friend, not your priest.

And for those Christians looking for a book that makes Christianity look easy, fun, and filled with happy endings with the intention of converting people, this is definitely not the book you want to read. There are already plenty of those kind of books on the bookshelves. This is a warts-and-all look at the role world religions, especially Christianity, play in the world. And the question will hover throughout this book: *Do we seriously need religion?* My ambivalent experience with religion is a microcosm of what the world is going through right now in this age of fast technological, scientific, ecological, and social change. We all feel tired of the social divisions, global conflict, and violence that politics and religion make around the world. As we sit at the dinner table with our families, stressed out, having panic attacks, and glued to our phones, we all have a growing sense that there's something missing in our life. That there is something poisonous about this superficially connected world that is so connected to man-made things as well as manipulated, algorithm-based cyber-places. Religious violence and bigotry are obnoxious, but so is the feeling that we are losing connection with nature, with our planet's health, with our own peace of mind, and with our neighbors. We've learned that the multi-national companies that provide our digital life are just as prone to trying to manipulate us as any religion or cult. Who is doing better at manipulating our minds globally? Religion or Facebook? Religion is in crisis, but so is our emotional and psychological well-being. We all feel it. It's the same feeling you get after eating six Dunkin' Donuts at one time: something inside of you feels poisoned and unhealthy no matter how great it looked initially.

Seriously! Let's not make this book (that is destined to be a classic and will be treasured for generations to come) solely about me! Let's make this book about you! About how religion is annoying you, inspiring you, uplifting you, hurting you, and breaking you. My hope is that it will cause YOU to reflect on your atheism, your agnosticism, your disillusionment with religion, your Christianity, your Buddhism, your anything-ism. I'm not trying to convert you. That's not my job. If there's a God up there that created the universe, he or she is surely more capable of reaching you than I can in a few pages. While it's true that I am incredibly muscular and have a full head of hair, I'm not a messiah nor do I have a messianic complex. I'm just a little pilgrim, a simple wayfarer, and a Hall of Fame quarterback who has led the Seattle Seahawks to six Super Bowl championships over the past seven seasons. Trust me.

Let's Go Deep

What specifically do I want to examine about faith and religion in this memoir? I believe there are a number of questions we need to ask at this point in the 21st century: why we have it, why we lose it, where do we use it, and does it matter? I want us to explore these specific fundamental questions: *Why do human beings tend to believe in the supernatural? How does religion give us an identity and a purpose? Why do religions become poisonous so often? How do religions deal with suffering and evil? Why do religions seem to be obsessed with keeping people out? And how do they build such incredibly tight communities? Why do religions often inspire us to do good works? Can religion and the intellectual life co-exist? Why has religion lasted for millions of years and will it survive the 21st century? Would it be better if religion went the way of the Dodo bird, or bell-bottoms, or Wesley Snipes' movie career?*

On a broader level, I want to introduce the idea that human spirituality and religion is something we should at least understand and respect, even if we don't fully embrace it. This book is for the curious, and for any religious or non-religious person who has ever been frustrated, hurt, and disgusted by religion. I also want readers who are confident in their faith to respect people's struggles, doubt, and disillusionment. Finally, I want to teach you a bit about the history of religion, where religion and spirituality stand globally, and why our lizard brains find the need to always flirt with supernatural belief. If, as I say, we are in a religiously charged time, we will need to learn how to dialogue and understand each other better. If we are not able to achieve this together, dear reader, then I hope this book sells a lot of copies so I can pay off my student loans in time to pay off my son's forthcoming student loans sometime before the year 2075. If that's all this is, then it's a win for me.

There's no way my path will be your path—nor should it be. I'm just sharing select parts of my limited personal faith journey to get you to reflect on yours. You may end up in the exact same place as where you started: as an atheistic, child-eating, murderer who stomps on flowers and cripples puppies for fun. There's nothing I can do about that. You be you! So, take a leap of faith, and keep reading. I don't have all the answers, but I am starting to believe that it's possible to have a life of faith *and* doubt, with no religion required.

1

A Pint of Guinness with God: Why We Believe in the Supernatural

Before we go back in time to the beginning of my modest, but chocolate-filled life, we start in 1995. Confused about what to do with myself after my lifelong plan to be a missionary had fallen apart, I began to feel abandoned by God. So, I issued him a challenge. What resulted would be the spiritual hinge upon which the rest of my life would swing. This is that story.

Is there really a God? And if there is a God, are we able to interact personally and intimately with this being? And if we can interact with this being, can he tell us which horse to bet on at the Santa Anita racetrack and which line is the fastest at the supermarket check-out counter? The last two are too miraculous to believe. But I do believe I actually met God once.

It happened at one of the lowest periods of my life. Lower periods that would suck even more awaited me in the future, but I did not know that then. I thought this was bad at the time, and I definitely was lost and off-track.

I was a young 24-year-old person with high hopes, but nothing post-high school had gone according to plan. My first run at college was a miserable experience. My mother, who was also my best friend and hero, died of cancer. And a second run at college had also not been a very happy experience. I loved learning, but I was so gloomy that I made Kurt Cobain look like Richard Simmons on cocaine.

But it was the loss of my dream job that finally derailed me. It was a job I had been wanting for 14 years and I felt gutted and lost. I grew up in a religious family and with a specific religious goal in mind. But as a young person, I didn't necessarily take my own personal spiritual development that seriously. As I got older, it was a process of asking hard questions, processing what a life of faith means, and honestly examining other religions and worldviews beyond my own. I start at this midway point in my life because of a supernatural encounter.

Why Do We Believe in the Supernatural?

Ironically,[3] thanks to the latest discoveries in science, psychology, anthropology and biology, we have learned that human beings are born hardwired to believe in the supernatural. It is not something that we pick up from our parents or society, as we previously thought. It is meant to be there. Surprisingly, it is discarding the supernatural in favor of a strict materialist scientific worldview that is the leap of faith away from human evolution. We humans are not only born to believe in a world beyond the one we see, but our brains look for patterns that explain both the material and the non-material world. If it doesn't take the form of religion, it takes the form of superstition, astrology, a belief in ghosts, a belief that we are still in touch with dead loved ones (or that "we feel their presence" and "they are still with us"), that we have a special intuition we can't explain, that something in

---

[3] I hate to say "ironically," because there is no need for faith and science to be so divided and antagonistic toward each other. A true believer and a true scientist should not be threatened by each other.

our life was not a coincidence, that there's an alternative universe, or alien life forms, etc.

If you look closely, you can see it. Athletes develop superstitious rituals. And every human in every culture and in every tribe is also born with a sense that bad actions will ultimately result in punishment and that all of our actions are being monitored somehow by someone or some force. Religions like Buddhism, Taoism and Hinduism that do not highlight an all-knowing, personal God chalk it up to fate, destiny, *karma* or being bound to the laws of harmony. Even atheists and secular scientists feel a strong sense of right and wrong, of consequence, and of someone or some natural law watching them and keeping score of our actions. And we all take tremendous, illogical leaps of faith and have a propensity for self-delusion. This is all true whether you are religious or not.

One approach by some scientists and atheists to this all-pervasive spiritual sense is to suggest that it is a hold-over from our more primitive hunter-gatherer days. That as we continue to evolve, our supernatural belief will become a useless appendage or drop off like our fuzzy tails. But a growing body of psychology and evolutionary science is realizing that the belief in the supernatural, in religion and in gods actually has a ton of evolutionary benefits that keep humans and their societies healthy and in balance. For instance, my caveman ancestor Ug Nachtigall (God rest his soul), could use that belief in the supernatural to form healthy dietary habits proscribed by his religion, get along with his larger community as they established moral norms, keep his selfishness and survival-instincts in check, and mobilize for large civilization-building activities. Basic survival and great advances in civilization and technology required being able to not only live in tight community, but to have a shared understanding of ultimate reality.[4]

Ug Nachtigall lived in dangerous times that were pre-scientific. But anyone who has watched a loved-one undergo chemotherapy and radiation treatments for cancer knows that our own treatments and knowledge seems pretty limited, even now. We don't have effective technologies to clean up oil spills and we just discovered a Black Hole that scientists say, "should not exist." We don't have good answers or solutions for many 21st century diseases and problems; and in fact, we can now see that our dear friend technology has actually produced new, exciting products that are tearing our societies and families apart in ways we never thought possible. Consequently, we see waves of people in our modern world reverting to yoga, holistic medicine, meditation, unplugging from technology, creating smaller ecological footprints, turning to veganism or paleo diets as they realize our modern societies are not so all-knowing as we thought; and that people in the old days were not as ignorant as we thought.

Religions have provided helpful beliefs and practices about how to grow food, how to respect nature, how to procreate and produce a family-line, how to bury people, how to avoid food poisoning, and how to treat your neighbor and community with respect, amongst many other things. Furthermore, religious communities tend to lead to greater productivity, community-spirit, and selflessness than secular communities of similar size and structure: A classic

---

[4] The more one looks at history, anthropology, and now ecology, the more one discovers that it is our modern technologically driven 21st century society that has brought a lot of imbalance to nature, to our farming practices, to our food-gathering, as well as many other areas. Precisely because we are so disconnected from nature, our technological wisdom can create global disasters that Ug Nachtigall never would have dreamed of.

case being the religious Jewish Kibbutz movement in Israel which survived and produces at far greater levels than the near extinct secular Jewish Kibbutz. That religious element provided a check on selfishness and greater communal bonding.

So, the first thing to realize about religion and belief in the supernatural is that we are born with it, and it is not necessarily a primitive human construct that can be easily discarded. Throughout human history, we were highly dependent on religion, and even today, we are born hard-wired to believe in the supernatural.

A Religious Childhood of Airplanes and Daydreaming

Ever since I was eight years old, I had this really extravagant, outrageous dream of being a missionary to Asia. Like Marco Polo, my hero (who may or may not have actually lived - historians are not sure), I wanted to travel the world, live in Asia, and feed lepers, or at least grow rice for starving people. I didn't know how to grow rice. Heck! I didn't even eat rice, but I had this desire to help in a big way.

Maybe I would help poor kids with bad haircuts go to school or collect abandoned orphans from dusty third world train stations or build a church out of straw and paper-mâché. I had no idea what a "missionary" did. I just knew that I wanted to tell people far away that there was a God who cared about them and who could make all of your life better, or at least help you find a job with a good dental plan. I was clueless. I just wanted to be a positive force for good in the world like my parents, like Mother Teresa, Indiana Jones, and all the famous rock stars who sang "We Are the World." I could help lost children, feed the starving, or move them out of their humble little mud huts into much bigger, well-built mud huts with a lovely sun deck made of manure and a satellite dish. It was all a mystery. There was no theology or career plan. Just this impulse to travel a lot and help people less fortunate than me.

It sounds pretty noble and sweet. Don't get carried away. I'm sure that I would have also punched you in the mouth if you tried to steal from my bag of M&M's or play with my Millennium Falcon. There are no saints among us. We are all a bag of mixed motives: some genuinely kind and gracious, others totally self-serving. I'm no different.

I also had another more self-serving goal. One that was even older than my desire to be a missionary—whatever that was. I wanted to ride on a lot of airplanes. My earliest childhood memory is from when I was two years old. I was playing with a battery-powered 747 toy on the floor of a shopping center. The plane would spin around, make noises and light up. I was already fanatical about airplanes and rode on my first one also at the age of two. Even my tricycle when I was three was in the shape of an airplane. It had a tail with a logo that said "Boeing 727" on it; and unlike other tricycles in the neighborhood, mine had wings that stuck out. The chicks dug it. I also collected little metal die-cast airplanes beginning at the age of four, and the first audio recording of me that my family has is just after I turned three when I demonstrated into the recorder for my grandparents, the sound that an airplane jet makes. I also drew airplanes constantly as a small child and invented my own airlines creatively named "Patrick Airlines." It eventually merged and code-shared with my other imaginary airline and became "Aviansa Airways" (a blatant rip-off of the Colombian airline Avianca). Fortunately, I stopped drawing pictures of the logo of my imaginary airline when I was 24 years old. True.

Then I had an even crazier, more audacious dream. I wanted to travel to all of the continents of the world. But I didn't just want to visit them once. I wanted to visit these places multiple times, over and over again. I wanted to visit these places as much as people in the suburbs visit downtown. I wanted to make so many visits that I would know my way around each place at the level of a local. I wanted to know Tokyo, Paris, London, Bangkok, Rome, Singapore, and Sydney like the back of my hand. I wanted them to practically be second homes to me. That is a tall order—yet incredibly, it happened! These places and many more do feel like home to me and I've been to them and to a large number of other countries and cities, many, many times over.

Those are pretty big goals for a very small kid who couldn't tie his own shoes. But I was always prone toward obsession, whether it was in the areas of travel, or following my favorite rock bands, or devouring books—I always wanted to know and experience as much as I could, like "The Wanderer" on the last track of U2's *Zooropa* album.

Certain that my destiny was to live a life of adventure in Asia, I began to educate myself on everything there was to know about China and Japan, in particular. I loved reading the *World Encyclopedia* as a kid, and I became a news junky at age eight tuning in faithfully to see Jane Pauley and Bryant Gumbel on the *Today Show*. As a weird little kid, for fun, I memorized the layout of cities and provinces in East Asia. I drew maps and skylines of cities like Tokyo and Sydney. I studied the air routes, collected books of airline schedules from around the world, and I would even call the Asian airlines and Qantas on the phone and make reservations for flights to Taipei, Tokyo, and "Peking" (you could do this in the 1970s without buying a ticket or being penalized). I would call up the airline and successfully reserve a ticket on a specific flight. Either they thought the high voice on the other end was a woman, or they went along with the little kid, because I was routinely able to book flights to Tokyo, Rio de Janeiro, and Sydney without any consequences. The reservations automatically expired in 24 hours if you didn't purchase the ticket.

Everything in my life was geared toward those goals from a young age: to be a missionary, to travel the world, and to get to know these exotic places in-depth. As a kid, waiting felt like an eternity.

But finally, after I graduated from college, I applied for my dream job: missionary to Asia with our denomination, the Church of God (Anderson, Indiana). I had been anticipating this "forever" and was excited that it would now be happening since college was finished.

Shortly after graduation, I was back in my home of Portland, Oregon and received a letter from the mission agency telling me I was on my way to Japan. Tokyo, no less!! My father and sister were ecstatic! At that point, I had been obsessively plotting for this moment for 14 years! We jumped around the house in celebration.

But exactly 24 hours later, I received a letter saying the original letter had been a mistake. The job should never have been offered and was meant for someone far older and more experienced than me. I was devastated. My dream job got ripped away, and I only got to enjoy my long-awaited prize for 24 hours. My sister and father were heart-broken and angry too. As far as I was concerned this derailment might be permanent. My problem-solving skills and perspective in my early 20s were not my strong suit. This was a catastrophe, I decided. And it was one of *many* moments in my life, where I would be disappointed, frustrated, and angry at the incompetence of a religious organization.

Instead of climbing Mt. Fuji and feeding rice to starving businessmen in Tokyo's financial district, I took up a number of "McJobs"—as Douglas Copeland called them: dead-end jobs that pay poorly and help you survive until you can actually get a career of some kind. I delivered pizza and was forced to put an enormous Domino's sign on top of my car— something that didn't tend to impress girls as much as my airplane tricycle. I worked at a clothing store, at a bank, as a telemarketer for secured credit cards, and at a health club as a janitor, which included cleaning the bathrooms. My dream job was gone, and as I took a wide variety of jobs, I realized that I sucked at all of them. My lack of talent in every job was truly something to behold. At one point, I was repackaging boxes on an assembly-line in Portland and was so bad at it, the Frenchman working next to me was convinced I was mentally disabled.

I hit a new low in my young life when I found myself in a large warehouse in Beaverton, Oregon stacking bags of environmentally friendly kitty litter. As I loaded "Cedar Kitty" onto a forklift, I marveled at how far I had fallen. I was supposed to be riding a boat down the Mekong Delta, climbing the Great Wall of China, dating a Geisha, or buying sushi from a Japanese robot. Instead, I was slaving away in a warehouse to make sure wealthy people's cats could relieve themselves in an environmentally friendly way. (This was the Pacific Northwest, after all. Even felines had to do their part to save the environment.) Stuck in Portland, at this rate I felt I would be lucky to get past Troutdale, let alone to China!

I began to consider other options like the Marines and after an embarrassing display of weak upper-body strength while doing pushups, I decided not to relive my humiliating 7th grade P.E. experiences at Fowler Jr. High in a military uniform while being shot at in the Middle East.

My mother had died of cancer during my college years and my father had moved back to Costa Rica and my sister had moved to Uruguay in South America. I was alone with my family all living far away and with no financial assistance in case of emergencies. While at my latest job in car insurance, I decided maybe I would need to go to graduate school to get qualified enough to live overseas. I decided to save money to go visit the history departments of Trinity College in Dublin, University of Oxford, and the University of Birmingham in England. I would get some time off of work, fly to London, meet up with some professors at each school and see if I could find a new way of moving toward my goal.

A Date with God in Ireland

There were no lepers in my future, so I went to the land of leprechauns: Ireland.

I had never been good at praying, but of course, that is not something a religious person admits—especially if you want to get hired as a missionary. It's a common problem, however, particularly for those with wandering minds like mine. Prayer always felt a bit self-serving, forced, and formulaic to me. We didn't pray often in my family and I also found it hard to concentrate. I usually have songs in my head 24 hours a day. It's like I have a radio on in my head every single second of my life. If I'm in a church, I probably have Led Zeppelin's "Over the Hills and Far Away", in my head, not "Amazing Grace." If there's a song about faith in my head, it's probably by George Michael. If it's an extremely reverent moment in church, I probably have The Cure's "Fascination Street" playing in my brain. It might even be LL Cool J's "Doin' it," which is a real problem. The point is, church music doesn't work for me unless it's Bach.

I've since found out that certain personality types struggle with prayer more than others. There are also personality types that struggle with reading the Bible—and reading period! And, of course, many personality types struggle with the extroversion required to get super emotional in church or share openly about their inner lives (like all of Sweden). A lot of churches demand a very high level of extroversion which doesn't fit everyone. I attended a church once that demanded everyone go out on the street and preach with their Bible in their hands. That sucked! It's a confrontational in-your-face style that really impacts large segments of American Christianity. It was pioneered by the 19th century frontier revivalist Charles Finney (1792-1875). It's an approach I have always found distasteful (more about why that is in Chapter 5).

Those of us raised in the evangelical church often feel like we are supposed to be absolute all-stars at every spiritual discipline there is, and if we are not, it's pretty much a source of secret shame. At the age of 24, I didn't feel very spiritually mature or strong, but I did want to make a big difference in the world: both to genuinely help people and to, more selfishly, make a name for myself.

Coming home from a hard day's work covered in kitty litter has a way of making you question your life. I'm sure you've been there. It was a season that led me to desperation and actual, sincere, prayer. I was clearly at a crossroads in my life. I took yet another job and saved money. This trip to the U.K. and Ireland was one that I hoped would provide a new clear path.

As I planned my trip, I thought about how I would like to fit in a stop on the west coast of Ireland, which had always seemed like a mystical place at the end of the Earth. When I was growing up in Oregon, my favorite place in the State was Ecola State Park, a beautiful, woodsy beach 90 minutes from Portland that had a big cliff that dropped off into the ocean. I used to like to walk around there and remembered one special night in 1984 when I was walking along the beach listening to the U2 song "Drowning Man" on my Sony Walkman. As I looked around my favorite beach and listened to this Irish band, I thought to myself, *One day I want to travel to the other side of the world and see the west coast of Ireland—to see the Irish version of Ecola State Park. Big cliffs, strong winds, green fields.*

I had read about the Cliffs of Moher located in County Claire—a 7-mile-long piece of coastline on Ireland's west side with cliffs that dropped straight down 800 feet into the Atlantic Ocean. The pictures were stunning. One of the most western points in Europe, the Cliffs of Moher looked like the very edge of the Earth itself. It felt like something I should strive for: a symbolic accomplishment to show myself that I would see every corner of the Earth.

As I thought about my upcoming trip to England and Ireland, I began to pray on my knees a strange prayer. I prayed: *God, I have no idea what I am doing with my life. My plans have fallen apart. I'm not sure what I should be doing. What I wanted so badly is not happening. I feel alone and you are silent. Now, I'm going to the other side of the world. In fact, I am going to the very edge of the world, about as far away as I can get from this spot. I'm going to the Cliffs of Moher and I want you to meet me there. Show me that you care. Show me that you are real and with me. Meet me at the Cliffs of Moher!*

What a strange prayer. I know I am a total weirdo, but even for me, this was bizarre. I just felt this inner impulse to challenge God, to test him, to see if he is really a God that meets people or if he is an imaginary being; a belief passed on to me by my parents, like Santa and the importance of flossing.

I had been told by a friend that anyone who goes to Ireland has to visit an Irish pub and order a pint of Guinness. I didn't really know anything about Guinness, but I read that there was a pub along the River Liffey that the rock band U2 liked to frequent. That pub was called Dockers and was next to Windmill Lane Studios where U2 had recorded three of my all-time favorite albums: *War*, *The Unforgettable Fire*, and *The Joshua Tree*. Could God be like U2, a deity that would actually hang out and share a pint with a fan boy? I challenged God to meet me, to see if he was truly going to show up.

I set off on my trip and flew from San Francisco to London. As soon as the plane landed and the sun came up, I headed into downtown London (my favorite city in the world) directly to the Irish tourism office. Speaking to a nice Irish lass, I pulled out my maps and plans for this special trip to Ireland. I had various meetings with professors scheduled in Oxford, Birmingham, and Dublin. Time was as tight as my budget, but I had planned meticulously and the girl at the desk was double-checking all my plans.

"Yes, that's right!" she said as she looked at all of my papers laid out. "You take the ferry from Holyhead, Wales to Dun Laoghaire, Ireland. Then you catch a train to Galway on the west coast. Then you take the bus to Lisdoonvarna and connect to another bus that will take you to the Cliffs of Moher." I double-checked addresses, prices, and hours of departure. It all looked good. Satisfied that I had eradicated the potential for any mistakes on this important appointment to meet God, I visited my favorite places in London before setting off to the University of Oxford.

A couple days later, I crossed the Irish Sea, arrived in Dublin, met my college appointment at Trinity College and stopped by the Irish tourism office; this time the one located in the Irish Capital. I spoke to a lad there, presented him with my plans, and explained to him that I was on a tight schedule.

"That's right," the young man at the office confirmed. "You catch a train to Galway on the west coast. Then you take the bus to Lisdoonvarna and connect to another bus that will take you to the Cliffs of Moher." I triple-checked addresses, prices, and hours of departure. Once again, it all looked good. Time was tight. My plans had to be perfect.

"Make sure to get on the 8 AM train if you want to get all of those things done," I was told. Good advice. There was no way I was going to miss my appointment with the Almighty who created the Heavens and the Earth in six days, or 4.5 billion years, or as fast as it takes to make a tuna sandwich. I made sure I was up by 6:30 AM.

I still had no idea what meeting God at the Cliffs of Moher would mean. As I headed off to the train station, I wondered what would happen when I actually arrived at the Cliffs of Moher, put on my headphones and listened to that U2 song "Drowning Man." Perhaps, there would be a very big lightning strike—God announcing to me that He is there in all of his power. I would tremble and fall on my face, doing my best Moses impression. A bush would burn, an earthquake would shake the earth, Morgan Freeman would show up. Was that going to be it?

Or perhaps I would get to the Cliffs of Moher, put on my headphones, and an old man with a cane, a white robe, and a long, flowing beard would walk up to me and start saying a bunch of Yoda-like things: "Met you I have, young Patrick. Now sod off, you will!"

Or perhaps, as I got to the 800-foot cliffs, I would fall over the side, accidentally kill myself, and meet God that way: kind of like those pathetic souls who die while trying to take a selfie for their Instagram account. I seriously had no idea what on Earth I was doing; I just felt sure that God would somehow provide a dramatic moment and make his presence known. He had better show up, or he would have to answer to me! I'm a 6-foot, 6-inch, 268 pound African American with hands that are registered lethal weapons.[5] I'm not to be trifled with.

I arrived at the train station on time and got some stunning news.

"You missed the train!" the man behind the ticket counter said. "The train left an hour ago, at 7 AM"

"What? But I was told it left at 8 AM!"

"No. You got some bad information. That train runs at 7 AM now," he told me.

"So, when's the next train to Galway?"

"It leaves at 2 PM!"

"What!!" I screeched. I told him, "I needed to get to the Cliffs of Moher today!" I gave him all of my information, my plans, my route, and my times. I omitted the fact that I had a lunch-date with God Almighty, lest that seem presumptuous and a sign of serious mental illness. I was too young to rent a car, and probably would have killed myself driving on the wrong side of the road. I needed to arrive in Galway early, so I could get all the transfers and make it by sundown. I was in a hurry!

As the man behind the train ticket counter looked at my plans, he had worse news. "Actually, these plans won't work. It's March. There are no buses from Galway to Lisdoonvarna and there's no bus from there to the Cliffs of Moher."

I was stunned. How could the guidebooks have all been wrong? I was known for my travel planning. This was my *thang*! And what about the Irish tourism office in London and the one in Dublin?? They had assured me all of this looked right! How could I have gotten this far only to have it all fall apart now? I had to be back the following evening to make sure I caught my boat back to England and make my appointment in Birmingham.

---

[5] I am not a 6-foot, 6-inch, 268 pound African American, for the record. The hands part is true.

I was crestfallen. What was the point of going? I'd basically see Galway and just have to turn around right away on the first train back. This was turning into a disaster. I suddenly felt incredibly stupid for thinking I somehow was going to be meeting God at a special summit meeting on a cliff surrounded by fields of sheep. *What an idiot! The power of a vivid and overly mystical imagination!* I thought to myself. This was magical thinking at its worst. How utterly foolish of me to think that, somehow, I was going to meet God at a particular place and time.

"I guess I'll take the 2 PM train then," I said, disheartened. I had no other plans, so I would just see Galway and come right back.

I spent the next few hours waiting in a café at the train station mostly stewing and feeling frustrated and angry. When the train pulled out of Dublin, I picked a seat in the middle of one of the railway cars. The train was almost entirely empty, and nobody was sitting in my particular coach.

It was a three-hour train ride from the east coast where Dublin is located across Ireland to the west coast where Galway is situated. The train made a couple of stops, but no one came into my car. I was all alone and that was a good thing because I was being a grouchy grouch! I looked out the window and it was a very gray and foggy Irish day. Visibility was low and the country looked bleak—the kind of place where a potato famine might occur and lead to millions of people emigrating to the United States. It was lifeless, gloomy, and depressing.

About half-way through the three-hour journey, the train stopped and picked up passengers. A young man came into the car where I was sitting and sat directly across from me. This annoyed me to no end because there were many other seats to choose from and I was in a horrendous mood. *Why did this guy have to sit directly across from me? God help me if he tries to strike up a conversation!* I thought to myself. *I'll shove a potato so far up his...*

The train rolled on and the fog didn't lift. I continued to stew as I looked out at the fog.

As the journey continued, I could see that this young man sitting across from me was often staring at me. It was deeply annoying, and it made me turn away from him more as I looked out the window. *Please don't talk to me,* I thought to myself. *Unless you want me to ram a box of Lucky Charms up your nose!!*

But then it happened. He spoke!

"So...are you a tourist?" he said in a most stereotypical Irish brogue.

"Uhm, yeah," I said in a monotone, hoping he would catch the hint that I was not interested in talking.

"Where are you from?"

"From the U.S." I said keeping my tone as disengaged as possible. This guy was distracting me from my massive pity party. His happy-go-lucky, leprechaun tone made it worse.

"What a great country! I hope to visit sometime!"

I nodded as if to say, Yes, that's great. Now leave me alone.

"So, do you like Ireland, then?" he asked.

At this point, I decided to let loose. If he wanted to talk, then we would talk.

"Well, yes, I've always wanted to come to Ireland. I've been very excited about this trip. My mother was of Irish ancestry and always wanted to visit, but she never made it. She died of cancer. I had all these plans to go see the Cliffs of Moher and I've been working on them for a long time and even checked and re-checked them and they were all wrong!" Of course, I left out the divine appointment with God that was on my calendar, lest he think I was insane or an American from the deep South. I told him about my time-crunch, my financial crunch, and all the misinformation I had received, and let out a big sigh.

"Really?" he said in a chipper tone. "How interesting! You see, I'm a tour guide!"

I froze. "What????"

"I'm a tour guide, and I live in Galway, and when we get there, I can get my family car and drive you to the Cliffs of Moher!"

I was completely stunned. Suddenly, my dark mood lifted, and I was happy to have this guy in the train with me. I was incredulous, but it seemed to all be true! He was about my age, a young tour guide starting out who lived in Galway. This was incredible!

Thank you, God! You always come through!! I knew you would!!! I thought to myself.

His name was Bartley and he and I talked for the next hour and a half about all sorts of things. We had a lot in common, he was one year younger than me, and he was a genuinely lovely guy. When we got to the train station, he got me some food and drink for free and told me he would be right back. "I'm going to call my family, tell them that I need the car, and then we will go to the Cliffs of Moher!"

How exciting! As I ate, I marveled at how amazing and miraculous this moment was. I was going to see the Cliffs of Moher! I would meet God!

But as I finished my meal, Bartley came back with a long face.

Uh-oh.

"I just got off the phone with my father. Apparently, there was an accident involving our car and some sheep and the car is not working. I'm afraid we can't go to the Cliffs of Moher."

A car and some sheep? Are you kidding me? I was back to being stunned. No way! After all of this, it just ends like this?

"I'm so sorry Patrick. What I can do is take you to a hotel where you can stay and catch the early train back tomorrow morning so you can get the ferry."

"Thank you, anyway." I said, once again feeling depressed and stupid for thinking this could work out and that miracles can happen for ordinary people like me.

Bartley showed me the statue of JFK in the park and walked me to a very nice hotel and dropped me off at the top floor in a beautiful room. "How much is this going to cost?" I asked.

"Oh, it's free. I'm a tour-guide, you know. You are a VIP."

I was impressed. A small consolation prize. He then took me to a movie starring the hideous Pterodactyl-mouthed actress Julia Roberts.

"I'll be by tomorrow at 7 AM and I can walk you to the train station. I want to be able to say goodbye." That was nice of Bartley.

"Okay," I replied and thanked him again.

I retreated to my room. Grateful to have such a nice place, but sad that I had gotten teased only to find out that the rendezvous with the Lord Almighty, Creator of the Heavens and the Earth would not be happening after all. Almighty God. What a slacker!

The next morning, I stood outside of the hotel at 7 AM.

Much to my surprise, Bartley showed up in a black sedan.

"I borrowed a friend's car. I can drop you off at the train station, but first of all I need to stop by my work."

"Okay," I agreed.

"Too bad we can't go to the Cliffs of Moher," he said in a forlorn manner. We continued chatting as we made our way to his office complex. He disappeared inside for what seemed like a half-an-hour.

Eventually, he came out running yelling, "Feck this! I've taken the day off! We're going to the Cliffs of Moher and then I'm driving you back to Dublin!"

"'What? Really??"

"Yes, we are getting you to those Cliffs of Moher!"

I was ecstatic! How could I have ever doubted God?? He is always so faithful! He rescued the Israelites from slavery! He helped St. Paul survive a shipwreck! He helped Luke defeat Darth Vader in *Return of the Jedi*! God was waiting for me, a pint of Guinness in hand—unless he really was a Southern Baptist! It was all going to turn out! What an amazing adventure!

For the next hour, we drove across County Claire through hills and valleys. This was 1995, so Ireland did not have many new houses at all, like it does today. We passed by brick cottages with thatched roofs, large groups of sheep roamed the hills and tiny roads, and a hovering fog covered mountains. Bartley was playing traditional Irish music the whole time and the cool weather and fog made the whole trip seem other-worldly. It was the mystical Ireland of all of our imaginations.[6]

We were now only about 30 minutes from the Cliffs of Moher, and a new problem arose. Bartley drove the car up to

---

[6] This was before Ireland became the Celtic Tiger of the 2000s. At this time, Ireland was one of the poorest nations in Europe and some in Ireland even viewed it as third world. Houses were old, infrastructure was bad, and the economy was very weak. About ten years later, Ireland boomed, everyone bought a new house, U2 started building a skyscraper called U2 Tower, and then it went bust in 2008. Today all of these places I am writing about look very different. On return trips, everything looks modern and wealthy, and it's hard to find the kind of old houses and cottages that I saw everywhere on this trip. Ireland was also very white. Nobody looked like me. Today, Ireland is filled with immigrants from all over the world and I look like your average Irish fish and chips server...and kitty litter packer.

the top of a hill on one of Ireland's small winding roads. Below was a valley that was mostly underwater. The road completely disappeared, inundated by Ireland's worst floods in more than a decade.

"Oh no!" Bartley said.

Not again! I thought.

"Last week we had really terrible floods here. This road is still completely washed out and this is the road we need to take to get to the Cliffs of Moher."

Unbelievable.

"I'm afraid we won't be able to go to the Cliffs of Moher, Patrick."

Where had I heard that before? What a disappointing God, who never shows up for us! His own son ends up on a cross! What was I supposed to expect?

We turned around and began our way back to a road in the north that would eventually connect with a highway to Dublin. But Bartley was unsettled. After a while, he had an idea!

"You know, there is one other little road I know. I can't promise you that it's not washed out also, but we could try it. It's a long shot, but let's try it."

At this point, I was just silent. I wasn't falling for this malarkey again. I needed to prepare myself for the inevitable disappointment. I felt like Charlie Brown trying to kick the football. God was Lucy.

We drove about 20 minutes down another small road and then suddenly, before I could say, *"I'm a faithless moron,"* the Cliffs of Moher appeared in front of us in all of their 7-mile glory. At the time, there was no big parking lot with a modern, fancy welcome center like there is now. The Cliffs were pretty raw and natural with very little tourist infrastructure surrounding them. Ireland was much poorer, with weak infrastructure, and a more underdeveloped tourism industry. The rain was pelting down, and Bartley pulled up to the modest parking lot.

"Right up there," he pointed to our right. Up the hill about 80 yards, the edge of the known world awaited: the 7-mile cliffs, and the 800-foot drop-off on Ireland's west coast were now only a short walk away.

The rain was coming down and the fog was all around, but the most enormous smile erupted on my face. Bartley began laughing. "You should see your face!" he said. I couldn't contain it. I was so giddy. I must have been glowing!

I put my hoody over my head, put on my earphones underneath, and pushed play. I had a CD Walkman. U2's song "Drowning Man" began to play with its quiet, building, Irish cool, grey sound. I walked up the hill in the rain until I got to the edge of the truly massive cliff where there were no guardrails or fences holding me back. Right in front of my feet was the massive drop-off. The visuals were stunning. It looked like the very edge of the world. I had made it!

There was absolutely no one at the Cliffs that day. No tourists, no tour buses, not a single person, not even Bartley who remained in the warm car a hundred yards away. It was just me. Right as I got to the edge of the cliff, I heard the lyrics from "Drowning Man" in a new light:

Take my hand
You know I'll be there
If you can
I'll cross the sky for your love
For I have promised
For to be with you tonight
And for the time that will come

These winds and tides
This change of times

Won't drag you away
Hold on, and hold on tightly

The storms will pass, it won't be long now
His love will last, His love will last forever
And take my hand, you know I'll be there
If you can, I'll cross the sky for your love
Give you what I hold dear

Hold on, hold on tightly
Hold on, and hold on tightly
Rise up, rise up with wings like eagles
You'll run, you'll run
You'll run and not grow weary[7]

The U2 lyrics quoted a famous Bible passage from the Old Testament: Isaiah 40:31. As the lyrics rang through my head, I swear, the skies directly over the cliff opened up. This was the only time the sun shone on the entire trip. The parting of the skies was dramatic, the fog lifted, and, for a brief moment, I saw the eye of God winking at me. He had kept his promise. My doubt, my frustration, my anger, my confusion, and my feeling lost had all been part of His plan. This was what it was like to know and experience God. The life of faith ultimately means losing your way, admitting powerlessness, and being rescued at the last minute by something far bigger and more loving than you can imagine. It's about vulnerability, and having your pride crushed into the ground. It wasn't the arrival point; it was the journey.

[7] U2. "Drowning Man." *War*, Island Records. 1983.

Replacing Religion with Faith

Organized religion has a bad rap and deserves it much of the time. But the life of faith is mysterious. It is also absurd, miraculous, and frightening all at the same time. It is about understanding that as John Lennon once sang, *"Life is what happens to you while you are busy making other plans."* It requires arriving at moments in your life when you have this tremendous realization that you are not in charge. That there is something that exists that is far beyond your control. It can happen on a mountaintop, at the birth of a child, in the tragic death of a loved one, or at the edge of a massive cliff. No matter how hard we try to systematize, dogmatize, and proselytize the life of faith into some concretized official religion, it forever escapes our plans, expectations, and understandings.

Religion for me provides the trappings: the institutions, the official theology, the rituals, and the designated community you are to be a part of and journey with. I grew up surrounded by the structures of religion. But faith is something else.

Faith involves getting on the train that is headed to Galway, when it seems that there is no reason to do so and you don't have the time, money, energy, or belief to want to try. Faith involves the willingness to be surprised and proven wrong. Faith is about deeply knowing and feeling why you are affiliating with a particular religion. Perhaps now at the Cliffs of Moher, I had graduated from a life of religion to a life of faith, something that I truly took ownership of, even though "ownership" meant surrender and letting go.

Ironically, religious people most of all, can take the mystery and magic out of faith—reducing it to formulas, chants, and legalistic behaviors that are rooted in a need for predictability or fear of doubt. Religious institutions can also co-opt faith and claim to be God incarnate—when they are often perfect examples of man at his most messy and corrupt. And communities of faith, sadly, can often be places where people discover new wounds and methods of self-condemnation instead of freedom, joy, and surprise.

When people express anger at religion, it is not necessarily because they want to live an immoral life, but rather they can see how often it seems very man-made and self-serving. But faith is something different. Faith always surprises and forces you into a journey where you do not know how it will end. Religion is about institutional self-propagation, certainty, and self-preservation, while faith is about struggle, doubt, awakening, and humility. Faith is always worth the journey and leads to a mysterious finale with a beautiful view, one you never could have predicted. It can even end with a pint of Guinness with God at the very edge of the world.

Is Religion Primitive?

I am not the first person in history to attempt to touch divinity on Irish soil. Religion began thousands of years ago because there was a fundamental belief as well as a lived, shared experience by our human ancestors that the Natural World and the Supernatural World should not be divided, but rather belong together. NW+SW = **ultimate reality**. The two are intended to be constantly interacting. Only in very recent human history, originating in the Christian European West ironically, have societies viewed humanity as being so self-sufficient and wise that they don't need to believe in a supernatural realm or seek wisdom from that realm. This is a new development and one that should be questioned as much as we question a televangelist asking for money.

I traveled to another part of Ireland once where a Neolithic ancestor of mine, Uggy O'Nachtigall, had a similar transcendent moment. Not far from Dublin in Ireland is Newgrange, a Neolithic tomb that is older than the pyramids in Egypt or Stonehenge. Every December 21st at 8:58 AM a beam of sunlight goes into the mound of Earth surrounded by stone, passes through walls and hallways and goes into the resting place of the dead. It lasts for 17 minutes and beams onto the crypt inside. It marks the ending moment of winter and reminded the people of the certainty of death and the possibility of renewed life. It is miraculous to think that after 5,000 years in rainy, damp Ireland, it is still airtight, and no water has ever seeped in. In order to build this amazing structure that includes ninety-seven grey five-ton stone slabs, the "primitive" people had to haul the stones from the far away Wicklow Mountains. They also had to understand the sun and the stars, the land that they lived on, and they must have been extremely familiar with how to build structures able to withstand 5,000 years in the elements. They knew engineering, farming, geology, astronomy, as well as how to mobilize their community. These were not primitive idiots.

A similar thing takes place at other religious monuments, such as the temple at Angkor Wat in Cambodia. At the spring and autumn equinoxes, the sun rises over the central spire as tourists from around the world look on. Built as a Hindu monument by the Khmer people in the 12th century, the now Buddhist shrine sees the sun balance on its top spire at the precise moment of seasonal change. The elaborate sculptures and Hindu artwork that stretches along the walls for more than half of a mile show the natural and the divine intersecting.

Neither the Neolithic people of Ireland, nor the Khmer people of Southeast Asia were superstitious meatheads simply blessed with vivid imaginations. Rather they were humble people who understood that much about this world and the universe we inhabit is incomprehensible to our small, human minds. **NW+SW = ultimate reality**. While they made complicated calculations and designed massive engineering projects that have survived far longer than most countries, they still had the humility to know that they didn't know everything. And the pyramids, Newgrange, and Angkor Wat were not about inventing answers out of thin air just to answer difficult questions. Whatever they found in the natural world, like the Sun, was used to discover the unknown. To further give light (literally) to what little we know about ourselves.

And that, my friends, is why we have religion. Because something far outside our temporal world, and something deep in our inner world, seek to connect.

2

Life is Like a Glass of Chocolate Milk: How Religion Gives Us Identity and Purpose

Born in 1970 to a mother that didn't want me, I found myself fortunate enough to be adopted into a wonderful family, but not without some unexpected complications. This is a story of near-death, rescue, church, and chocolate.

Nobody really knew when I was born or where. I didn't really find out myself until I was 18 years old. We always celebrated my birthday on November 7th, which was the same date as the Russian Bolshevik Revolution. One year, my sister Marcel made a cake that was decorated with Soviet imagery and propaganda. Another year there was a Michael Jackson cake, and another year, there was an aircraft carrier. We were a weird family! We were mostly certain that I was born in 1970, and I grew up thinking that I was born in the capital city of Costa Rica: San Jose. Later I was told that I was actually born in a little town in the south-central part of the country called "Compton." No, just kidding, it was a little village called San Pablo de Leon Cortez. In the old days, it would have been a small, disconnected and remote town.[8]

---

[8] Today, with improved roads, it is a relatively short drive from the capital city. but it's a trip I have never made for fear of running into a bunch of Patrick clones and a hysterical, impoverished birthmother who wants me to take her to Disney World. One of me is enough for this small planet already under considerable strain environmentally and otherwise.

I grew up believing I was dropped off at an orphanage in Santa Ana because my mother "couldn't take care of me." Only as an adult would I learn that my birth mother had actually had an affair and I was the love child. She already had two boys with her husband (my half-brothers that I've never met) and was rejected by her lover whose last name is one that originates back to Basque, Spain. Apparently, she made no effort to take care of me, and would leave me on the porch for days at a time, unattended. The neighbors grew concerned and eventually reported her to the authorities. They found that I was extremely sick. I was dying of malnutrition and dysentery. They took me to the *patronato* in Santa Ana, where I was expected to die shortly.

The story I was told was that "God had a very special plan for my life and saved me." My parents believed that was true, but it was also a nice way for my adopted parents to spin abandonment. I was always told I was a gift and that "our family wasn't complete without you." I grew up viewing adoption as a positive story—which it is. But from an early age, it thrust upon me a sense that I was going to have to grow up quickly and do remarkable things for God in order to pay him back. I was saved miraculously, therefore I had a massive debt I had to work off in some spectacular way. It was like a cosmic student loan program. I owed God big time! While my parents certainly did not intend that, I internalized this deeply as a small child, for better and for worse. We are born with a natural propensity to believe in the world of the supernatural, but our parents also influence our beliefs greatly. This usually leads to a time of questioning as one gets older. People begin to either own their own particular spiritual beliefs or reject them.

This story that I was told was positive in that it gave me a sense of purpose and motivation to think big from the time I was very small. *I'm going to save the world, feed lepers, build huts, etc.* But it also unintentionally created a tremendous amount of pressure on me. This is actually how many Christians feel about their faith. They feel grateful they have been "saved," but live in fear of not doing enough for God or living well enough to make their salvation legitimate and permanent. It mostly goes unspoken. In my case, I literally felt I owed God my life and that the clock was running.

A few months into my dramatic, but malnourished little life, a group of American nurses passed through the orphanage on a tour. The group was led by a registered nurse living in Costa Rica named Jene Nachtigall.[9] Jene was from Cincinnati and had been living with her husband Harry in Kenya, East Africa before moving to Central America. She had delivered over 200 babies in the African backwaters and treated people with all kinds of illnesses. Her husband Harry was the headmaster of a little village school in Emusire about two hours north of Lake Victoria. He was a white headmaster who staffed the school with black Africans at a time in the late 1960s when white colonialists were skeptical that Africans could truly run their own institutions. The Nachtigalls were progressive and ahead of their time. They were on the right side of the civil rights movement, women's equality, they were fine with being a multi-ethnic family, and were strongly anti-colonialist. Not only was Harry the first to trust and empower black Africans and East Indians to run the school, but 40 years later I was able to visit the little village school in rural Kenya and report to him that the school was still running, and still led by an all African staff— including an impressive, young Kenyan principal.

---

[9] The name "Nachtigall" means "Nightingale" in German and is considered very beautiful in Germany. Only in Germany and Austria do people on the street pronounce my last name correctly on the first try.

Harry and Jene had a 7-year-old daughter, Marcel, who had been raised in Kenya and was used to eating ants and eating raw sugar cane. She loved Kenya, spoke Swahili, and thought she was a black African. It wasn't until they moved away from Africa when she was six years old that an American pointed out to her that she was, in fact, a white person. Further proof that kids are born colorblind and only turn into racist pigs when we poison them.

On this particular day, she went with her mother Jene on the tour of the orphanage. As Jene led the tour, little Marcel Faith Nachtigall strayed from the group. She walked into a room and found a sickly little baby that was just *"two big black eyes."* Skinny and with a distended stomach from malnutrition, I was too weak to make sounds or move—much like I feel now after going to the gym for 30 minutes. She was smitten with this sickly creature and returned to her mother and said, "Mom, I found a baby I want to take home."

Tragically, it was right at that point that I died. The funeral was held a week later, and no one attended. I hope you have enjoyed this book. I've written others, please check them out!

That was a joke!

I did manage to survive, barely.[10]

Jene told her daughter Marcel that they couldn't just take a baby home. But the more she thought about it, the more the idea appealed to her. She had suffered a series of miscarriages and they had desired to adopt a Kenyan boy, but it had not come to pass. My name was Jafét Ramón (which is still my official name in Costa Rica to this day). I had two last names as well—the one of my mother, and the

---

[10] I used to make that joke in a certain high-tech, modern Asian country that shall remain nameless. Because the people were so literal-minded, but also had a strong belief in the supernatural, they assumed I was telling the truth and became convinced they were speaking to a ghost. True story.

one of her filthy, no good, lover who dumped her. Jene told her husband Harry about this dying child their daughter Marcel found and how she was insistent that they needed to take this baby home. But when they inquired further about baby *Jafét* (pronounced like "Ha" as in laughing and "fet" as in Boba Fett), they learned that he was probably going to die any day, or at least be a dim-witted bore. The prognosis was not good.

The adoption agency was concerned that these Americans were taking an interest in the Dirty L'il Bastard (DLB). Jafét was sickly, was going to die soon, and it would be scandalous and news-worthy if they handed over this child to *gringos* and then the child died a few days later. There was no way they wanted to go through the embarrassment of having Americans adopt a child that then, shortly thereafter, died. But Jene was relentless. She continued to visit the orphanage pressing them to let her take the baby who would grow up to have delightful hair, despite his early anemic appearance.

Jene could be a bulldozer, and when she set her mind on something, that was it. She adopted forests way before saving the environment was cool. She treated the first AIDS patients when no one would touch them. She started a nursing home in an impoverished part of the Oakland inner-city because it was a need not being met. She knew how to get things done. She pushed and pushed until the orphanage director relented—tired of dealing with the crazy American nurse.

"Okay, but you better be prepared because he will die soon," the director warned in frustration.

Jene, however, was convinced it was the right thing to do. She felt strongly that God was telling her to take this baby, even if the child would only live a few more days or weeks. As much as we harp on religion and its tendency to make people do bad things, the reality is that the vast majority of the time, religious faith propels people toward doing amazingly selfless things. People of faith often choose to do the illogical, selfless thing, and that is important in this world. Those that decide to strap themselves with explosives and blow up children in the name of religion are the extreme minority. After having saved many other children in Africa, now she was saving me. That's the primary face of faith, not war or terrorism.

Papers were signed, clothes were purchased, and sickly little Jafét Ramón was renamed "Patrick Ramon Nachtigall Clark." I was now the proud possessor of a Spanish, Irish, German name but still looked like Colombian coffee-picker Juan Valdez. Mom was Irish and named me after her sister Patricia. Harry was the son of a Prussian German father with a family whose origins we've traced back to the Odessa area of Ukraine. And Harry's Hungarian German mother was a harmless vampire from Transylvania. Today, Transylvania is located within the borders of Romania—but still has a large ethnic German community. Years later, I would visit Hungary often, live in Germany, and have my deep spiritual encounter in Ireland. It would be an odd new circle, full circle. But that would be many years in the future after I learned to walk, talk, and moonwalk.

Religion and Spirituality Gives Us Orientation Purpose and Identity

One of the primary reasons religions formed is because it gives individuals and communities orientation—i.e. understanding our place in the universe, as well as giving purpose and identity to our daily lives and responsibilities. Ug Nachtigall was a caveman who was born with a strong sense that there was more to the world than what he could see. Ug's fellow cave*people* (politically correct term) were humble hairy creatures and began to explore the world they knew to get in touch with the world *they didn't know*. They were forming an understanding of ultimate reality that would reflect the way human life clearly exists in two realms: the visible and the invisible. There was the known and there was also the mysterious, and they were clearly linked—Ug could feel it, and so do we thousands of years later.

But Ug and his fellow cavepeople also had a sense that all was not right in the visible world. Pain, suffering, selfishness, greed, and mosquitos were a reminder that both the outer world and our own private inner worlds could be dangerous places. Ultimate reality included "the sacred" and "the profane." Being "whole/in balance/saved/enlightened" or whatever religious term you want to choose meant bringing more of that sacred into the parts of the world that were profane. This meant that religious laws, rituals, symbols, and beliefs would be needed that could keep Ug from becoming an ignorant, selfish, and lost one-dimensional figure, in a multi-dimensional universe. It also added a number of evolutionary survival benefits that I discussed in Chapter 1.

That is what symbols and objects like a reclining Buddha statue, a Tibetan prayer wheel, a Mayan pyramid, or a Native American pipe represent: a link between the known world and the unknown world, joining the sacred and the profane. The Christian crucifix is a particularly good illustration as it has a horizontal piece of wood and a vertical piece of wood that literally intersect. And then on that wood is claimed to be a man that is both divine and human in order to reconcile the profane to the sacred. Furthermore, the cross was a symbol of death and our finiteness that became a symbol of life and our eternal nature. That's a pretty good example of religious orientation about ultimate reality.

Purpose is another key factor in religious belief. In Hinduism, the sacred law *Dharma* which is found in numerous Hindu texts gives a person upon birth a set of duties and obligation for this life. It has shaped not only billions of individuals personally, but also gave rise to the Vedic Age (1500-500 BCE) in the already ancient Indus Valley civilization. Out of that period, great gains were made in agricultural technology, writing, the use of iron, economic prosperity through trade, and republics that were every bit as sophisticated as ancient Greek democracy.

On the Great Plains of North America, Black Elk of the Oglala Sioux had a vision that lasted 12 days. In his vision, Black Elk saw that various powers were being bestowed upon his people from a higher realm: the power to renew life, the power to heal, the power of the cleansing wind, the power to know and understand, the power to kill, and the power of prophecy. Black Elk said: "It is from understanding that power comes: and the power in the ceremony was in understanding what it meant; for nothing can live well except in a manner that is suited to the way the sacred power of the World lives and moves."[11] For the Oglala Sioux, living well would mean understanding these powers and responsibilities. They had a strong sense of their place in the world, but it was an integrated world where man and nature, the spiritual and the material world were all one. That has been the default setting of human beings for millions of years. The Chinese religion Taoism teaches that the unnameable is the beginning of Heaven and Earth with the Tao representing the ultimate reality, which cannot be described, but which is the origin of all things. For Muslims, God came into the world as written word, the guidance of the *Quran*. It was only the weird, Christianized Europeans who came from an "enlightened" heritage that created strong boundaries between the spiritual and material world (see Chapter 7).

---

[11] Vine Deloria Jr. *'Introduction,"* *Black Elk Speaks: Being in the Life Story of a Holy Man of the Oglala Sioux.* As told through John G. Neihardt (Lincoln, NE, 1988). P. 208.

For Jews, honoring one God (YHWH) above others, keeping a covenant with YHWH, and being fruitful and multiplying, has given the Jewish people a globally-renowned (and often resented) resilience and success born out of their strong sense of purpose and a clear identity. Their honor for the sacred name of the one true God, "Yahweh," is so great, that God's name is never spelled out because it is too sacred. Instead, it is written "YHWH." In the Hebrew Scriptures, YHWH tells Abraham (the religious founder, formerly known as Abram): *"I will make of you a great nation, and I will bless you and make your name great, so that you will be a blessing."*[12]

Orientation, purpose, and identity. That's what religion brought me when I showed up into the world, and that is why even today, 85% of the world's population are part of a religion.

Living La Puree Vida

Things began well-enough. I began to recover slowly. I was a year old when I was finally able to roll-over on my own, a skill that I have since lost. I apparently loved Kentucky Fried Chicken and their mashed potatoes, which possibly explains my deep adoration for American chain restaurants, no matter how tacky. But after putting on weight and becoming a smiling, super-contented baby, I was taken to a doctor who was very worried about me. In his opinion, my stomach-lining had taken such a beating that I should not be eating solid foods until the age of six, otherwise I could die. Most likely this was an incorrect diagnosis, but it had lifelong consequences for me. Suddenly I was restricted to only two

---

[12] Genesis 12:2. (NIV). The Book of Genesis is part of the Jewish *Tanak,* (Hebrew Bible) and for Christians is the first book in the "Old Testament." They added a sequel called "The New Testament."

foods: Gerber baby cereal and Gerber baby food (the fruit puree in the glass jars). To drink, I was allowed milk, but I only wanted chocolate milk. That was my daily food intake until I was six, with very, very few exceptions. It was like being sent to a penitentiary for toddlers. Eating the same meal over and over would ultimately lead to a ridiculous eating disorder.

I have tons of memories from my childhood in Costa Rica. My parents worked for the Church of God, a denomination that claims to not be a denomination and that claims to have no headquarters, but actually has headquarters in Anderson, Indiana.[13] There are nearly one million people in the Church of God in nearly 90 countries. It is not a group of shouting, dancing Pentecostals, nor is it a group of very conservative Southern Baptists. It is quite mainstream and was founded around 1880. It was ahead of its time on issues of race and women in leadership. It also rejected the kind of denominational divisions that have riddled Christianity, preferring for everyone to just work together and view each other as "brothers and sisters in Christ."

I had no real idea what on Earth my parents did. I just knew that our house was full of people all the time, that they were always helping those in need, and that we traveled a lot. My parents worked with the churches that were located throughout Latin America. That meant lots of travel throughout Costa Rica and to other Central American countries like Nicaragua, El Salvador, Panama, and Guatemala.

All of this occurred during the Cold War when Central America was a playground for the two superpowers—the United States and the Soviet Union. Costa Rica wisely abolished its military in favor of investing in education. The

---

[13] Long Story. I won't get into all of that. See my book *Mosaic* if you're curious how that works.

rest of the region was overly militarized, poor, not well-educated, lacking a middle class, and increasingly violent. During my childhood, border crossings were always dramatic. In those days, crossings always involved machine-gun wielding soldiers scanning your documents for hours and giving you dirty looks. They often seemed to love the power they had, and harassing my American parents was probably a treat for them. The tension at the border crossings was all normal to me and would come in handy years later when I secretly smuggled Bibles into two communist countries: Cuba and China. It all seemed oddly familiar years later when I dealt with border crossings.

Our trips were often very dramatic. We would drive through wild jungle, get stuck in mud during torrential downpours, and drive our Land Rover through rivers. One beach we visited called Nosara required that we cross 52 rivers! There were no bridges over some of the rivers and the water could rise up almost to the level of the driver as we pulled our Mazda van tied to our Land Rover across raging waters. The car would shake back and forth violently making it look like both cars were on the brink of tipping over and being carried away by the strong current. But all of this was normal for us. The childhood of missionary kids often makes the abnormal and exotic seem very routine indeed. If you are fortunate enough to grow up in a "third world country" (underdeveloped country), the exotic experiences become like an immunity shot that makes travel to strange and dangerous places far easier than it is for the average traveler. In fact, sometimes you can have a hard time seeing the "shocking" third world aspects of your country: the dirt, the poverty, the smells, the strange inconveniences or dangers— it all becomes totally normal and it doesn't even register as strange, scary, or different. This happened to both my sister and me.

We visited little churches in the jungle; some that were just pillars made of wood holding up a corrugated tin roof. That left a deep impression on me: that church was about people, not buildings or institutions. The words Jesus spoke: "Where two or more are gathered in my name; there I will be," was how I first grew up thinking of the church. People, not buildings.

We also met pastors who didn't have enough food for their children. One of the few times we ever saw my father weep was in El Salvador when he met with a pastor who had to decide each night which child he was going to feed that day. We saw extreme poverty and were not frightened by it. But that doesn't mean that it wasn't disturbing or sad. It just meant that we were comfortable in those settings and engaging those people. They were our friends and our equals, not charity cases.

We slept on the floor, or in hammocks on these trips. We were often in bug and bat-infested chapels, and we stopped to eat lunch by raging tropical rivers.

We climbed Central American volcanoes and looked right down at the craters where there would often be boiling water the color of green sapphire or deep aqua. My father would occasionally go down into a crater—something that frightened me terribly because of my fear that he would not come out. Dad had quite an adventurous streak. None of this stuff scared him. He was later known as a mild-mannered schoolteacher—a math, computer and science nerd of the highest order. But when I was growing up, he was truly the real Indiana Jones. Dad would fearlessly drive across raging rivers, explore volcanoes, and zip-line across rivers before zip-lines were a thing. Clearly, at an early age, I wanted to imitate my father's life of travel and adventure. Certainly, that played a part in my wanting to be a missionary. I would eventually surpass all of his exotic travels while managing to remain unable to change a car tire or kill a ladybug. I got his love of travel. Unfortunately, I did not get his bravery and practical skills.

Costa Rica was very much a "third world country" at the time—not at all like it is today with its booming tourism industry, tech sector, and upwardly-mobile population. It was still the most developed nation in Central America, but power-outages, bad roads, and poverty were much more a feature of daily life than they are today. But our family loved it there. It was probably the happiest that my parents would ever be in their lifetimes.

The church grew quickly with my parents' assistance. A local pastor and his wife, Julio and Alicia, became my parents' best life-long friends and were the head pastors of a church in a dangerous and poor part of San Jose. That's another thing about religion. It often motivates people to forgo their own security and put themselves into dangerous places and situations to better humanity. Non-religious people can do that as well, of course.

My parents started a skating rink in the church, which was a pretty innovative thing for a church to do in the mid-1970s. My sister and I loved it. There were skating competitions and it was a very cool place to hang out. It brought in a ton of youth and we all roller-skated all the time. Roller-disco was perfect for music by KC and the Sunshine Band. It was the mid-seventies and we all dressed like the Brady Bunch, although that show was not on television in Costa Rica. I was good at skating, but my big sister was better. She was better in school, better in dancing, better in various foreign languages. I looked up to her tremendously and liked to just follow her around and get in with her friends.

All of this took place in a large church facility called the Christian Center which was meant to serve the community and not just be a church serving itself. Today, many churches are trying to recover that idea. Once again, my parents were quite ahead of the curve—by 50 years or so! Christianity needed to be about serving others with no strings attached, as opposed to building up an institution or converting people just to make ourselves feel good or "right." To my parents, people were never objects to convert or numbers to count. Faith was primarily an act of service and action, not dogma. You lived the faith, more than you talked about it. That rubbed off on me in a big way.

Numerous groups of kids from Anderson College (later Anderson University) would come down and do projects around the country with my parents. Our house was always filled with guests and we had parties that included singing and people playing instruments late into the night. It was like Charles Manson and the Family, but in a nice, non-creepy, safe way. Or like the Beatles in India with the Maharishi, minus the four brilliant musicians. I would often wake up at 3 AM and join the party for a while before going back to bed. The house was always filled with laughter, music, and my dad pulling out his glorious trumpet for a solo performance of "Cristo Es La Peña"—a very cool, catchy song.

These American groups often brought me miraculous gifts like peanut butter, a candy called "M&M's" and Kraft Caramels. These candies were absolutely amazing to me. Baby food and chocolate were all I ate—with the exception of these sweet, special candies. I developed an extraordinary sweet tooth.

But nothing was as amazing as the things we would see on our trips to the United States. There were, for instance, machines that would take a coin and spit out Pepsi Cola *in an aluminum can!* To me, it was the most high-tech thing I had ever seen in my life. Robots come to life! The sound of the can dropping and coming out of the opening was pure exhilaration! They also had cars in America that had something called "air conditioning" which could alter the temperature dramatically on a hot day! They had roads with no potholes and up to six lanes! People had screens on their front doors, so the door could be open but not be open at the same time! Nobody had metal bars on their windows and doors like we did in Costa Rica. And people had cute little mailboxes with a red metal flag and the mailman would get your mail! Most impressive of all was that nobody would steal your mail! It would sit in the mailbox all night and nobody would steal it! Unbelievable!

There were also these things called "shopping malls" that were stores enclosed under a roof with that thing called air conditioning. And there were black mats that you could step on that would open the doors automatically leading into the grocery stores. America was filthy rich, awesome, and super sophisticated, but we all loved life in Costa Rica and had no desire to ever leave.

I attended Country Day School, a private school filled with ex-pat kids, elite Costa Rican kids, and the children of a criminal from the Nixon administration who was in exile in Costa Rica. I played drums in school and was already hooked on Abba, Elvis Presley, and Paul McCartney & Wings. My parents listened to the Carpenters, John Denver, and the groovy, soul sounds of the Stylistics. My sister listened to Bachman Turner Overdrive and the Four Seasons. The radio was filled with English songs like "Take it to the Limit" by the Eagles, "That's the Way I Like It" by KC and the Sunshine Band, and "Make it with You" by Bread. Even at that age, I was hooked on secular music and had zero interest in church music or any Christian artists. Back then, there weren't really Christian rock artists (the good old days!). There was also a ton of music on all the time from artists from Spain like Mocedades, Camilo Sesto and Julio Iglesias. To this day, I barely know the words of any Christian songs in Spanish, or in English for that matter. The guilt about that would come later in the 1980s when I was taught in church that rock n' roll was evil and some of my favorite bands were supposedly putting hidden messages from Satan onto their records. Sigh.

One of the targeted "satanic" bands was Styx. My sister and I would play Styx's album *Paradise Theatre* backwards to supposedly hear the words "save me Satan." Anyone who listens to the opening notes of the famous Styx song "Babe" should figure out pretty quickly that they are far too wimpy to be into devil worship.[14] And later in junior high school, we decided Billy Idol was evil. I unwound his *Rebel Yell* cassette tape and tied it to the back of my bicycle, determined to destroy Satan's awesomely produced and super catchy evil music. A victory for Jesus! My commitment to get secular music completely out of my life lasted about a half-hour. I was down with Billy Idol, Def Leppard, and everyone else with a pentagram on MTV. I couldn't give it up.

Starvation Diet

In my early school years, music and Satan were not the problem. I was in elementary school and I was still eating baby food and drinking chocolate milk! Every day, my primary meal was chocolate milk. It was delicious, filling and "healthy." Even after I began eating normally, the chocolate milk thing never went away. When I turned six, the doctor said, *"Okay, Patrick can eat anything he wants now."* *"Great!"* my parents said. The problem was that Patrick didn't want anything other than chocolate milk—unless it was M&M's or a Milky Way from some group of college kids from the U.S.A. The baby cereal I ate only because I had to. All I wanted was chocolate for every meal, all the time. My

---

[14] Seriously! Listen to the first one minute of that song and ask yourself if that is the sound of Satan or the most beta-male song ever written!

mother introduced me to chocolate candy bars, and she insisted to her dying day, that chocolate milk and chocolate bars kept me alive.

It was true. There were no vegetables, fruits, or meat going into my mouth, ever. All I ate were chocolate bars and chocolate milk. My parents tried to get me to eat new foods, but I refused. Not only did I not want anything but chocolate, but I was deathly afraid that eating any food was going to make me throw-up to death. I was convinced that one bite of an apple, a piece of chicken, or even a peanut would lead to my instant death by vomiting. I was sure I would go out like John Bonham of Led Zeppelin. I had peaked at the age of two when I was able to eat KFC. Once the doctor put me on this super restrictive diet, it stunted my ability to learn to eat new foods and taste new flavors.

Forty years later, I would learn that it is often common for abandoned children to be picky eaters and/or develop eating disorders. I've met quite a few adopted kids who are very particular about their food like me. But in my case, it was worse. The doctor had made me feel that *any* food could kill me and so I was deathly afraid of all foods. Not only that, but at the age when kids are adding to their palate and adding different kinds of tastes and textures, I was stuck on chocolate. I didn't even know the taste of bitter, salty, or sour. All I knew was sweet and chocolaty in those early years.

Eventually I graduated to soda crackers which, in time, would lead to an addiction to Ritz crackers. But that was it for the non-sugary stuff. Not only did I live in fear of food, but foods actually looked like frightening insects to me. There was nothing about food that looked delicious. For me, looking at a hamburger, a pizza, or an orange was like looking at a spider, a praying mantis or a cricket. That's great for Cambodians, but not for me!

My gag reflex was triggered just looking at anything that wasn't chocolate or crackers. It would not be until my 2nd decade of life that I would be able to begin to eat such exotic foods as peanut butter and jelly sandwiches with the disgusting crusts cut off, McDonald's french fries, and that super exotic and unusual food: pancakes with maple syrup (with no disgusting slab of butter on top).

My sister was sympathetic, my mother was puzzled, and my usually calm and mild-mannered father was mostly annoyed. Every once in a while, he would bring the hammer down and put one single bean on a plate and say, "You are not leaving this table until you eat that bean!" Of course, I did not. Not even being put on a medieval torture rack or, worse yet, being forced to watch *Hee Haw* and *The Lawrence Welk Show* back to back would be enough for me to put that disgusting creature in my mouth. Dad thought I was being stubborn. But in my head, he might as well have been saying, "You will not leave this table until you cannibalize your sister, cover her in bug juice and vomit yourself to death. Then you are free to go." There was zero chance that I was going to touch or even look at that hideous bean, or slice of apple, or grape, much less eat it. Zero! Usually at the 9 PM or 10 PM mark they would give up. I'd leave feeling victorious and, of course, utterly demoralized and totally ashamed for being afraid of a single bean.

I spent many hours hiding in the bathroom or pretending I was asleep at dinner time. I conveniently always fell asleep at mealtimes when we visited relatives. I thought I was being pretty tricky, disappearing every evening. "Oh, he fell asleep at 6 PM, let's not wake him during dinner," I imagined they would say. Usually, my parents would let me sleep. Obviously, my parents must have known it was all avoidance, a ruse to get out of having to eat food in public.

It got worse, however, because our house was often full of visitors. At every single meal with visitors they would ask, "Why isn't Patrick eating?" Mom had a few excuses she used regularly, "He already ate," "He's not hungry," "He's fine," or "He will eat later." I was humiliated for myself, and I was humiliated for my parents. Over and over, guests were relentless and would keep badgering me or my parents. They would then inevitably say, "Here, Patrick," as they held out some insect-looking vegetable or fruit. "No thanks/No gracias," I would reply. But they would always keep asking. "You don't know what you are missing!" they would say, making me feel like the biggest loser in the world.

It was even more humiliating when they would start scolding my parents in front of me, which would happen all the time. "Why are you letting him not eat?" "Why aren't you forcing him to eat?" "Why don't you make him eat with the rest of us?" "How is he going to get nutrition?" "How will he grow?" People were so judgmental and hard on my parents, but my parents continued to defend me in public.

I looked on with such envy at every other human being in the world. They could eat *gallo pinto*, or spaghetti (evil red worms), and McDonald's hamburgers without batting an eye. They all loved food. I hated it. Popcorn, steaks, tamales, chow mein—everyone could eat everything. But for me, three times a day, I had to be reminded what a bizarre, freaky, idiot I was.

Once people knew my secret, they would never drop it. "Are you eating anything yet, Patrick?" "Do you eat apples yet?" "But apples are so good!" "How can you grow big and strong if you don't eat?" That last comment would make me wonder if I would be a midget. I really feared that! I assumed I would stay the size of a 2nd grader for my whole life. The criticism was constant, and it went on for decades. Even after I began eating everything and even getting overweight in my adulthood (I lost the weight folks!), people would still ask those questions. Even in my 40s when I had my very last meal with my dad before he died, he was still saying to me, "You eat fish? I didn't know you eat fish! Hey everyone, he eats fish!!! He never used to eat fish! I remember when he was little, and he didn't eat fish!" Okay, Dad. Zip it!!!

My mother worried about my health. Jesus had made some comment in the Bible like "man cannot survive on chocolate milk and chocolate bars alone." I felt like it was some punishment from God, like St. Paul's thorn in his side. I prayed that it would go away. Why am I cursed? Why do I have to have the stupidest problem in the entire world? Who on Earth is afraid of food??! I had to be the only person on planet Earth who couldn't eat anything. It felt like it was my destiny. I could not imagine anything, not even a candy apple or a lemon pie ever being appealing to me.

But maybe it was also proof that I was special. Maybe all that stuff about me having a special purpose or destiny was true, and my subsisting on 1,500 calories daily of pure sugar was proof that I was meant to survive and live. But how on Earth was I going to keep up this façade? One day I'd want to have sleepovers and my buddies would need to eat. What would I do? Or what if people at my birthday party wanted to eat something more than chocolate cake.[15] How was I going to go to college? Would the school cafeteria have candy bars and chocolate milk? Could I travel to the six continents of the world—which was my dream—ultimately subsisting entirely on Milky Ways and Hershey Kisses? Did I think I was going to be given Nestle's Quick by tribes in the Amazon? What about dating girls? Was I just going to take them to See's Candy store on every single date? How could I ever get married? What girl in the world would go out with a guy

---

[15] I stopped having birthdays at age five and began to ask my parents to please take me to the airport to watch airplanes instead.

deathly afraid of a piece of lettuce? And what would happen when I had a one-year old kid in the future who could eat more than me?

"Daddy, eat your vegetables!"

"No, I'm scared, son! But you eat yours!"

The humiliation was going to be never-ending. It was mortifying.

My mother took me back to the doctor.

Mom: "He is not eating anything."

Doctor: "How's his energy level?"

Mom: "He has constant energy."

Doctor: "How is he doing in school?"

Mom: "Great."

Doctor: "Is he ever sick?"

Mom: "Never!"

"He's fine. He will grow out of it. Don't worry about it." The doctor said leaving my mother and I puzzled. Now that I was over the age of six, apparently there was no danger, and I was free to eat whatever I wanted.

Inexplicably, I seemed to be completely fine living on chocolate milk and candy bars.

In fact, I was completely addicted to chocolate milk, and even today as an adult, chocolate milk is like heroin for me. I could relapse at any moment. If I take even the smallest sip, I fall off the wagon. No joke! I never tire of it and look at it lustfully in grocery stores.

Despite that secret eating disorder, I was a perfectly healthy, energetic, hyper, happy boy as long as I was away from a table or restaurant. And I had a strong sense of purpose, destiny, and a feeling of being greatly loved by my family and by a larger community. That, in a nutshell, is what religion does for human beings. Orientation, purpose, identity. And it is not easy to replicate outside of religion. Football clubs, Fraternities and Sororities, the military, and even atheist churches (yes, they are a thing!) have a very difficult time providing an existential solid framework around a person's *entire* life. The fusion of the sacred and the profane, the physical and the material, the temporal and the eternal, the visible and the invisible taps into our deepest core as human beings. Despite my eating disorder, I still felt my life was important, had meaning, and that there was a divine purpose for me. Was that just religious indoctrination or are we all here for a purpose?

But What If We Have No Souls and There is No God?

It is possible to have orientation, purpose, and identity without religion. Plenty of people choose not to be religious and live full, happy, and meaningful lives. There is a wave of neo-Buddhist Atheism that is becoming popularized by sharp thinkers like Sam Harris, Yuval Noah Harari, Richard Dawkins, Robert Wright, the late Christopher Hitchens and Neuroscientist Robert Sapolsky which contends that there are no gods or God. Not only is there no God, but no soul and no self. We can call this a scientific materialistic worldview, "physicalism" or "naturalism"—the idea that the physical world is all there is in the universe. Evolutionary psychology teaches that human culture and the human conscience (the ability to know right from wrong) are just the result of evolution.

These thinkers believe there is no consciousness (no soul, no self). Not only that, according to many of these new thinkers, advances in neuroscience are starting to show that human beings are just a collection of neurons, synapses, genes, molecules, atoms and impulses to such an extent that we have no free will at all. Our soulless, non-conscious, selfless physical body is just constantly and involuntarily reacting to various physical stimulants. "What we call sensations and emotions are in fact just algorithms," Harari writes in *Homo Deus: A Brief History of Tomorrow*.[16] I am a big fan of the aforementioned scholars and thinkers. They have a number of ideas that are important and should be wrestled with for those of us who actually believe we are here and have a consciousness, but some things for now leave me unconvinced (which I will discuss in Chapter 8). I hope you will continue reading this book through the final chapter, although if those brilliant thinkers are right, you will not be consciously making that choice because you are just a collection of neurons, synapses, genes, molecules, atoms, and impulses that has no free will. It also means your negative reviews of my book on Amazon.com shouldn't hurt my feelings since neither of us are really here.

The idea that there is not a self is an ancient idea from the Indus Valley taught thousands of years ago. Long before Sigmund Freud (1856-1939) told us about the dangers of our out of control egos, Buddhism pointed out how our notions of self are an illusion that leads to suffering. But even in the *Mundaka Upanishad* of Hinduism, or the work of the Sufi philosopher Ibn Arabi (1165-240), or the Cosmology of Taoism, or ancient Judaism, or any other religion, there was always the underlying belief that there is *a* source. The reality we know is both spiritual and physical and emerges from something bigger than ourselves and not simply out of randomness and nothingness. The conclusion that there must be a primary source was based on intelligent logic, not ignorant superstition.

Whether we truly have selves and bodies or not is a matter for later discussion in this book, but at this point in my story, I am in Costa Rica almost half-way through elementary school and my physical body still refuses to eat "real food."

---

[16] Harari, Yuval Noah. *Homo Deus: A Brief History of Tomorrow*. London: Harvey Secker, 2015. P. 86

Now free to eat whatever food I wanted, I continued my diet of constant chocolate and baby food and continued to get clean bills of health from every doctor I saw.

My father on the other hand, was a different story. Only in his mid-30s, he had a sudden stroke, ended up in the hospital, and our days in Costa Rica came to a surprising and rapid end.

3

The Immigrant Song: Why Religions Become Poisonous

After my father's stroke, we moved to the United States where I became a legal alien still unable to eat a single french fry. We lived in a super-rich part of the San Francisco Bay area but attended an African-American church in the 'hood of Oakland. My world became extremely multi-cultural and the vision to become a missionary became clearer.

I stared at my plate.

"You are not leaving that table until you eat those two pieces of rice," my mother and father said to me one evening in the kitchen of our San Francisco condominium. This would happen to me about every four weeks. The monthly food challenge that I would always, humiliatingly fail.

I stared at the two little grains of white rice. I licked one of them. It tasted like absolutely nothing. They were so small. Maybe I could put them in my mouth? Maybe I could swallow it and not even feel it, and then be free to get up from the table and be left alone. Of course, the answer was "no," because to me, the two pieces of food looked like little white larvae—little worms that were going to multiply and eat me from the inside out. Worm-a-Roni: The San Francisco treat!

Other than the monthly eating challenge, I loved our new home in Marin County, just a few minutes from downtown and across the majestic Golden Gate Bridge. I was in the second half of my elementary school years and in the process of becoming an all-American boy. We had relocated to San Francisco to be closer to my father's elderly parents who were former Church of God missionaries and, in the case of my grandfather, was actually an ordained pastor also. My father returned to teaching in downtown San Francisco on Nob Hill and my mother returned to nursing, this time in a convalescent center in Terra Linda.

Marin County is pretty famous in California. It's the Beverly Hills of the north. It is what you see in all those pictures of the Golden Gate Bridge that don't include the city—where instead you see the bridge head into a mountain. Behind that mountain was our home in a town with a Spanish name: Corte Madera. Marin was full of very wealthy liberals, new age gurus and hippies. It was the second richest county in the United States at the time, and also had its fair share of famous people. Robin Williams lived just about four miles from our home in the scenic coastal town of Tiburon. He was a graduate of my sister's high school: Redwood. Clint Eastwood had a home in the adjoining town. Steve Perry, the lead singer of Journey, lived in a canyon not far away from us. Journey was my favorite band at the time, and they were at their peak with the *Escape* album. Most exciting was the fact that George Lucas' Skywalker Ranch was in Marin County near Lucas Valley, and Industrial Lights & Magic was based in Marin. We were the home of Star Wars! What could be cooler than that?

The Nachtigalls were not rich, however. We mostly lived in condominiums with high rent. At one point, my father had to take a before-dawn newspaper delivery route for a brand-new newspaper called USA Today. In addition to the early paper-route and the all-day teaching downtown, he also took a carpool each day. The U.S. was in the middle of an oil crisis. Dad would then return home at about 4:30 PM and play 90 minutes to two hours of sports with me every day (baseball, football, and tennis)! He was an amazing father! I still find it so amazing that he had the energy and commitment to give me so much time every single day to play with me the sports I loved. Our times together were the highlight of my day, and of my life.

My mother often worked the nightshift—which probably didn't help her health ultimately as nightshifts are now known to be very hard on the body and cause illness. We didn't have much, but as a kid, I didn't know that. It never bothered me to get used toys, broken football helmets, or other hand-me-downs. And, Lord knows, the family saved money on the grocery bill with me in the house. Chocolate candy bars were only 25 cents back then.

My parents were no longer missionaries and never really would be again. Their 13-year stint in Africa and Latin America had come to an end. I think from then on, they worked just to get me and my sister through school and college, not out of a deep love for their jobs. It's something I didn't fully understand or appreciate until I had my own child, and my parents were gone. I look back now and see a million ways that they submitted their own desires and wishes to the higher good of giving opportunities to their children. I wish they were around for me to thank them.

My parents never worked in a church again either. But we did go to church. They were always looking for places where they could be of help, in churches or as community activists. We checked out a church in South San Francisco, but my parents always gravitated to where the greatest need was, so we ended up going to church in the 'hood—45 minutes away in crime-infested Oakland, California.

It was an African American church in a rough part of town in a very tough city that had a high crime rate, drugs, gangs, and broken families. In those days, Oakland and even what is today Silicon Valley were the jokes of the Bay Area. Fremont, Los Gatos, Oakland were all places that we made fun of. It was awesome to *not be* from those places and to be from Marin. Today, millionaires and billionaires live in Oakland and San Jose. These are the places where the world's richest companies are based, including Apple, Google, and Facebook. We listened to Casey Kassem's *American Top 40* countdown on the radio on the way to church every Sunday and on the way back. The number one song was always announced as we would be returning to the shores of Marin after church at about 1:57 PM. "This week's number one song is "Tragedy" by the Bee Gees," Casey would say in his staccato voice. Then my Mom would complain about their falsettos, capped teeth, and tight pants designed to show off their "peepers." My mother's hilarious anti-Bee Gees rant was one we grew really familiar with. She loathed them.

We always stopped off at McDonald's on the way home where I would order McDonald's animal cookies and a chocolate milkshake. Sometimes in my mind, I would pretend cookies or cupcakes were real food like hot dogs and hamburgers just to make myself feel better. Once I got to 6th grade, I had graduated to McDonald's chocolate chip cookies and a strawberry milkshake (because it didn't have any real pieces of strawberry in it—or *anything* real for that matter). Prior to that, I was seriously afraid of the non-chocolate chip part of chocolate chip cookies. *It must taste like disgusting bread, or someth*ing, I thought to myself—as if I knew what bread even tasted like. But I did try chocolate chip cookies eventually and this was incredible growth in my opinion. I was learning to eat more diverse food!

At church, I was the only non-African American kid other than my sister. But our family was so colorblind, I really didn't notice that we stuck out at church, or that it was unusual for us to be there, commuting from 45 minutes away. Ours was a struggling black church in a bad part of town. There were fiery, long sermons with a lot of yelling, call and response, and the people saying, "that's right!" "uh hum," "preach it" and "amen" all throughout the sermon.

Unfortunately, we didn't have the killer black choir that other churches had. In fact, the music was led by the only other white person in the church other than my family; a woman named Pat who sang very flat in a whispery voice. How could this happen in a black church?? The brothers and sisters must have been tormented by being the only black church in America with music you didn't want to listen to. You could tell they really wanted to takeoff musically, but had to hold back for the musically challenged, white music director. They were like a pack of racing greyhounds at the track with their leash tied to a picket fence. To get around this, the black pastor would often break into song throughout the Sunday service and become the temporary music director which would allow us greyhounds to run the musical track, so to speak. The church never really grew in all of our years there and the only song I learned was "This is the Day," which I learned in the African American style—exuberant, fast, and with a motherlode of clapping. It was a shock to hear the more sedate, white version years later. It sounded like a funeral dirge in comparison. Coming from Latin America and now in Oakland, I had still not heard the awful "Yacht Rock" adult-contemporary sounds of the white Anglo-American church. Even though I was not a fan of any kind of church music, I still thought all church music was supposed to be loud, rambunctious, and full of action.

While religious music continued to not register in my brain whatsoever, I did, however, fall in love with R&B, funk, and soul music. Chic, Prince, Parliamentary Funkadelic, the Gap Band, Michael Jackson, Kool & the Gang, James Brown,

George Benson, Kurtis Blow—any kind of African American music with a throbbing baseline interested me. The Bee Gees were in their prime and ABBA were still around and always had great underrated bass lines in their songs like on "Lay All Your Love on Me." We never sang that one in the Oakland church, but I'm sure if Pat wasn't in charge, the brothers and sisters would have knocked it out of the park.

Growing up in Costa Rica, but raised by American parents, meant I grew up bi-culturally. I was always part American and part Costa Rican. But now in San Francisco, I grew up multi-culturally. It wasn't just the African American church that we attended that exposed me to different cultures. My elementary school classes were filled with first generation immigrants fresh off the boat. Like me, they were mostly foreigners that looked different trying to learn what it meant to be an American. Alberto had just arrived from Italy, Michelle from Japan, William and Kyong Soon from South Korea, Bahram from Iran, etc. And my next-door neighbors, the kids I played with after school, were Russian, German, Israeli, Australian, Iranian, from England, and American Jews. All of this, I'm sure, played a part in my development. I grew up being used to relating to and feeling comfortable with people from different parts of the world and seeing the commonalities. It prepared me for the life I would one day live.

Like me, most of them were not illegal aliens, they were *legal* aliens—waiting for the day years in the future when they would get to take the oath and get U.S. citizenship. What a lot of Americans don't realize, especially those strongly against immigration, is that foreigners get Americanized extremely quickly. The U.S.A. is exceptional at creating an American culture that topples people's original culture. It assimilates people far better than any country, including those in Northern Europe. The speed at which all of us foreign kids became experts on the NFL, the Brady Bunch, Star Wars, Warner Brothers cartoons and American video games like Asteroids and Galaga was astonishing. Within weeks, we talked like kids that had lived in America our whole lives. You would never have known that we were new to the U.S.A., or in many cases, had parents who couldn't speak English.

One of the smartest things my father ever did for me, a new immigrant, was teach me American sports immediately after arriving to the U.S.A. He didn't want me to be left out on the playground or be the last one to be picked for the team. Every day he would teach me the rules of football, baseball, basketball, tennis, pool, ping pong, and every other sport he could think of. We would often play until sunset, just him and me. Of course, he let me win constantly. To this day, despite all of the exciting adventures I have had around the world, and all the amazing experiences in my life, my time as a child playing sports with my dad is probably the greatest memory of my life. It is a magical, sacred time to me. The images flash in my head weekly of that time we spent together every day. He would often say:

"One day, you won't want to play with your old man. You will want to be out playing with your friends, and that's okay." I used to always want to cry when he said that. I would quickly respond:

"But Dad, you are my best friend! I'm never going to want to play with anyone else!" But of course, he was right. Once high school rolled around, I was never around. I was always out playing with my friends and rarely saw him.

I didn't realize how exhausted he was from his very long workdays, but he never said "no" to my requests for time to play sports together and his plan worked. I was an extremely good athlete in elementary school—extremely good. That was, until puberty destroyed all of my athletic aspirations later in 7th grade. I went from being a star athlete to the tiny, anemic kid who couldn't get his locker open in the span of three months. But those early years of supreme athletic prowess were glorious. I assumed I would grow up and be the star athlete of my junior high and high school. It never occurred to me that it would depend on my size and strength as I aged. Maybe years of only eating Three Musketeer bars were finally catching up to me.

My sister's experience going from a third world country to living in one of the richest and most materialistic places on Earth was a negative one. She hated the United States and always wanted to return to Costa Rica. She looked like an all-American blonde, but she was not an American girl. In her mind, she was Costa Rican. The truth was more complicated.

We were both TCKs (Third Culture Kids). We were children that had grown up in countries outside of the home country of our parents—their passport country. We were neither American nor completely from another country. We were both, but also kids that lived in-between two worlds and created a third culture – all our own. It would have spared us a lot of pain and confusion to have known that we were TCKs, but it is not something that would become widely studied or understood until the 1990s. This was the 1970s and it was an area of study that was still in its infancy. My wife Jamie (also a TCK) introduced the concept to me when we first started dating and it was a revelation for me. It explained so much about who I am and why I think the way I do. It also explained why any place in the world feels like home within a few minutes, if I want it to. For my sister, she can do the same. But in her heart, she always longed to go back to Costa Rica.

We also now know that moving a teenager from one culture to another is rarely a good idea. My parents did it because of my father's stroke and also because my sister needed to prepare for American university, and they thought an American high school would be a better place to prepare for that. But in hindsight, moving a teenager cross-culturally is always high risk and not recommended. Too often, the repercussions are very negative for the child.

I was in the United States now, and the number of different candy bars available was mind-blowing. My palate began to grow: Charleston Chews, Reese's Peanut Butter Cups, Junior Mints. I was really challenging myself food-wise! I was also delving into the world of crackers, which was exciting. However, I was not doing very well with cereal. I was afraid of Froot Loops because the association with the word "fruit" scared me. Same with Apple Jacks. I wish I were kidding. I was the only child in America desperately afraid of sugary cereal.

Unfortunately for me, there was a new product available in the American supermarkets called "Breakfast Squares." They were basically packages of two brownies that were filled with vitamins, nutrients, iron and other things I was never getting and that make chocolate taste gross. My parents instituted a rule that I had to eat two packages of Breakfast Squares a day.

Initially, I was able to handle it. Sometimes they almost tasted good. But it wasn't pleasant. Daily I had to eat these iron-tasting things. It lasted for a couple of years and then they went out of business. Great, right? Wrong! They got replaced by a new product called Carnation Breakfast Bars which were chocolate on the outside, and some kind of peanut butter crunch with nutrients, iron, and other things on the inside that made the bars taste even worse than Breakfast Squares. Since they were "chocolate," I had no excuse! I had to eat those stupid things every day and couldn't go out and play until they went down my throat in front of my parents. I loathed the taste of these "chocolate bars." It would take me an hour to eat them.

Every day in elementary school, the first thing I would do at lunch is throw my lunch away—minus the chocolate milk. When I was at home, if I didn't have to eat in front of my parents, I started flushing Carnation Breakfast Bars down the toilet during the mealtime. My mom caught on, so I started to bury my Carnation Breakfast Bars in the soil of our potted plants. I was amazed when she managed to find them in the plants. I thought I had hidden them so cleverly. Suddenly, I didn't entirely associate all chocolate with joy and yumminess. Carnation Breakfast Bars were destroying my chocolate-filled life. I cursed the idiot who invented these.

My mother would often have us take a Sunday off from church and we would have outings all throughout the Bay Area. She would always say to us, "You don't need to be in church to worship God." We were constantly traveling around San Francisco, the Bay Area and taking our many visitors to see all of the sights. We would go to the Golden Gate Bridge hundreds of times—above it, below it, across it. Fisherman's Wharf, Pier 39, Alcatraz, Coit Tower, the Cannery, Stinson Beach, Muir Woods, the top of the Bank of America building, the campus at Berkeley, Napa Wine Country, cable cars, ferries to the city and hiking around Angel Island. We were experts on the Bay Area thanks to my Mom. I still love going back every four years or so to relive it all.

The China Vision

One of my friends in the neighborhood was a Jewish boy named Ricky. We spent a lot of time together. He was a top student, and his family was very artsy, sophisticated, and intellectual. One day his mother invited me to go to a movie.

"Sure," I said, expecting it to be *Popeye, The Black Hole, Sophie's Choice*, or some other kid-friendly movie. It turned out to be a documentary called *From Mao to Mozart*. It was about a famous violinist named Isaac Stern who was invited to the secretive People's Republic of China to play his violin and meet music students. Ricky was a violinist, so his mother probably wanted him to see this movie about the Jewish violinist Stern making this groundbreaking trip into Red China.

Stern was the first American to get into China after a long period of the nation being closed to foreigners. The movie came out in 1979. Mao Zedong had died in 1976 and China had just spent the last 20 years in chaos. The disastrous Cultural Revolution which followed the deadly Great Leap Forward had set the country back decades. Instead of being a Communist paradise, China was a nation of repressed, mostly starving people. China was on the brink of experimenting with free market capitalism for the first time, a move which would ultimately transform the country and the whole world (and that I would eventually get to witness first-hand)! But this was before all of that and was one of their preliminary contacts with the West after this period of being completely closed.

As we sat in that movie theatre watching these exotic images of China, I was completely thunderstruck. The scenes of the dramatic, jagged mountains, the green rice paddies, the villagers carrying straw on their back walking alongside water-buffalo—all of it had me riveted. Only the documentary *Wham in China!* would eventually surpass this! It probably helped that the very first frame of the movie is of an airplane landing, and it's amazing it had such an impact on me because so much of it is about Stern trying to teach Chinese musicians about how to play classical music properly. Boring!

I had grown up with books with Chinese characters in my house, photos of Mao, and lived in San Francisco surrounded by Chinese people. But something awoke in me that day, and I became obsessed with all things Asia—specifically China. That's when I made up my mind that I would go to China, I would live in China, I would help people there, and I would never come back to America. My future was in China—as far away from the USA as I could get. On Bugs Bunny cartoons, when Bugs would dig a hole in the ground he would end up in China. It was clearly the farthest place away on the planet and I had to become a part of it. From that moment on, I never had a doubt that my life and China would be inter- woven. When and how, I didn't entirely know. I just knew that was my destiny. The irony that I wanted to spend the rest of my life feeding poor people in China, but was afraid of eating rice myself, was completely lost on me. Slowly but surely, my dream of being a missionary was becoming more and more clear.

Religion and the Power of Self-Delusion and Mass-Delusion

Like a kid who wants to live in China but is afraid of a piece of rice, human beings are able to block out reality pretty easily when we want to. In San Francisco, we always received visitors from all over the world, and as a kid, I loved playing the tour guide (and I still do). The most amazing story from our tour guide days was when we had a friend visit us from El Salvador. He was a die-hard Marxist, so he distrusted the United States and capitalism. He believed all the communist propaganda that was put out by the various Marxist groups in Latin America. We took the El Salvadorian to the famous viewpoint on the tip of Marin County so he could see San Francisco and the Bay on full dramatic display. It's perhaps the greatest city view in the United States. The El Salvadoran

Marxist looked at the incredible vista of the Bay and the city and proclaimed it *"not real."* He insisted the tour we were giving him was fake. He chose to believe the Marxist propaganda that the United States was a poor country with beggars everywhere and not nearly as advanced as the Soviet Union. Capitalism was a failure, according to him, so he refused to see what was right in front of his very eyes. Choosing to believe that we were working with the U.S. government and had created an elaborate visual deception.

I'm not exactly sure how we could have possibly pulled that off—to make an enormous fake bay, with a fake city, and a big fake red bridge that we walked across; but he insisted. There is a great lesson in this: a human being's capacity for self-delusion is incredible. Particularly when ideology, politics, and religion get involved. People can decide what they want to believe and then create their reality to make it fit. This is a danger for religious people, atheists, scientific-oriented people—basically anyone that lives and breathes. Literally hundreds of studies, beginning with some revolutionary studies in the 1970s at Stanford University show that when people decide on certain important facts to them; they are likely to stick to those "facts" even if they are proven wrong. The emotions count more than the facts. Debating academic scholars do this, atheists do this, doctors do this, political activists do this, religious people do this. We all do this! It can be particularly dangerous in politics and religion.

European cognitive scientists Hugo Mercier and Dan Sperber argue that the primary role of human reason is to enable us to collaborate and live in groups; not solve-problems and make discoveries. This is a terrible evolutionary trait, because it means that if we are hunter-gatherers living in the Kalahari Desert, we have the capacity to decide that the killer lion outside of our hut is not there.

Fake news! There may be eight key facts pointing toward the fact that there is a lion that wants to eat us as a light afternoon snack, but we will cling to the more comfortable idea that it is just an unusually loud kitty cat. Religious people can easily believe false narratives to make them fit their theology, while an atheist Marxist like our dear friend, can decide that the giant Golden Gate Bridge he is walking across is fake. This should bring humility to both the atheist and to the person of faith.

Another experiment at Yale University had students explain how everyday devices work, things like toilets and zippers. It turned out that the students (and all of us people) are completely ignorant about the most highly used, mundane things around us. We think we can explain systematic theology and the origin of the cosmos, but we don't even know how a toilet works! The reality is that we all have a shockingly limited amount of knowledge and depend on others to fill in the gaps constantly. But as humans, we are not self-aware about this. We over-estimate how much we personally know, and how much we know as a species.

Our fear of immigrants is like this. Usually, for instance, the strongest anti-immigration opinions in the United States, Poland, Hungary and in other countries are held in places where there are virtually no immigrants. It is ethnically homogenous town, cities, and countries that are most likely to fear foreigners and believe that they are "destroying our land." Facts and experience don't factor into their opinions. It's a willful blindness for emotional reasons. But what we see time and time again, is that the communities that embrace multi-culturalism have the most dynamic economies—even in very rural parts of the United States. The small, midwestern farm town that is embracing multi-culturalism is always going to have a stronger economy than the ethnically homogenous one that is resisting ethnic integration.

When ideology and Christianity or any other religions mix; it too can cause completely irrational, dogmatic, beliefs. We are used to hearing of militant and fundamentalist Christians and Muslims, but the world also has fundamentalist Hindus and militant Buddhists. We have also seen genocide-loving atheists like Stalin, and non-religious, materialists like Kim Il Sung create their own religion based on themselves.

We are currently going through a time around the world where the fusion of Christianity and nationalist ideologies around the world is changing many churches and religious people for the worse. Protecting the already decided "truth" becomes everything, and the pursuit of real truth which always involves *agape* love ("loving your neighbor as yourself and seeking *their* highest good") becomes secondary. Cognitive scientists show us that repeating a false story over and over is enough to make us believe it is a reality. Joseph Goebbels and the Nazis knew this too. Repeat a falsehood over and over and it will be accepted as truth. Reality and the Christian faith can become twisted into a pretzel to create a new reality based on a lie. We see this with the nationalist Christian movements spreading across the globe, but it clearly happens with secular, atheist Marxists as well, like our San Francisco-denying friend from El Salvador. It happens with Buddhists, Muslims, and Hindus. Our Marxist friend was ignoring the reality in front of his very eyes. Karl Marx was right about one thing: religion can be a powerfully negative tool. But so, can any ideology. Karl Marx said, "religion is the opiate of the masses." A more correct statement might have been "self-delusion is the opiate of the masses." I should have said to our friend from El Salvador, "I don't believe you are a human. You are clearly a robot. A well-constructed Marxist robot built by slaves in El Salvador, but a robot nonetheless." Of course, I didn't think to say that because I was in 5th grade and probably playing with my Greedo doll.[17]

Then there's the fact that secular, atheistic regimes of the past as well as nationalist regimes often became religions themselves; utilizing rituals, symbols, festivals, martyrs, parades, sacred locations, holy pieces of literature, and myths that were both based on celebrated true events as well as completely invented events. For instance, Mao Zedong in China was treated as a god, and everyone was required to venerate his photo daily, and carry his Little Red Book of quotations memorizing all of his sayings as if it were a Bible. Going to Tiananmen Square during the Cultural Revolution to see Chairman Mao was like going to Vatican City to see the Pope. Mao's "Long March" during the revolution was based on a historical incident, but turned into an impossibly massive, magical event. Secular saints like Che Guevara were highlighted or fictitious patriotic peasants were intentionally manufactured out of thin air to help people believe in the cause. In North Korea, their brand of state totalitarianism mirrors the Christian Trinity in that there is the Father (Kim Il Sung), the Son (Kim Jung Un), and the Spirit (*Juche*). The Nazi's primary symbol, the swastika did not originate in Germany, but rather is a symbol that was utilized heavily by Hinduism, Buddhism, and Jainism. And all of these non-religious movements had a promised religious utopia or nirvana they were aiming for: A Communist world where "the workers of the world unite," a restored Germanic Nation, Chairman Mao living on "for Ten Thousand Years," etc. Even when we try to create non-religious societies, we make them religious. Even our beloved entertainment myths

---

[17] Han Solo shot first, by the way.

Star Wars and *Harry Potter* utilize the unseen powers constantly in a religious manner. We borrow all of the religious trappings and try to create something sacred out of the material. Interesting isn't it? Things that make you go hmmm.

Atheists and strict materialists like to point out that religion is filled with manufactured symbols, saints, rituals, and infallible truths that cannot be challenged. Religious intellectuals point out that even non-religious, atheistic movements end up taking on the trappings of religion or borrowing them outright. So, why do even non-religious movements like Nazism, the Bolshevik Revolution, and even European soccer clubs start to take on so many of the trappings of religion?

I think it goes back to what our cavepeople ancestors figured out early on: The Natural World and the Supernatural World should not be divided, but rather belong together (**NW+SW= Ultimate Reality**). If something is going to have deep, true meaning for a human being, it is going to be linked to the unseen world, to the unexplainable, to a higher realm. That's just across the board whether you want to be involved in religion or not. That's how we are wired.

How Religion Critiques Itself

Liverpool is one of my favorite cities to visit in the world, and not only because I am a huge Beatles fan. It's a wonderful, vibrant city with a massively cool vibe. It's a good place to see how non-religious things can take on a religious flavor. Living in Europe, I am always impressed by the religious fervor that one finds by the supporters of football clubs. LFC (Liverpool Football Club) has their long traditions, their chants, their songs, their celebrated heroes from the past, their social clubs, their sacred day (Sunday in

England), their beautiful cathedral (Anfield), and as I saw on one of my trips, they even have their martyred saints. I found this out when I stumbled into the Liverpool Cathedral with my work colleagues while the Liverpool FC supporters were having their annual mass for those 96 people killed at the "Hillsborough Disaster." This was a moment in the 1980s when fans were crushed to death during a match. Every year a mass is held for those LFC supporters that lost their lives. Religious fervor is the only way to describe the energetic, whole-hearted fanaticism of LFC fans.

If humans are hardwired to try to combine the seen and unseen, the natural world and the supernatural world, isn't it extremely dangerous that we also seem to be easily prone to self-delusion and following dangerous mass movements?

Yes! Jim Jones, the San Francisco preacher and cult leader lived during the time that we were there. Shortly after we moved to S.F., he took his followers to Jonestown, Guyana where he led a mass suicide by 918 followers, including 304 innocent children. And then shortly after we moved to Oregon, the Rajneesh led by Osho (the cult leader formerly known as Bhagwan Shree Rajneesh) took over the town of Antelope. So basically, the moral of the story is: don't let me move to your hometown. Bad things follow.

Our propensity as human individuals to be stupid idiots who will do and believe anything for a single moment of temporary comfort, knows no bounds. Of course, religions can tap into this, but so can Facebook, Netflix, ice cream, sexuality, and every other thing imaginable. This is why Taoism emphases *Wu-wei*, meaning non-action or not going to extremes. It is also why religions spend a lot of time emphasizing concepts like dying to your ego and embracing love for the universe as in Buddhism, or not to speak untruth as in Jainism, or not harming others (*ahisma*) in Hinduism. Taoism teaches to respond to injury with kindness,

Confucius (not a religious figure) taught that one should treat others as you would want to be treated prior to Jesus, and Jesus in the New Testament is a gentle, cute, hippy figure until he confronts religious people taking things too far. That's when he goes medieval and cranks it up to eleven! He once said:

"Woe to you religious leaders and legalists. You are a bunch of hypocrites! You are constantly shutting the door of the Kingdom of Heaven in people's faces, when you yourself do not live there, nor will you let anyone else enter! Get out of here before I kick 100% of your ass! And I'm not talking about your donkey!"[18]

In fact, Jesus' critique toward religious people is so harsh, it is said that if a pastor preaches straight through the Gospel of Matthew in the New Testament of the Bible, she can expect to lose half of the church. Jesus doesn't spare the self-proclaimed "holy people."

Religions need internal critiques to prevent religious abuse and sanctimony designed to manipulate and hurt others. I love the fact that Jesus in the New Testament is always super patient with the Roman soldiers (who will later torture him and kill him), with the prostitutes, with a woman about to be publicly executed for adultery, he's even super-nice when he is dying on the cross naked, with nails in his hands and feet and is getting made fun of by a guilty criminal. He only seems to unleash a can of whoop-ass on the top religious leaders and on his own disciples when they misuse the faith that he is teaching. Check it out! Jesus completely loses patience with the religious people because they are constantly violating the whole point of true faith. That's

---

[18] That's the New Patrick Version (NPV), but you can read the original in the New International Version or any other version of the Bible. It's Matthew 23:13. I think the reason we Christians water this stuff down is because it is aimed directly at us. We only want cute and cuddly Jesus.

pretty cool and pretty profound. It's fantastic that these stories were included in the Bible instead of edited out to protect religious institutions. All those harsh words toward religious figures could have easily been cut out.

One of the reasons we hate religion so much is because we look at the wars, the disturbing rituals like female circumcision, the violent movements like ISIS, and our uncle who insists we are going to hell because we drank a glass of wine or saw a Tarantino movie. Yeah, there's a lot of stupid stuff out there, but when we look at it selectively in the comfort of our air conditioned homes, with running water and flushing toilets, it's easy to miss the other things religion brings, and why it is maybe worth the danger.

Let's go back to my cave-ancestor Ug Nachtigall. Let me remind you that Ug lived in a world filled with danger and complexity. He needed to know which plants and berries not to eat. He needed to know how the seasons affected the wild game he was hunting. And eventually his wife taught him the benefits of bathing at least once a year. In other words, for all of human history, the most important thing for humans to gather was a community that could transfer information to one another. That's what religions do so well. You may say, "Well, that was fine because back then we didn't have Google! We are not primitive idiots now. We have a wealth of information that doesn't require ancient religious codes, so bugger off Patrick!"

Actually, Google is a perfect example of the limitations of knowledge without morality and religion. We are not entirely sure of what Silicon Valley is doing to our humanity and whether it is good or bad. Remember the old joke was that a college degree in philosophy was great for "pondering the meaning of unemployment." Ha! Good one! But now as we have 24-hour surveillance, great leaps forwards in artificial intelligence, cloning, and robotics, as well as algorithms which are trying to monetize us every second of the day, it's becoming a different story. Philosophers, ethicists, and religious ideas are now a valued commodity. In other words, human wisdom that takes into account ultimate reality is necessary in this material world. Even tech corporations in Silicon Valley are figuring this out. Suddenly, the philosophy major doesn't seem so irrelevant and useless.

Karl Marx: "Religion is the Oppressor of the Patrick"

We got to know San Francisco extremely well and it is still one of my favorite places on Earth and one of my many "homes." My mother's forced family outings were deeply tied to faith. Faith that the world was beautiful. Faith that learning was a good thing. Faith that different people and ideas were also good things. And faith that it was valuable to be exposed to things outside of church and Christianity. To go see the redwoods, or visit the Japanese Gardens, or to visit some farm near Point Reyes was all a form of worship to her. Seeing beautiful things and experiencing the joys of life and nature was also worship. I had learned that church could be just a bunch of people under a tree praising God. Or it could be a drive through wine country. That freedom to view other things as worship impacted me. Nobody in church was really saying what my mother was saying back then. In fact, it was often the opposite.

In the church, there was a strong message that only Christian music could be good. Everything else was "worldly." Missing church was a sin. "Real Christians" get up at 5 AM to read their Bible while they are eating Grape Nuts. The Bible is their favorite book and has the answer to everything! Going to PG and R rated movies was wrong because of the language, violence, or sexual innuendo. Certain books were off-limits, and some were banned. The more I was exposed to American evangelical culture, the more it seemed that it had a real hatred and fear of the world. If something wasn't drenched in God-stuff and Christianity, then it was not good; and quite possibly was very dangerous to your soul. Cherry-picked scriptures were always chosen to back that idea up. A Christian had to show piety in all these outward ways to show (prove) that they had truly changed their life and were living for God. You had to watch the right movies, read the right books, and use the right spiritual language. The language was key. There was a form of talking: a "Christianese" talk that we were all expected to speak.

Evangelical Christianity often promotes a dualism that borders on the Gnostic. Gnosticism was a spiritual movement that arose in the first and second centuries that believed that all earthly matter is evil, and only the spiritual realm is good. This is actually a heretical view in traditional Christianity, but American Christianity (and the evangelical Christianity it has exported around the world), has retained this very dualistic view. Evangelical Christianity can easily become a religion where everything in the world is bad, stained, and ugly. Only things that are clearly linked to God, like the Church and the Bible, are good. It means that a lot of things should be off-limits. It may mean not reading Stephen King, not seeing *Pulp Fiction*, not listening to David Bowie, not dancing, and instead speaking Jesus talk all-day long, or at least a lot of the time. Only then are you truly "on-fire" for God. My parents thought that was weird, and so do I. Christianity is about God entering the world. American Christianity is Neo-Platonic, often wanting to just keep Heaven and Earth totally separate. But as I said in the very first chapter, the understood nature of reality is that the seen and unseen, the sacred and the profane, the material and non-material have always been understood to be connected. Most American Christians don't see how much they have been influenced by secular or gnostic thinking.[19] They think they are being extra holy, but are actually adopting a secular, scientific dualism. As Homer Simpson would say, "D'oh!"

Outward piety was something our family was really bad at. I have always carried a lot of guilt about not seeming to be a very religious person. It was only as I began to write this memoir that I realized that all four of us in my family really sucked at this. We didn't really pray before meals (or candy bars in my case), we didn't have family Bible studies, we didn't ever really use religious language, and we all listened to secular music and I even went to R rated movies with my parents. When the *Jesus Christ Superstar* movie came out in 1974, while evangelicals in the United States boycotted it and were appalled at this "sacrilegious" acid rock opera about Jesus' last week, my Dad responded by taking all the youth of the church to see it. In his opinion, we needed to be able to see truths in secular art and not run in fear.

Just as my mother didn't shy away from reading Marxist tracts and Mao Zedong's books in order to understand communist ideology even if she didn't agree with it, our family just didn't believe it was necessary to dismiss the secular world and view everything as dangerous, earthly, and a temptation. I was taught to engage the world and have confidence that my faith was not so fragile that an encounter with different belief systems and non-religious people and things would destroy me. It never did.

There would be many times, however, even up to today where I would feel judged by Christians for my music taste,

---

[19] This is a really important point and one that I flesh out in detail in my book, *In God We Trust: A Challenge to American Evangelicals*. Honestly, this footnote is not meant to be here for self-promotion purposes. This under-written about and not widely discussed "Americanization of Christianity" is one of the most important things evangelicals need to grasp and the entire focus of that book. Oh, by the way, the book prevents aging!

my books, and my lack of outward piety and "holiness." I learned early on that the evangelical church is obsessed with comparison and judgment. It's a religious system that has believers constantly measuring their own spiritual life and pious actions against that of others. It also easily promotes judgment because there are certain movies, songs, forms of dress that are acceptable or not acceptable. This conscious and subconscious monitoring of each other's actions is not something found in every religion or even in other forms of Christianity. It comes from the fact that evangelicalism demands a high level of accountability from its adherents, usually to the people of their local church. This can be a potent force for good; a positive peer pressure that can be life-changing and help people overcome life-long struggles with the help of a loving, supportive community. But the flipside is that it can also turn into a hyperactive judgementalism that is in constant monitoring mode. Many evangelical Christian communities have a hard time finding that balance.

Some forms of Christianity, like Lutheranism and Eastern Orthodoxy, can have more of a 'live and let live' attitude. And many East Asian religions like Shinto and Buddhism are not very concerned with whether other people are acting religious or not in their private lives. They are very low pressure (although a Japanese child or teenager may be very pressured by their parents to partake of annual Shinto rituals). But usually the religions that mobilize people the most, and that have the most fervor; are also going to be religions that demand a lot of conformity and ritual. This is certainly the case in the vast majority of indigenous and tribal religions that have very high expectations of conformity. Something like a male or female circumcision ritual or the scarring of the face, or the first lion hunt helps the tribe foster a unique identity, marks the member of the tribe as one of their own, demands sacrifice by the individual, and differentiates the tribe from other tribes so that they can be united in survival. In general, the more a religion demands from someone, the more religious fervor and commitment there is.

Our Human Tendency to Create Insiders and Outsiders

I did not have a lot of friends in San Francisco. I was shy at first, but eventually opened up. In 4th grade, I got into my first and only fight. Boys never forget their first fight—especially when they lose. It's imprinted in their memory forever—a stamp of male failure and impotence that survives to your deathbed.

One of the worst things religions can do, is create stark divisions between insiders and outsiders. It's something that we learn to do at an early age—irrespective of whether you are religious or not. For reasons of self-protection, survival, and selfish pride, we love to make sure we are on the "in" and others are on the "out." My first fight taught me that.

His name was Jimmy Will[20] and he was the elementary school bully. He was not particularly tall, but by 4th grade, he already had pectorals. He looked tough and brawny in his Toughskin jeans and Oakland Raiders t-shirt. He always had a mean, angry look on his face. I always kept my distance from him on the playground and was glad that he was not in my 4th grade class. I was afraid of Jimmy Will.

One day I was running at full speed across the playground next to the monkey bars and my feet got caught up in something and I tripped. Unfortunately, I had gotten tripped up with Jimmy's feet and we had both fallen hard to the

---

[20] I've changed his name to protect his reputation and because he might find me and hurt me.

ground into the playground bark. I got up and Jimmy got up. He had a sneer on his face and walked right up to me.

"What did you do that for?" he asked in a mean, tough way. He pushed my chest. "Wanna fight?" he pushed my chest again. "C'mon, do you wanna fight, you wuss?" He pushed me again and I fell off the elevated playground and onto the pavement below. A large crowd gathered around looking down at me with Jimmy's pectorals hovering over my head. I was scared and humiliated. Luckily for me, Jimmy then walked away. It was my first fight, and I hadn't even gotten a shot off.

I never forgot that. I was pretty dismayed when I got to 5th grade and learned that Jimmy was now in our class. By then, I had become more popular and the cool kids in the class were my friends and Jimmy was on the outs—a loner. I saw my opportunity for revenge so I decided to start a club that would meet at recess in one of the big trees on our elementary school playground. The club was called the IHJWC: The I-Hate-Jimmy-Will-Club. I gave everyone a title: President, Vice-President, and I even designated someone to be the Treasurer for some reason, even though we had no money. I was "the Senator." I have no idea what that meant or why I did it, but we were a real club. We spent recess climbing the tree and talking about how much we hated Jimmy Will. Constructive stuff! It was my first experience with leading a mass-movement for evil purposes by demonizing another human being! Go me!

Word got back to Jimmy and he would come to our tree and ask if he could join. He wanted to join the I Hate Jimmy Will Club! And he was Jimmy Will! Bwah! We enjoyed telling him "no." No one more so than me. I finally got my revenge.

Word also got back to our teacher Ms. Harrington, who was my favorite teacher in elementary school, and probably my favorite of all-time. She was furious and she came out one day to the tree yelling at us expressing her extreme disappointment at us and our cruelty. We couldn't just claim "fake news." We had been caught being super mean. I was horrified to have disappointed her. The IHJWC was immediately disbanded.

In hindsight, I wonder who was hurt more. Me, from having been pushed off the playground? Or Jimmy for having a whole club formed by me dedicated to expressing our hatred for him? I've definitely learned in life that words and emotional rejection are far more painful to us than physical pain. I don't like who I can become. And that is one of the reasons that I believe a life of faith is necessary. There is something in our human heart that is so quick to anger, so quick to wound people, and so willing to go to selfish places that make us lose perspective of ourselves, the people in our lives, and our own life overall.

Jimmy and I became friends and I learned more about his background. His parents were divorced, and his life had not been easy. His father was a drug-dealer and his 30-year-old mother looked just like Steven Tyler of Aerosmith does now! Jimmy had reasons to be angry. He had become a bully, but life had bullied him. Learning to see the person behind the caricatures we create is one of the most important skills we can develop as human beings. That is another thing that the Christian faith insists on: viewing everyone as God's children—no one person more or less valuable than any other person. It forces us to see the good, when all we want to do is see the bad.

More than 30 years later, I would return to Marin County and take my 5th grade son Marco to see the very tree where the I Hate Jimmy Will Club had met. I was in 5th grade at the time and now my son was in 5th grade. I wanted him to see the tree of shame and learn about the huge mistake his father made. I explained how, out of my pain and fear, I had decided to respond with anger and hate, and what a mistake that was. I told him about how throughout life we are going to have people that hurt us and our desire will almost always be to find ways to hurt them back, when we should rather try to find the source of their pain and feel compassion for them. This is not a test I regularly pass, but my hope is that my son will do better. So far, he's been far better at this than his old man.

4

Death and Suffering are Really Not Fun: How Religions Deal with the Dark Side of Life

1987 was the happiest year of my life. High school was filled with amazing friends, constant laughter, and a great church. Everything playing on the radio was fantastic and the acne was under control. And then in the last days of summer, my mother got cancer.

Do religious people have to be boring, humorless people who are prohibited from reading, singing, dancing, or doing anything that isn't expressly religious and "holy?" A lot of people seem to think so, and many religions expect very rigid standards in certain areas. But, of course, these vary by religion, sect, and even by the particular mosque, temple, church or synagogue. Jews are known for their life-affirming celebrations and Hindu celebrations can break out spontaneously on the streets of India in what look like scenes straight out of a Bollywood production. The vivacious music, vibrant color, and dancing is one of the most beautiful things about India.

While my family came from a faith tradition that can often become legalistic with lots of rules for "living a life of holiness," it was never really like that for us. It was more a matter of the heart, personal convictions, and obeying Jesus' Golden Rule. He said, "Do unto others as you would have them do unto you and share your McDonald's french fries even when they are hot."[21] In other words: my mom taught me to mind my own business. Neither she, nor I, had a lot of tolerance for adults becoming religious behavior nannies acting like the Iranian religious police who constantly check to see if Iranian Shia Muslims are breaking the law.[22] But many Christians do take it upon themselves to constantly be the morality police.

The truth is that all religions have a broad spectrum of acceptable and unacceptable behavior. There can be prescribed rituals, dress, ceremonies, dietary laws, and behaviors that must be followed and other things that must never be done, taboos. Expectations in certain Buddhist sects are very high, while in others, they are virtually non-existent. Some Muslims demand that women remain covered at all times from head to toe when outside, while Muslim women in Indonesia may hit Jakarta nightclubs dressed to kill as much as any woman in the singles hotspots of London or Paris.

The Amish Christians use a horse and buggy and usually do not believe in being hooked up to the power-grid, while other Christians are simulcasting their church services around the world on the internet every Sunday. Even issues of morality can vary significantly. Some churches think all alcohol is evil, while others use alcohol in the service in their most sacred ritual, holy communion. In my denomination, we have both sides of the spectrum. One side would be aghast at the thought of Christians drinking, while the others would have no idea why alcohol would even be an issue. And they are in the same religious branch and movement and don't always know that the other one also exists within it!

---

[21] NPV-New Patrick Version

[22] Saudi Arabia's religious police are known as the Committee for the Promotion of Virtue and the Prevention of Vice. If ever there was an organization that has super-boring New Year's Eve parties, this is it.

A Christian Sarah Silverman?

My mother was irreverent and always border-line politically incorrect. I'm glad I am not like that! She was a very funny woman. She was like Mother Teresa meets Sarah Silverman. When she was not secretly taking food to single moms, working with AIDS patients, or adopting trees in the forest, she was making inappropriate jokes, being irreverent, and straddling the border between entertaining people and being sacrilegious. The truth is that I am sure that much of my sense of humor and sensibility comes from my mother Jene. Anyone that truly knows me well, knows this is how I talk as well. But unless they knew Jene, they probably don't know the source. I think she was my hero and at an early age I imitated everything about her—except for the dressing as a woman part. That came later.

Jene loved to pull practical jokes on all of us. She would throw water on my sister from our balcony while she was getting a suntan. She would make jokes about my acne when my friends would come over, and I would tease her about her age. She once planted a *Playboy* magazine in the carry-on luggage of a traveling evangelist friend so that it would fall out when he was on the plane with his wife and cause a scandal. It worked!

Jene passed notes in church, like a teenager. She would call people on the telephone putting on a fake Russian accent and claim to be the Soviet embassy. When she learned that one of her friends had a collection of ceramic cows, Jene showed up at her birthday party with a real live calf. She had convinced a local farmer to let her borrow the animal just to pull the practical joke. My mother also dressed up as a clown and shared the stage with the Governor of Oregon. She stood behind him making faces at him behind his back during his speech. At the dinner table, she would make jokes about my mild-mannered dad having a venereal disease. This was normal stuff in my house!

She loved to tease us. Dad bore the brunt of the jokes, but she also really loved to mess with me. She had an ironic sense of humor before irony became cool in the 1980s. When I was in high school at my beloved Tigard High—when I was most conscious of being cool—I would accompany her to the grocery store, and we would inevitably end up going down different aisles and get separated. In such a public place, it was a perfect time for her to embarrass me.

"Sweet pussy willow!" she would cry out at the top of her voice! "Where are you?"

Panic would set in. I recognized that voice and wondered how many people from my high school might be in the supermarket. I would go running at full speed to find her.

"Sweet pussy! Where are you?" "Pussy willow!!"

"Mom!" I would say in an extremely stern whisper. "Will you be quiet!! You are embarrassing me! I'm here now! Stop calling for me."

She would play dumb with a little gleam in her eye.

"Chicken of the sea! Where are you??!!"

If movies were good, we would go to them—it didn't matter if they were R rated. I got to see my favorite movie of all time, *Excalibur*, four times when I was in 5th grade. It was rated R, had violence, a rape scene, and witchcraft (By the way, all of those things and much worse are in the Bible in spades!). Parents were definitely less protective in the 1980s than they are now, and back then even PG movies often had bad language, nudity, and violence before PG-13 was introduced. But I also think that my parents really valued good art and good stories and trusted us kids to be sophisticated enough to handle it. I'm so glad they did that.

That didn't mean that she was a fan of the nude scenes. She seemed to like to talk loud in the movie theatres—to be the person that annoyed everyone. As a teenager in the movie theatre with my mother, I wondered, *Is she just clueless? Does she not know how loud she is talking?*

But as an adult I realized it was all part of her own little in-joke, tormenting her kids.

We went to see the Robin Williams movie *Moscow on the Hudson* about a Russian who defects to the United States. We were all extremely fascinated by the Soviet Union and my sister was a Soviet Studies major who would end up studying in Moscow and Leningrad a year later. We always went to movies that were about global issues or world history, movies like *Gandhi* or *The Killing Fields*.

There was one particularly long nude scene in *Moscow on the Hudson* and Mom made sure to express her displeasure and embarrass us at the same time in front of the whole audience at the cinema.

As Robin Williams and Maria Conchita Alonso got *en-flagrante* in a bathtub practicing all-forms of sexual congress, my mom loudly said:

"Oh, here we go!"

The sound of *"sshhhh"* came from the audience. She didn't care.

"They have to throw in a nude scene," she said with disgust.

"Mom be quiet" I would say, dying of humiliation.

"Oh look! They have to show us her boobies!" She would say loudly.

"Mom!" My sister and I wanted to crawl into a hole and die.

"Now he has to play with her nipples. Here's the boob shot. Of course, they have to show boobs. What's the big deal about boobs? They all look the same! If you want to see boobs, come with me to the nursing home. I'll show you all the boobs you want."

"Mom!!!! Shhhhh!!!!" I was ready to commit hari-kari.

"This is how they get people to show up. Throw in a nude scene. Here we go!"

The crowd stirred some more, my face turned an appalling shade of red. It was impossible to be a teenager and enjoy a nude scene with your Mom embarrassing you in front of a couple of hundred strangers.

We continued *not* to listen to any kind of Christian music in our home. My father always played trumpet at church, but in his private time he preferred Herb Alpert and the Tijuana Brass, the sounds of Glenn Miller and Tommy Dorsey, and *Muzak* versions of the Beatles and The Carpenters. My sister was into many things including Queen, Boston, Kansas, U2's *War* album and I co-opted a lot of her musical tastes and inherited her albums. It was hell when she went into her *Urban Cowboy* phase. My life was all about The Police, Duran Duran, Wham!, Journey, David Bowie, Roxy Music, Frankie Goes to Hollywood, Culture Club, Prince, Michael Jackson, A-ha and lots of other far more obscure '80s Brit pop bands and artists. My Mom mostly listened to my music. She particularly liked Terence Trent D'Arby and his funky James Brown-like sound and George Michael. She would dance in front of me. It was very cute.

She absolutely hated the Bee Gees and Rod Stewart. Her embarrassing comments would soon follow:

"Look at how tight their pants are!"

"Mom!"

"They want everyone to see what's in their pants! They are saying, 'look at my pee pee!'"

"Mom!"

"They all have capped teeth! Look at those capped teeth. And they have falsettos and sing like girls!" Then she would imitate the Bee Gees distinctive breathy falsettos. She would have my sister and I laughing hysterically. She despised them. I loved them. Still do.

My mother and I were incredibly close. We rarely fought and loved to hang out together. There was one subject that would lead us to absolute knock-down, drag-out fights: the television show M*A*S*H.

Mom insisted that the show was funnier in the second half of the series run when Harry Morgan joined the cast as Colonel Potter. I was adamant that the show was much funnier in the early years when McLean Stevenson played Lt. Colonel Henry Blake. We went back and forth on this serious issue and it was nearly a fight to the death.

The point of all of this is that with a mom like mine, it never occurred to me until junior high school that being a Christian meant that you had to have a "G-rated" sense of humor, that non-Christian music was bad, that only certain films were good to see and that good Christians were people with very bland artistic tastes. Safe, white-washed Christian movies, Christian rock songs with unrealistically triumphant lyrics, and books and stories that promise a happy ending where God solves every little problem were common in American evangelical culture. I knew my mom was a Christian not because she cited Scripture every five minutes or sang hymns while she cleaned the house. I knew she was a Christian because she was always helping people—and making them laugh!

But as I became a teenager, I became more exposed to American Christianity's Manichean thinking about the world: you are either on one side or the other; a creature of God or a creature of the world. It was a form of religion that I would never be able to fit in, even though I would try.

We moved to Portland, Oregon in 1982. Leaving San Francisco was a complete and total drag. The reason we left was because of a measure called "Proposition 13" which was gutting the Marin County school system. All sorts of music, sports, and art programs were going to be slashed and schools would close and merge. My parents wanted us to settle somewhere with good schools. My sister had graduated from Redwood High School and I had finished elementary, so they moved us to the Tigard school district where I attended both Fowler and Twality junior high schools.

We had driven through Portland once before in 1980 and found it to be rainy, dreary, and frighteningly woodsy. It looked like the kind of place that was full of smelly paper mills and nothing else, a far cry from the gorgeous scenery of Marin County and the Bay Area. We were not excited. Portland was so far off-the-radar then.

But Portland was about to experience a massive renaissance. Nike, Intel, Tektronix and many other companies were going to completely change the city's landscape. A film industry was going to grow, it would turn into a land of microbreweries, coffee houses and bookstores. The beautifully managed downtown would be a model for the rest of the country of how to keep the center of town relevant and exciting. By the time I graduated from Tigard High School it would be the most livable city in the United States and 10 years later it would be an expensive, hip city with a global reputation. It would also be where I would find my best lifelong friends.

Junior high school was a disaster. I was the second shortest kid in 7th grade and shared my locker with a Vietnamese kid who was *the* shortest kid in the school, although he seemed to not care. Neither of us had friends and it took me until November to learn how to open my locker. I had to carry all my books around or meet my locker partner/only friend to get into my locker. I had a callous and a permanent Band-Aid on my finger. There was some bullying at Fowler Junior High School, and I was atrocious in every single class. Every minute of the day I would be playing albums in my head from start to finish. Mornings started with chocolate milk, I ate no lunch as I preferred to hide in the library and read *Business Week*, and then a big chocolate milk and cookies, crackers, or a chocolate bar awaited me when I got home. I was thrilled when I was moved to Twality Junior High because there I could be miserable and depressed without being bullied. It was also there that I picked up my first three life-long friends: Mike, Alan, and Scott. They would be the first of many Tigard friends that I would keep for life and that would become my extended family.

While I had very few friends in junior high school, at church it was a different story. Once I went into the doors of the Tigard Church of God, I was the most confident kid in the world. There was acceptance there. I was valued, I had friends, and the adults were like protective aunts and uncles. I had a double life: total loser at junior high and a happy confident kid in church.

My mother knew that I was pretty traumatized in junior high. I had always felt special and confident in school. Suddenly in junior high I was a "nobody" in a school of 800 kids—all cooler than me. Maybe that's everyone's junior high experience, but we don't know that as kids. And it is amazing how once you are a nerd, you never really quite get over it. Mom continued to work the graveyard shift in Oregon so that she could be there when I got home. It was true. I really needed her in those years. The graveyard shift was brutal and is horrible for your health, but she never complained. She continued to work at a convalescent hospital until she switched to the state insane asylum—Dammash State Hospital—more politely known as a psychiatric institution, and one of the locations where the movie *One Flew Over the Cuckoo's Nest* was filmed in 1975.

Jene was no evil Nurse Ratched. She worked on the violent ward—the most dangerous part of the hospital and did it with her customary smile and sense of humor. The things that would happen on the violent ward were pretty horrific. She rarely shared any details, but what she did share stuck in our minds forever.

One Thanksgiving she brought home some of her mentally insane patients to our house for dinner. It was certainly the most awkward Thanksgiving dinner ever. "George Washington" told us all about how he crossed the Delaware River while a woman with blue teeth talked gibberish about her child ostrich. My mom was utterly unphased, of course. "It's no different than being with you guys," she would tell my dad and me.

Mom had been abandoned by her mother. She grew up in a farm in Kentucky with two younger sisters and her father. One day her mother just walked out and left, leaving Jene to be the mom of the house. They moved to Cincinnati and she raised her sisters. She had to become very responsible at an early age and it showed. Underneath all the humor was a very serious woman who had known loss, had learned to serve others ahead of herself, and knew how to care for everyone that crossed her path—no matter their race, ethnicity, sexual orientation, political orientation or nationality. She went to Anderson College where she met my father—part of the Beatles-like "Trumpet Trio" that rocked the campus between 1955 and 1959.

My dad was one of the three good looking guys in the trio. She thought he was stuck up. She ran for Homecoming Queen and lost by one vote. Harry forgot to vote. She married him anyway.

Now I can see how Mom's early abandonment by her own mother must have played into our relationship—two abandoned children trying to find a family. Jene's one big fear was going insane. She always said that she hoped she would die before she ever lost her mind. I suspect mental illness might have run in her family and her work exposed her to the worst conditions of the human mind. It's also probably no accident she went into the mental health field. We often try to reconcile our past by reliving it in a more positive way. The former drug-user becomes a drug counselor, the traumatized child grows up to be a therapist, and the victim of tragedy becomes an activist to prevent those types of tragedies. This is how we humans end up acting out our deepest felt needs. Religions at their best, encourage people to rise above past traumas and reinvent their story. And one of the key reasons we have to ask ourselves if suffering has a purpose, is because so many people have gone on to be positive forces in the world after enduring a painful and traumatic life experience. Nothing breaks our hearts for others like having our own hearts broken.

Tigard High School was amazing. The complete opposite of my junior high experience. My life was better than *Ferris Bueller's Day Off*. I found many friends who would end up being my lifelong tribe. About a third of them were Christian and the others were not. They were all equally fantastic, funny, smart, and taught me a lot. They opened my world up intellectually and artistically. My parents' gamble had paid off. Tigard High School was a wonderful place with an abundance of smart kids, excellent sports teams, and a top-notch theatre program. It was an incredibly talented class of people who have all gone on to do extremely well. And nobody was funnier than my crew. Caleb, Peter, Andy, and I were often inseparable spending just about every day together: the fab four, better known as *"the Nürdz."* Josh, Howie, John, Eric, and Greg joined us in our ironic, comedic merriment over the years. Mike, Alan, and Scott were part of "the Comedy Club." Alicia was the queen Empress of Nürdica. Diana, Stephanie, Mary, Jami, and Shelby were *the Nürdz's* female counterparts. And it seemed that it was three years of non-stop laughing, high school hi-jinx, and occasionally, schoolwork. *"I just remember my sides always hurting from laughing so hard,"* my friend Caleb said to me once as we walked along the Santa Monica Pier in Los Angeles, 21 years later, reminiscing about those great days. Nobody made me laugh harder than Caleb who showed up at our graduation rehearsal dressed as an Arab sheik for absolutely no reason at all.

Have you ever felt that life was too perfect? That you were a little too happy, so some tragedy must be on its way? That's how I felt the summer before my senior year. I always had a feeling that one of my parents would die while I was young. I had always thought it would be my father. I felt that it was a premonition, but it was probably just my own abandonment issues and the fact that dad had suffered a stroke in Costa Rica. But I always had a sneaking suspicion that the bottom would one day fall out and my days of happiness would be over. That would prove to be the case.

The summer of 1987 was unusually sunny, and I spent every day that summer with Caleb, Andy, and Pete. We were constantly playing baseball, basketball, going to record stores, and trying to find girls. Everything was a joke and life was one big competition to see who could come up with the best one-liner or act out the most comical thing. I put thousands of miles on my parent's rust-colored 1985 Chevrolet Cavalier—putting that car through absolute torture with my unnecessarily reckless driving. I never appreciated the way my parents gave me so much access to the car. I utterly destroyed it; one of the many things I wish I could apologize for now.

One day after having spent the day with the *Nürdz*, I drove back home in the late afternoon and my sister Marcel was in the driveway with a strange look on her face. It was the look of bad news. I got out of the car and she said, "Pat, did you hear? Mom has cancer."

My very first thought was, *I knew it.*

My second thought was: *She's going to die. There's zero chance I get to keep my mother.*

At first, Mom and Dad were relatively hopeful. Cancer treatment was not as good as it is now—which is still not nearly good enough. Mom would need to have a mastectomy. Being my mother, she decided to throw a "Farewell Boob Party," *at church*! Everyone had to show up to the party with something made out of half of a brassiere. As usual, Mom made a joke and kept everyone laughing. She lived to bring others joy.

She put on a brave face. We all did. We all acted like she would beat cancer—even though I never really believed it. My response was to just try to never think about it. Eventually, she would go through chemotherapy, throw up, and be mortified as clumps of her hair would fall out.

She continued to work hard, do the graveyard shift without complaints, and I kept on living my selfish life— trying to avoid thinking about what could possibly happen. Rarely did I let reality fester in my mind for very long. Winter of my senior year, I went to see the movie *Beaches* featuring Bette Midler with Kelly, a very nice girl I was dating, and another girl. I didn't know that the movie would have a tragic end and I certainly wasn't prepared for the emotional punch of the closing song "Did You Ever Know That You Are My Hero?" When the movie finished, I went silent, tried to drive everyone home, and absolutely exploded into massive sobbing. The movie had penetrated my little safe bubble of denial.

I had a couple of other outbursts in those final months of high school. My Mom had decided to let a foster child live with us. She told me this as we were driving across Tigard after school and I absolutely freaked out.

"How can you do that to me! I'm only going to be home a few more months! And now I have to share my house and my family with someone I don't even know!" I was hysterical and sobbing hard. My mother gave me a funny look—as though she knew something far deeper was happening, and then she said, "Okay, we won't." Poor foster child who needed love. My selfishness won out. The girl didn't get to share our home. That could have been the best thing to ever happen to her, to live under the same roof with my amazing parents.

One day I showed up at my friend Pete's house sobbing my head off. Both of us were mourning the end of high school realizing that our tribe was going to be broken up in June. I didn't realize it, but I was also mourning my mother and the separation that would happen when I left home to go to college 2,300 miles away in Indiana.

High school came to a glorious end and our family celebrated with champagne because I was never taught that alcohol sends you automatically to hell. My sister and I celebrated my graduation by going to Costa Rica—which she paid for by selling her beloved MG car. And that August my mother dropped me off at college.

I chose Anderson University because it had a travel program called Tri-S which enabled students to travel all around the world for very discounted prices. It's something I ended up not taking advantage of even once. My parents had met there and the mission agency for the Church of God was located across the street. I thought I would put in my four years and get shipped off to Japan or China. Lifelong dream accomplished!

Saying goodbye, however, was not easy. My mom and I had a moment when my mother dropped me off at college for the last time before she flew home. Her voice broke and she said: "I don't think I can do this." I was annoyed. "Mom! Yes, you can!"

But now that I am a parent I understand. I also wonder if she thought she might die while I was away at college, or if my going to college so far away would mean that our days together were now extremely limited. I didn't catch on to any of this, of course, caught up in my own little world as I was.

She pulled herself together and ribbed me one last time. As I walked toward the dormitory with my first two college friends, Mom yelled out the car window:

"Honey! I packed your underwear! You have new underwear! I got you underwear!"

My new college friends laughed at me. Mission accomplished.

I was ready to take college by storm. My triumphant journey to China and the world would begin here and total domination would ensue.

I lasted a mere 16 weeks and I was done. Midwestern evangelical culture was a complete shock to my system. I felt like I had nothing in common with the people who claimed to be of the same religion as me. It was partially true, and partially sanctimonious. It was the analysis of a naïve and immature 17-year-old. I returned back to Oregon utterly miserable. My dream of being a missionary seemed over and my mom was dying.

The Problem of Evil and Suffering

Why is there suffering in the world? And how can a loving God or any gods that are good allow death and cruelty to be such a big part of human existence—especially if they created everything. This is a question that has haunted humanity since the first caveman got a hangnail. Gottfried Wilhelm Leibniz (1646-1716) was a German philosopher and mathematician during the time of the Holy Roman Empire (which, as has often been pointed out, was neither holy, Roman, nor an empire). This man, who wore a wig that made him look like Brian May of Queen, dealt with an issue called "theodicy:" If God is so good, wise, and all-powerful, then why does he allow evil, suffering, and Korean boy bands?

Many theories have been proposed by world religions. They have taken this question extremely seriously and each religion has entire libraries of books dedicated to the subject. There are not flippant answers and summing up all of this in a few paragraphs is difficult, but there are some important different general approaches that we can examine.

For many in tribal religions, the answer was that angry gods dominated the heavens and human beings need to be punished and forced to behave. For Buddhists, it is that all suffering and even all of life is an illusion. The goal then is withdrawal from the world in order to extinguish desire so that you feel no more pain. And for many Christians, it is an issue of free-will. In other words, God does not impose his goodness on humans, but allows them to decide for themselves. Our bad decisions can lead to suffering and death, but they can also lead us toward becoming faithful and better people. There's also the idea that true goodness can only be understood, valued and appreciated if it can be juxtaposed against evil—or at least against bad television sitcoms.

As we look deeper, we can say that for the most part, Hinduism and other Asian faiths are not that interested in figuring out who exactly or what exactly started this beautiful but also messed up world and why there is so much suffering. Finding the answer is viewed as theoretical and a waste of time but learning to deal with it is not.

Hinduism, Jainism, and Buddhism blame suffering on the ignorant actions of finite beings as they go through the process of life, death, and rebirth. Despite the very non-western and non-scientific view of creation, God, and suffering, Hinduism does not blame God. God's essential nature is perfect intelligence and bliss. It's possible to find portions of Hindu teaching that grant creatures freedom and offer a promise of final bliss. The ultimate source, Brahman, gets off the hook. Nevertheless, the bottom line for Hinduism is that people are dominated by their greed, their desire for wealth, physical pleasure, and their need to get a ton of likes on Facebook. Hindu scriptures—*the Vedas, the Brahmanas*, and the *Upanishads* teach that suffering is the essence of the universe as it is filled with killing and being killed. Hindu rituals act this out. At one Hindu temple I visited in Kolkata (Calcutta), India, I stood in the temple surrounded by Hindus as a black goat was brought into the cement square, where I was standing. In one fell swoop, the goat's head was cut off, his horns hit the cement with a thud and the goat's blood sprayed up on my socks. This is our universe of conflict and we must accept it.

The toughest pill to swallow is that when we see an infant killed in a bombing, or a child molested, or a woman raped—under the Hindu system this is *karma*. It is deserved for sins in a previous life.

Buddhism, which originated from Hinduism, also blames suffering on humanity's negative actions and negative state of mind, but not on the self because there is no self. The whole individual "self" thing is an illusion, as many modern-day atheists argue. Instead what we are is part of everything else and interconnected to the whole universe. Once we realize that we are part of everything, then we will no longer step on ants or kill mosquitos because we see that they are part of what we are, and we are them. Ideally, this helps

Buddhists avoid contributing to the suffering and mass delusion. The only way to truly escape suffering is to detach to such a degree that you become awakened as the Buddha was. If you reach the bliss of *Nirvana*, that allows you to break the cycle of birth, death, and re-birth that Hinduism keeps one trapped in forever. For me, there are a few things tough to swallow here as well.

First of all, the bombed baby, the molested child, and the raped woman are getting what they deserve from their life's previous *karma?* Those people may be hurt, and you may feel hurt by them—but ultimately, they all deserve it (and you deserve the pain you feel about your painful life experiences). However, your pain also comes from failing to realize that there really is no baby, child, or woman. Since there's no self, there's no real reason to feel pain about any of it. For most of us, it's a difficult thing to accept that our beloved child or even our faithful dog are not real enough for us to cry over if they are being tortured, maimed or killed. Not only is that level of detachment difficult, but most of us (on the deepest level that we can possibly feel), do not want to completely detach from our loved ones. Quite the opposite. We deeply feel fundamentally violated when we are forced apart from our dearest loved ones.

When the Buddha attained enlightenment, he was able to completely detach from everything to such an extent that he announced that he would never be reincarnated. He had escaped the cycle of reincarnation that bound all Hindus. But why would the Buddha want to do that? Isn't that in itself a desire? If everything is one, shouldn't he still be one with all the crappy stuff that he is supposedly leaving behind? What is the difference between those crappy things and the Buddha himself? Is he just super self-aware and conscious enough of illusion to escape? Sounds good. But we are not supposed to believe there is a self at all, so how can we reach or even have self-awareness?

Back to the hypothetically bombed dead baby, the molested child and raped woman who all deserved it—they are not really selves so we shouldn't really feel bad about it. Even classifying them as a baby, a child, and a woman is an illusion. They are all just part of everything. So really, there is no suffering at all. Sounds awesome, except that's not how any of us feel on a regular basis. The suffering we feel is about the most real feeling and concrete encounter with reality that we have in our lives. Most of you are suffering through this book I wrote.

Judaism and Suffering

The monotheistic faiths that believe in one comprehensive God who has a more intimate and proactive relationship with humanity (Judaism, Islam and Christianity), tackle the subject of suffering more aggressively since their God demands a lot of adherents and communities of faith. Consequently, the personality of this God and why he allows suffering becomes a pretty big deal.

All three faiths born in the Near East (today's Iraq, Saudi Arabia, and Israel), are different from the religions of the Far East and the Indian subcontinent in that they believe God wants to be known and participates in history. This is different from the gods of Taoism, Hinduism, and Zoroastrianism that are either remote, unknowable, or beyond appearing much in our temporal realm. Neither does this go along with the thoughts of Epicurus who believed there was no divine providence and that everything that happens, simply happens by chance. Nor does monotheistic thought agree with Aristotle who believed divine providence only extended to immutable aspects of nature, including the celestial stars, and the nature of animals (for survival) and humans (for rational thought). Actual individual involvement in the affairs of human beings is non-existent, according to him.

The monotheistic religions greatly disagreed. Christianity moved the farthest from this previous religious thought by arguing that the historical Jesus Christ was God in the flesh, participating in our temporal world to such an extent that he was born in poverty, was a refugee, was a blue-collar workman, and was unlawfully convicted of a crime and sentenced to death by an empire and uppity religious people. Jesus is portrayed more as a character in a Bruce Springsteen song than an all-powerful Great Gatsby. Furthermore, this modesty, suffering, and injustice suffered by Jesus was for a specific reason: solidarity with humanity's suffering that moves to salvation and restoration of the whole universe. This is quite the radical move in comparison to Epicurus, Aristotle and all other religions of the Far East. It's either patently absurd or deeply poetic; or both.

What does Judaism say? It's important to remember that the books of Jewish law (the *Torah* or *Tanakh*) are books— plural. Each book may take a different angle on the issue of suffering. Proverbs is filled with promises of good overcoming evil, Jeremiah is sad about the suffering and feels that full resolution will come with a new creation and covenant, and the book of Ecclesiastes appears to have been written by Eeyore of Winnie the Pooh: "All is vanity and everything sucks," says the wisest man who ever lived. Ecclesiastes has a very Far Eastern sensibility about it, but with a Jewish twist.

In addition to the variety of voices in the book, there is also the oral *Torah* that developed while the Jews were in Babylonian exile. More Jewish law and tradition emerged in the 5th century with the *Talmud* which consists of the *Mishnah* and the *Gemara*. On top of all this are centuries of brilliant rabbis and thinkers like the great Maimonides (1135 - 1204 AD) who believed that man's intellect is the mechanism YHWH has given us in order to know God, the universe, and ourselves. This is the purpose of life and the key to understanding why things happen. The more we know through our intellect, the more we will avoid suffering because we will accrue wisdom about how to avoid the painful things of life. Like St. Augustine of Hippo (the greatest Christian thinker in history), Maimonides believed that evil does not really exist, but is the absence of goodness. Some bad things occur in nature (like earthquakes, getting hit by lightning), then there are human evils like greed, violence, and intentional oppression of others (because of illusions of the mind like the ones Buddha talked about), and then human evils that are self-inflicted and are our own stupid fault (like deciding to run a red light and hitting an ice-cream truck and decapitating yourself). Ultimately, Maimonides feels that suffering helps the universe in the long run.

Probably the greatest piece of literature on the issue of why bad things happen to good people is the Jewish book of Job. It's an incredibly sophisticated piece of art that reads like a play. It's filled with irony, paradox, and very intentional phrasing and word choices (which are often lost in the English translations). Briefly: a skeptical figure shows up identified as "Satan" and talks to YHWH (God) and tells the Almighty that he has been walking around the Earth checking things out. And YHWH asks him, "Have you seen my awesome servant Job. He is the nicest guy in the world, and he is extremely moral and just an all-around upstanding guy." Cynical Satan says, "Well of course, he owns a cattle ranch, he vacations in the south of France, he shops at Hermes, he has seven hunky sons and super-hot daughters and he owns Google stock! Of course, he is good and raves about what a good God you are! But if you took all of that stuff away, he would not want to have a relationship with you. Take it all away and he will curse you and hate you!"

So, God takes up this challenge. The next thing you know, Job's cattle are poisoned by bad farming chemicals, his Google stock tanks, and his children are all together watching the Seahawks play when a tornado hits and wipes them all out. Job is emotionally devastated but remains faithful to God: "I was born buck-naked and that's how I will leave." But then his friends show up and start giving him different reasons why all this suffering has occurred. His first friend Eliphaz says it's because bad things happen to people that do bad things. Clearly Job was looking at goat porn or something and God rightfully punished him. Although, the book of Job tells us that's not true. Job was good. Job's response, however, is full of self-pity and amounts to "Life sucks, God is a meanie, and I'm screwed." Job's second friend, Bildad, shows up and really rains on the parade. "Dude, there is no way you didn't do some awful thing God is punishing you for. He is great to people who are good, and he just royally messed up your life, so you are guilty as sin."

Job turns into a Deist. "It's true God created things and is infinitely powerful, but he is nowhere to be found. He has no time for little peons like me, so I'm screwed. He is distant, far gone, and just doesn't care. Why the heck was I even born?"

Then Job's next friend Zophar shows up. "Well, you have a lot of nerve challenging God, you evil man. Turn yourself into the authorities and there is hope."

Job then responds with more sarcasm: "Oh, you guys are so brilliant and helpful! Thanks a lot! The bottom line is that God is all-powerful, and he does things like giving us droughts, tearing down kingdoms, humiliating godly people, and he likes to create light and then takes it away. If only God would let me present my case with Johnny Cochran as my lawyer, I would prove my innocence. Get in the ring, God!" He's kind of bitter.

Job's friends return and continue to rag on him for a few more chapters. They continue to argue that bad people suffer. Job starts to point out that it's not true that all bad people suffer! "Have you met a U.S. politician? A Russian oligarch? Don Corleone? Bad people have good things happen to them all the time!" Job's friends are not impressed and continue droning on, making the same argument and are joined by a sanctimonious know-it-all named Elihu.

Finally, toward the end of this drama, God shows up and doesn't answer the question as to why there is suffering. Instead he says:

"Hey Job? Where were you when the Grand Canyon formed? What hurricanes are forming now? How did you make a caterpillar turn into a butterfly? What's your take on nanotechnology or physics? Do you even know what that is? How about quantum physics? Why do things exist that defy gravity and what then holds them together? Why did George Lucas make *The Phantom Menace*, and why does it suck so bad? You don't know these things, right? That's because you are in no position to even understand the things I do and what my ultimate plan is. I care about you, but you can't see across the universe or create it. So, there's a lot about our relationship together that you will never understand, kind of like a two-year-old child who can't understand why his parents make the decisions they do and how selflessly they love him. I am with you; that's all you need to know and have the capacity to know. You had the most important thing, though—faith. Got it kid?"

Then God adds, "Hey Job. By the way, your friends are wrong, and they're jerks. But I'll let it pass."

At that point, Job feels a bit stupid, admits he doesn't know much, and forgives his friends. Then God gives him

Google stock and Amazon stock. He gets an even bigger ranch, Seahawks season tickets, and seven even more hunky sons and three even hotter daughters.

The Jewish rabbis in the Talmud and Midrash refer to *yissurin*: sufferings and afflictions that have a purpose and that offer redemption when we accept it. Suffering has a purpose that while difficult to understand, has the capacity to bring compassion, wisdom, and a better knowledge of God, ourselves, and our relationship to God.

Christianity and Suffering

Christianity puts the suffering question at the very forefront by making the entire climax of the Christian story a grisly, Roman crucifixion. Instead of denying that suffering exists, or that we are simply to detach from it, the four Gospels of the New Testament give four different brutal descriptions of a totally innocent Jesus of Nazareth getting his back flayed open, his skull cut with large thorns, and nails going directly into his feet and wrists. The graphic description is no accident. It's as if to say: "I get it. The pain is real." There's even some emotional abuse at Jesus' end when he gets jeered at, and even made fun of by a guilty criminal on the cross next to him.

"Hey, innocent crucified guy! You're a fraud and you suck!" says the guilty thief on the cross next to Jesus.

Seriously, it's a pretty inglorious moment for an incarnated God, as he hangs naked on a cross and sits, yes sits, on a spike! Crucifixions were even worse than we think.

Jesus makes it clear that bad things will happen in the world. He runs across people who are born with birth defects, he lives under Roman occupation, he most likely lost his father, Joseph, at an early age. And of course, his own disciples often don't understand him or make stupid mistakes. What Jesus seems to promise is that God has entered into human history to share in that suffering with the purpose of one day ushering in a new world, free of suffering. His resurrection on the third day after crucifixion then becomes a historical and symbolic event that suggests pain, suffering, and evil will be overcome. In the meantime, much like Job, Jesus presents our connection to God as being one that is intimate and has an ultimate purpose and direction. Portions of our suffering can be redeemed now, while other portions await a universal redemption. But it will be redeemed.

Later, his follower St. Paul (the first missionary) elaborates on that idea and suggests in a classic of literature, the Letter to the Romans, that "the sufferings we now endure bear no comparison with the splendor, as yet unrevealed, which is in store for us." He goes on to say, "the created universe waits with eager expectation" and that God is with us as evidenced by the historical presence of Jesus. Paul acknowledges that life is filled with suffering but argues that none of this can separate us from God, nor is it going to win in the end. That argument is found in my mother's favorite chapter, Romans 8. Whenever I was feeling down, she would always say, "Read Romans 8!"

Suffering in Islam

Islam teaches that the God of the Jews and the God of the Christians is its God too. Muslims believe, however, that those religions have distorted views of God. Jewish prophets, Moses, and Jesus are all honored in the *Quran*, but only Muhammed as God's final prophet was able to bring clarity about God. Islam also criticized and eradicated the polytheism of the Arab tribes. Its attitude was that monotheism had become extremely heretical and paganism was equally as bad, consequently it all had to be re-established by force.

Islam also has a long history of literature which deals with the issue of suffering, including the *Quran* and the *Hadith*— oral collections of the Prophet's many sayings. But Islam leans more toward the fatalism of the Far East. Allah is beyond reproach and not to be questioned. Everything happens because it is the will of Allah. *"If God wills it,"* is a phrase that you hear constantly in Arabic and in Middle Eastern countries. You also hear it a lot amongst Latin American evangelicals. The message that "God is in control," is very strong in Islam and the expectation of personally understanding God (as with Christians), or the vital necessity of arguing with the text (as in Judaism) is far less expected.

Human free will is less emphasized and there is also a stronger sense, unlike in Job or with the words of Jesus, that sin is always punished and so it's logical to believe that bad things happen to bad people. But that's not the whole story. The *Quran* and other Islamic literature also make it clear that humans have the duty to give to charity and care for others to lessen suffering. The writings of al-Ghāzalī or Ibn Taymiyya elaborate on themes of the relationship between Allah and free will, and the *Quran* cautions against the idea that all bad things are the result of punishment. Overall, the *Hadith* presents a God who does oversee everything and where bad things are often deserved. It's a mixed bag.

Living La Vida Crappy

So why is there human suffering and why do bad things happen to good people? I'm not going to lie—most answers to this question suck. But I will return to that later in this book. By 1989, my wonderful high school days were over, my best friends had all scattered and moved on to other things, my much anticipated move to college was an expensive failure, and I was thousands of miles from my denomination's mission agency and my dream of getting to

China. I was in my McJobs phase delivering pizzas, packing environmentally friendly kitty litter, and completely lost.

Mom had her mastectomy and we celebrated that the cancer was gone. Maybe things would get back to normal and I could get my groove back with Stella, or at least with Jene. Mom worried about my future. We still had our great friendship, although she wasn't crazy about my long hair and dangling earring that I had picked up in college. With so much free time, I would accompany her to places sometimes. I remember one day her forcing me to go visit a farm in Hillsboro, Oregon. Why? No reason. Just because the world is beautiful.

I was grouchy on that drive. I didn't want to go. I didn't even like rural places, had no idea how farms work, and hated most, but not all, country music. Nevertheless, I went.

As we drove, Mom asked me, "Do you think I'm going to die?"

Yes, I thought to myself. "No," I responded. "I think you will be around for a long time. You will outlive your two sisters. They are less healthy than you! They are the ones I worry about," I replied. The truth is I was scared to death.

Mom picked some random farm and asked some farmer if we could look at the animals. I reluctantly followed her. We walked into an animal pen and goats began nipping at my knees. It tickled and I laughed. It was amazing how a little bit of nature could break through the darkness.

I enrolled at Portland State University, a state school of mostly commuter students and an incredibly large population of Iranians. I called it "Persian State University." With most of my friends gone, me at a loss for what to study, and working dead-end jobs that would never get me anywhere near China, I contemplated a life in radio. I loved music. Maybe I should be a DJ. Of course, I have the world's worst voice for a DJ, but I didn't know that. Mom looked into a broadcast training program, but I made no moves.

I was still subsisting on chocolate milk, Ritz crackers, pancakes, candy bars and other ridiculously, sugary foods. I had added french fries to my palate which was an incredible victory. Finally, at the age of 19, I could go to a McDonald's and sort of look like I fit in—even though McDonald's hamburgers still looked like animal roadkill to me—which of course they actually are.

The Adventist Hospital in Portland had opened a program for young people with eating disorders. In the wake of Karen Carpenter's tragic death from anorexia, bulimia and anorexia were on the radar. I was scared of being sent off to an eating camp, but also very tired of being the only idiot in the world who wanted to live in China and was afraid of a piece of rice.

We went and visited the doctors. I was excited. It would be like summer camp, except they would force me to eat terrible things like vegetables, fruits, and meat. But they would fix me. I wasn't ready, but I was.

In the end, the doctors rejected me. "He doesn't have an eating disorder." They were probably right. I had a phobia, but they didn't explain that.

We then tried hypnosis. I was excited about that. Even though I was "knocked out" for the therapy sessions, I did feel a bit better when I returned to consciousness. Unfortunately, it only lasted three sessions because it was so expensive. I continued to get Christmas cards from the shrink for years.

And then Mom's cancer came back. It was no longer just breast cancer; it spread into the lymph-nodes and was headed for her lungs.

5

Power and Judgment at Calvary Temple: Why Religions Keep People Out

After leaving college early, from 1989 to 1991, I spent 2 years of my life training to be a pastor in a fundamentalist, charismatic church. The church changed me—in some ways, not for the better. This is that story.

Make no mistake about it, churches not only have the power to heal, they also have the power to hurt people—leaving them with wounds that can last a lifetime—and which can run as deep as those caused by divorce or parental rejection. For some Christians, "certainty" is their real religion, not the Bible nor Jesus. If anything threatens their certainty that they are right and possess the truth, they go on the attack and take no prisoners.

His name was "Three-Fingered Gary." That was not his real name—it was the name I secretly gave him after I met him for the first time. Pastor Gary had extended his hand with such force to shake mine that I was taken aback to see that he only had three fingers. It can be a bit awkward to shake the hand of someone that is missing fingers. There is the strong sense that one shouldn't make a big deal out of it, yet the mere fact that you have to think about your reaction makes the situation unnatural, like the feeling of soft skin pressing against you where fingers should be clasping on to you. Gary[23] was the pastor of a brand-new church plant. A church-plant is a church that is started by a bigger church. They send out a pastor and maybe some other volunteers from the church to begin a new church. This church was so new that the first time I showed up with my friend Rob, we made up half the congregation. The other two young fellows in the church were two sharp twenty-something businessmen that had recently graduated from a nearby college where they were players on the basketball team. Both of them looked the way we felt, unsure of what we had gotten ourselves into by showing up at this small church—Calvary Temple—which did not even have a building. We were, in fact, meeting in a conference room at a local budget motel.

Three-Fingered Gary actually had seven fingers. Gary, a handsome all-American looking young man of twenty-three years had brown hair, a bowl-haircut, and deep blue eyes. Raised a Catholic, he had been a star athlete at a local high school, and had become a rebel involved in drugs, alcohol, girls, and skipping school. In his late teens, Gary encountered Jesus Christ and his life was changed immediately. Saved by a church belonging to the New Creation Fellowship of Churches, Gary married his high school sweetheart, and committed himself to becoming a pastor.

By trade, Gary was a carpenter—just like Jesus. One of the men in his church operated a carpentry shop and employed men from the various NCFC congregations. Once Gary was saved, he found himself in a new job surrounded by men of God who were raising him up to one day become a pastor of his own congregation. By all accounts, Gary was an outstanding student of the Bible. He fell passionately in love with the Bible and had boundless energy for street

---

[23] All the names of the people in this chapter have been changed.

evangelism. Gary, who must have been quite an imposing figure on the football field, now had a Jesus-like countenance about him, but carried all the energy of a linebacker charging against the offense as he carried his sermons to people on the streets. Gary was aggressive about sharing his faith, but his bright smile, warm eyes, and jovial disposition disarmed people who otherwise might be hostile. He radiated niceness and positivity. Gary's zeal was infectious and inspirational.

How did Gary lose his three fingers? It happened at the carpentry shop one day while cutting wood. His hand slipped and three of his fingers were sawed off. As the story goes, blood spurted everywhere, and his fellow mates rushed to call 911. When the paramedics arrived a few minutes later they did not find a man screaming in pain. Neither was he in shock. Instead, Gary spent the entire time preaching to the paramedics about how they needed Jesus Christ in their hearts. He didn't care about his missing fingers, which if lost would forever alter his life, he just wanted them to know Jesus.

It didn't end there. Once they arrived at the hospital, the entire time that Gary was on the stretcher he was talking about Jesus to the people in the hospital. When the doctors attempted to put the gas mask on him to anesthetize him, he kept taking it off as he desperately begged the doctor to accept Jesus as his Lord and Savior. He was tenacious. And now a few short years later, Three-Fingered Gary was starting his church in a motel room and we were amongst the first congregants.

I do not know how the two yuppie ex-basketball players stumbled upon this new church, but I do know how Rob and I found it. We were both exiting a supermarket and heading toward Rob's car. As we approached the car, I saw a blue flyer in the middle of the parking lot. For some bizarre reason, I felt compelled to go look at it. Covered in mud and slightly torn, I was still able to read what it said:

> "The End of the World is Coming! Are you Ready?
> Come see a movie about what the Bible says about the End of the World"
> Calvary Temple
> Room 240
> Cascade Inn

Both Rob and I grew up in Christian homes and loved movies. I think we were also fascinated by the writings of people like Hal Lindsay, a Christian "prophet" whose predictions about the end of the world had to keep changing because Jesus was super late to his own after-party. At the time, we thought that there might be something to the predictions that the world was going to end soon and thought that at the very least, it would be something interesting to do.

I was nineteen years old and still reeling from the classic, naïve assumption that my Christian university would be filled with committed Christians who would be funny, interesting, and Christ-like twenty-four hours a day. When that illusion was shattered, I couldn't cope, threw in the towel, and said goodbye to a much bragged-about four-year dream of having the best college experience ever. I was humiliated and felt burned by Christian institutions. I even left my home church in Tigard, Oregon, although they did nothing wrong.

Some angry teenage rebels smoke pot, burn bras, and steal cars. I switched churches.

As a young, idealistic Christian, I became convinced that my Church of God faith was not representative of the Christianity that Jesus had intended. Our faith was dead, I believed, and what I needed to find was a church that "believed in God's power and took it seriously." In hindsight,

I can see that my college experience had left me wounded and that now I was projecting my anger on to the Church of God movement as a whole. It was a form of retribution. As I looked at the flyer, I thought, *perhaps this is a church where they take God seriously.*

After we introduced ourselves, the movie on the End Times started. It was atrocious. The acting was horrific, the dialogue wooden, and the simplistic eschatology ran counter to my Church of God theology which teaches that we do not know when the end will come nor should we be that concerned about it. After ninety long minutes, the film ended, and Rob and I gave each other knowing looks agreeing that the film was terrible. I'm sure that Brian and Craig, the sophisticated yuppies watching with us felt the same way. Three-Fingered Gary turned his chair so that he was facing the four of us. Next to him sat his adorable two-year-old son Matthew and his lovely wife Jenny. Gary then shared with us about the Gospel and asked us if we wanted to accept Christ. All of us bowed and prayed. That following Sunday all of us returned and Three-Fingered Gary officially became my pastor.

A New Church Home

The church grew quickly. Within a couple of weeks, we had twenty people in the service. We attended the Sunday service at the Cascade Inn conference room and went to Wednesday night Bible Study at Gary's apartment located in a low-income complex not far from the Inn. Brian and Craig, the yuppies, lived in the same apartment complex but eventually moved into a house. They soon brought their third roommate Chad—another sharp, corporate-looking guy. The yuppies invited a few of their friends who also looked like the kind of people that would not be following a plain-speaking, uneducated pastor a couple of years younger than them.

Nevertheless, they continued to show up and soon began changing their lives. The things they watched on TV, the way they spoke, the way they responded to things—all of it changed dramatically, filtered through the Word of God. I marveled at the transformation.

Pastor Gary's transformation must have been even more dramatic. Despite being only twenty-three years old, he had the demeanor of someone in his late thirties or early forties. Gary exuded confidence and was utterly devoid of self-consciousness about his disabled hand or his radical Christian faith. With his smile and overwhelmingly positive spirit, we all felt that Gary was a man in possession of the Truth.

Gary quickly taught us that it was important to go door-to-door, "witnessing." If we loved Jesus, then we needed to hit the streets and invite people to church. We were given flyers and spent our Saturday mornings and afternoons knocking on doors. Each team of two was assigned an apartment complex where we would try to engage people in conversation or leave a flyer. We would explain to them that we were from a new church called Calvary Temple and that they were welcome to attend our services at the Cascade Inn. It was awkward and not at all my style to go ringing people's doors and ask them "Have you accepted Jesus Christ?" It seemed to be what Mormons or Jehovah's Witnesses do—not what us 'normal' Christians do. But I had wanted a church that took the power of God seriously so here I was following a man who was preaching just that very thing.

My partner Craig was one of the yuppies. Although I was about four or five years younger than him, we soon hit it off. All of the young men were funny, cool, and hip. It kind of amazed me that they would be willing to do something as "uncool" as going door-to-door. But they did—at least in the beginning.

On one of our first visits together, Craig and I ran into a co-worker of his in one of the apartments. Her name was Allison and she was a young, single mother of twenty-three years. As we shared about Jesus and Calvary Temple with her, I could tell that Allison had a little crush on Craig. Consequently, I wasn't surprised when Allison showed up with her little daughter the very next Sunday. Allison was of a poorer class economically. It was obvious that just making ends meet was difficult for her and probably had been all of her short life. Shortly afterward, her father, who obviously had spent a lot of time doing things that had not gotten him far in life—joined the church. Allison's sister, also a single mother, joined the church as well. They all accepted Christ.

Brian also had a co-worker with a crush on him despite their twenty-year age difference, a forty-five-year-old divorcee named Kitty. Chad, the third yuppie roommate, brought his girlfriend, and soon we were a church of mostly twenty-something young people.

There were two key exceptions: Lamar, an African American man who had been a Pentecostal pastor in the past, and his wife Yolanda and their three young children. They always came to church immaculately dressed while the rest of us dressed more casually. Last, there was a brand-new convert named Randy. Randy and his wife Lindsay were cocaine addicts who also dropped acid frequently. Randy had played football in high school with Gary but had accepted Jesus after Three-Fingered Gary confronted him, and then Randy made an instant turnaround. Now he too was in the church, arms raised, and praising Jesus with as much exuberance as Pastor Gary.

That became the core of our church. An unlikely crew to be sure, but from that group the church would eventually grow to about fifty or more.

Pastor Gary was not a dynamic speaker. It was actually hard to tell his messages apart. They usually were about how great and powerful God is and how terrible Satan is. It was delivered in the style of Southern Pentecostal preaching. It would have looked very familiar to anyone from that background or from an African American church:

"He is the Alpha and Omega!"

"Amen!" Lamar and his family would cry out with claps, hoots and hollers.

"We glorify him!"

"Yes!"

"We magnify him!"

"C'mon preach it!"

"We praise him!"

"Hallelujah!"

"We need him!"

"Oh, thank you Jesus!"

"And Satan we're going to stomp on you!"

"We rebuke you!"

"And every knee shall bow, and every tongue confess that Jesus Christ is Lord."

And on it went. It was simple, but oddly very inspirational. We all followed Lamar's lead and let loose. Before long we were all Pentecostals, our hands in the air, our inhibitions gone. The sermons didn't have much meat, but we felt the power of God like never before. At the very least, we were all emotionally uninhibited like never before.

All of us became more committed. Some of us even took an extra step. Pastor Gary asked us one day if any of us wanted to go into training to become pastors just as he had done a few years back. We would be watched closely and within three to five years we would be sent out to plant a church. Two of us raised our hands: Randy, the former cocaine addict, and me. Now we would be even more connected to Pastor Gary.

Pastor Gary would often get up and pray before work from 5:30 AM to 7:00 AM and we were to do the same. This I hated. I've never been a morning person and don't even feel that I can think that clearly at that time of day. I often joke that I don't believe in God until after 10:00 AM. Nevertheless, I did it and castigated myself for not having better concentration like Gary who was always bright-eyed and full of energy and enthusiasm for the Lord's work early in the morning. I wanted to load a high-powered rifle, kill innocent people, adjust my pillow, and go back to bed.

We were also put to work setting up the speakers, microphones, and chairs in the Cascade Inn. Randy and I started doing the work we had seen Pastor Gary do, including cleaning the toilets. Pastor Gary told us, "If you want to get to do the big things, then you need to be willing to do the little things." It was a great lesson I never forgot.

In addition to door-to-door preaching, once a month we were asked to do street preaching. That meant finding a busy street corner or parking lot and preaching the Gospel of Jesus Christ into a microphone while someone else held the speaker. The first time I did it was at Tualatin, Oregon's big summer fair—the Crawfish festival. The thought of being seen by friends was frightening. Worse yet for me was the fact that we preached that everyone that did not accept Jesus would go to hell. I had a more nuanced belief of this theologically and had never felt that this was really the best way to reach people. Nevertheless, we were told to do as Pastor Gary did and Gary was bold. "Are you ashamed of the Gospel, Patrick?" I asked myself. "The Bible says that if we are ashamed of him, he will be ashamed of us." Peer pressure, the threat of damnation, and lots of shaming was never far away. Despite my hesitation, I did it because I felt like this was the true power of God and that to follow Jesus meant denying oneself—certainly one's pride.

I watched the other preachers from the New Creation Fellowship Churches that had come in support of Three-Fingered Gary and his church plant. Each one took the microphone and preached a quick fire and brimstone sermon. Eventually, they passed the microphone to me. It was my turn to publicly humiliate myself for Jesus, catch people's attention, and assure them that they were on the brink of eternal damnation. Fun!

"Folks, it's great that you are out here having a celebration and enjoying this beautiful day. But things are changing in our community. This used to be a country that took God seriously (not really true). We were a religious people. We were a people that cared about the things God cared about! I'm-a-telling-you that there's a day when none of this will matter and it will all disappear! We have to go back to God before he turns his back on us!" I shudder as I remember my simplistic take on U.S. religious history, but that's what I believed at the time. Any good student of U.S religious history knows that secularism, enlightenment-thinking, and low-church attendance have consistently been a hallmark of American identity and religious practice. But at the time, I assumed life prior to 1960 was like *Little House on the Prairie.*

I handed the microphone off to another pastor. He looked at the other pastors and pointed at me and said, "We've got a preacher here!" That affirmation felt good. I always loved theatre in high school. Maybe this is what I was supposed to do? None of the people from our very secular city in the Northwest joined our church that day. But I felt happy that I had overcome my inhibitions and my more nuanced, intellectual approach—which certainly must squelch the work of God in my life, right?

Religion Forcing People In and Keeping People Out

Christianity, Judaism, and Islam—the Three Monotheistic faiths—have high expectations about understandings of God. There is one God and that is indisputable. Of those three religions, two of them are very much "missionary religions." While Judaism does allow for conversion, it is not just a religion but an ethnic identity. One is Jewish if your mother was Jewish. In Islam, the world is divided between *Dar al-Isam* and *Dar al-Harb*, the world inhabited by Muslims and the world inhabited by non-Muslims. Purifying the world, initially by force in the Arabian Peninsula and beyond, was Mohammed's mission. Jesus gave his disciples a command to go into all the world and preach the gospel to all of creation. Saint Paul and his other disciples began the process of taking the message of Jesus in every direction from Jerusalem.

Eastern faiths do not have as much of a missionary/conversion impetus. Buddhism comes the closest and it was Buddhist missionaries who spread the religion from the Indus Valley into China where the Mahayana form of Buddhism is dominant. And even Zen Buddhism sects can make the effort to transport their form of Buddhism to places like Southern California or Berlin, Germany. But for the most part there is not really the expectation that the Taoist believer will go around trying to convert people to believing in the Tao. Religious beliefs and rituals are cultural issues or private habits. That's not to say that these less missionary populated faiths are always completely tolerant and not pushy about their beliefs. Hindu fundamentalists are incredibly intolerant, and Buddhists are not only killing Muslims in Myanmar right now, but some Buddhists sects have gone after each other violently over differences, as happened in South Korea when I lived there.

This mandate to convert people is what has led both Christianity and Islam to be viewed as imperialistic religions. Both religions have a long history of trying to subjugate people, taking over territories, and making their faith the dominant one. While the original Christian movement was very much one that spread non-violently in the shadow of empire and grew by the power of its unified communities and inspirational message; once Christianity acquired political power and wealth after the conversion of Constantine, the militaristic expansion of Christianity became a real thing.

But Islam, which came out of the Arabian Peninsula was militant and empire-minded from the start. Muhammed successfully disbanded the old tribal order—which was itself very violent; and Islam acquired land so quickly that it borrowed from the Byzantine and Persian empire systems to run its newly conquered territories.[24]

By the late 15th century, European "Christian nations" were on the brink of colonizing enormous portions of Asia, Africa, North America and Latin America "in the name of Christ."

Islam had conquered significant portions of Southern Europe, and when the Portuguese and Spanish empires liberated themselves, they had the audacity under the Pope's direction to divide the world for conquest with Portugal taking the east and Spain the west with the Treaty of Tordesillas (1494).

What followed was not much different than what the Muslims had done in Central Asia, North Africa, and southern Europe centuries before. Cortez converted the Aztecs, Pizarro converted the Inca, and the Portuguese went to Brazil and began importing slaves from places in Africa, like Angola. In some cases, the Muslim colonizers were even

---

[24] See Chapter 5 "Islam, Violence, and Territorial Expansion," in my book *Facing Islam Without Fear* for further information on this subject.

more civil than Christian colonizers. At the same time, Christians from the very beginning, men like Bartolomé de las Casas (1484-1566), and William Wilberforce (1759-1833) were early pioneers of the fight against slavery and genocide. My colleagues in Europe today are the Christian descendants of these believers that fought against human trafficking.

The point is that missionaries trying to shove the Bible down people's throats is a real thing with an ugly history. Calvary Temple's approach to sharing Jesus was far more aggressive and hostile than I was comfortable with. They didn't see it that way. As far as they were concerned, they were offering people salvation, not enslaving them on plantations in the name of Jesus. True, but you can also wield words and judgment as a weapon against people. What my parents had modeled to me was that actions were more convincing than just words. The old saying, *"Nobody cares how much you know, until they know how much you care,"* has always seemed very true to me.

No Questions or Doubt Allowed

Once a month, we had a week-long joint service with all the New Creation Fellowship churches in the Portland area. All of us crammed into a supermarket that had been turned into the New Creation Church in a town located twenty minutes away from our Cascade Inn. Pastors from throughout the region would come to preach each evening for a week. The sermons would be full of emotion as each pastor tried to outdo the other. Some were very repetitive while others had a real gift for getting us all excited. In addition to the sermons, there were calls for repentance, times for healing, and lots of speaking in tongues. Speaking in tongues, or *glossolalia,* is a supernatural moment when a Christian is praying and begins speaking in a language unknown to them. Many Christian churches do not believe in the public practice of speaking in tongues, but "charismatic" churches and people do. I grew up in a home that did not practice that at all. I'd never heard of such a thing. But at Calvary Temple, it happened often. Foreign languages would come out of people's mouths as they prayed. Inevitably, there were also moments of prophecy when someone—often the pastor—would have a specific message from God for a member in the congregation.

The head of this mother church for the Portland area was a man named Bill Block.

Bill Block looked every bit the part of the regional chieftain. He was, in fact, a frightening figure to me. He looked like a five-star general who spoke about spiritual warfare the way George Patton might speak about traditional warfare. Bill Block was a one-man Satan smashing machine. With his strong jaw, erect posture, and no-nonsense approach, when Block started preaching you had the sense that he could look into your soul and find any residue of secret sin.

The stories of Bill Block were legion. "One day in the Philippines," I was told by an awed congregant, "Block was preaching a sermon on a hill. Suddenly gunfire erupted all around him. Block didn't even move an inch. He just kept preaching the Word of God." It was a story reminiscent of the scene in *Apocalypse Now* where Robert Duvall's Pattonesque Colonel arrives by helicopter into a war zone in Vietnam and shows no reaction to the fact bombs are erupting all around him. "I love the smell of Napalm in the morning" he famously says as he surveys the damage. This was more like Pastor Block saying, "I love the sight of exorcising demons in the morning."

Another story we learned was that Bill Block was preaching on a street one day and a man came up to him cursing Bill and his God. The man then dropped dead right on the street. "You don't blaspheme the Lord or his servants," I was told. I believed it. I was scared and in awe of the man. I myself told someone around this time, "If Pastor Gary and Pastor Bill told me to jump off a cliff, I would do it." I meant it. Saying something like that is never a good sign (see Chapter 3)!

On one occasion, Bill Block came up to me, the young new apprentice, and said in his serious, intimidating tone, "I want to see how strong you are." He led me to the wooden pulpit at the front of the church while all the other men were watching and he said, "I want you to hit this pulpit with your fist as hard as you can." Without hesitation I clenched my fist and brought it down on that pulpit as hard as I possibly could. Immediately, the pulpit split in two. I feared for my life. Block looked at me with his eyes as wide as saucers and then let out a huge laugh. "Look at what he did! He broke the pulpit! I was only kidding!" How was I supposed to know? I was a believer through and through and ready to obey these men of God.

As the church grew, I fell into a pattern of work in and around the church. I often picked people up for church and dropped them off after the service. I cleaned the church and set up for the service moving chairs, hooking up cords, testing microphones. Mornings were spent on my knees and at the conference room before I headed off to work—exhausted before the day had even started. I attended every Bible study, every meeting at the mother church, and of course went door-to-door as well as preached on the street. We all brought friends and family and they were usually impressed with the exciting spirit of our worship services. It seemed that God was very near.

Satan also seemed very close to us. We were always "binding him" and casting him out and commanding him to leave. Occasionally an exorcism would take place, and someone would lie on the ground writhing around until the demon left them. I always found it frightening and wondered if demons lived inside of me. This was not something that I had grown up around in the Latin American, African American, or Anglo church.

Sometimes miracles would occur. Someone with the flu would suddenly feel better. Sore legs and knees were healed. People started to get "slain in the Spirit," meaning that one of the Fellowship pastors or Three-Fingered Gary would touch someone's forehead and they would fall to the floor. It was the kind of thing you saw at a Benny Hinn revival on television. Most fascinating to me were the prophecies that would be given to individuals. The pastor would have a private message for you that would be about something only God could possibly know. It was like seeing a fortune-teller. It only happened to me twice. The first time it happened to me I was thrilled.

A group of us were standing in the front of the church as a visiting Fellowship pastor prayed over us. When he got to me, he said that he had a prophecy for me. At the time, I still harbored that great dream that I had had ever since I was a small child—that I would get to travel all over the world and be a missionary. When the guest preacher touched my head and began speaking in tongues, he shared the prophecy, "Your heart's desire will come true, Patrick. You will go unto the nations of the world and be a missionary." I was flabbergasted and ecstatic. How could a stranger that had just arrived from out of town have possibly known that the two great dreams of mine were to travel all over the world and be a missionary? I took this as the word of God and indeed, in the years following, it did come true at a rapid pace. By the time of this writing, I have traveled to 80 countries and a large portion of those I have visited countless times. My life would one day be spent primarily on airplanes and airports on six continents to a ridiculous degree. But at that time, it seemed pretty impossible.

Three-Fingered Gary and I spent a lot of time together as we visited people in the hospital or people who were considering coming to our church. Gary talked and I watched and learned. Gary was a very good man. It was obvious he loved the Lord and I never saw him do anything that struck me as wrong. I had questions about the theology and structure of the church, but never any sense that Gary was anything but a real, sincere Christian. While Bill Block seemed totally unapproachable and intimidating, Gary was always all smiles, encouraging to me and showing me the ropes.

We had our fair share of adventures. On one occasion we decided to go street preaching in the parking lot of a large K-mart. Randy (the other guy being mentored), and I manned the speaker as Gary preached at the top of his lungs calling everyone to repentance. The manager of the K-mart was furious and came out yelling. He began to threaten us physically and we started running. Of course, Three-Fingered Gary didn't break a sweat nor did he stop his preaching. After all, he was the man who had tried to get the paramedics to repent as his three severed fingers lay on the ground covered in blood. The manager gave chase. It must have been a hilarious sight to see this preacher running and yelling scripture into a microphone while his two assistants followed behind him carrying a speaker and cords while dodging cars and the angry manager. Those were moments where I felt like we must have been really great Christians because we were being threatened and ridiculed for our faith. This was the bold, *real* Christianity that I had been looking for—or so I thought.

The first time I began to question Calvary Temple occurred in a Bible Study. We were told that one day all of us

Christians would be "raptured"—taken up into the clouds to meet Jesus. Meanwhile, the rest of the sinners would have to live on Earth where the anti-Christ would make everyone's life miserable. It was a last chance to gain salvation for the sinner.

I had a problem with this concept. At the time I did not know that these dispensational ideas came from J.N. Darby in the 19th century and were not part of classic orthodox Christianity as it had been understood for centuries since the time of Christ. All I knew is that it just didn't resonate with me. Why would God spare us suffering when Jesus, the Apostles, and so many other Christians throughout history had to endure it? It just didn't seem, well...Christian. When I raised that objection, I was told to accept it, period. Discussions and questions were not allowed at Calvary Temple.

This had happened to me in the Church of God as well. As a young, inquisitive teenager, I one day asked one of my Sunday School teachers if the story of Adam and Eve in Genesis was supposed to be taken literally. That seemed like a perfectly reasonable question considering that this story has many strange, possibly non-literal things such as a talking snake for instance. My teacher reprimanded me immediately. "I don't know why you would even bother to read the Bible if you don't take that story literally. You might as well stop reading it now." Discussions were not allowed, and I was hurt. It's also not the correct answer. The Bible is, in fact, filled with different types of literature, different genres, and uses allegory, symbolism, hyperbole, comedy, and many other ways of conveying larger points. In fact, the ancients were more sophisticated than we think. When they used symbols and metaphors that wasn't because the religion was made up. It was because the story they were telling was so true that the only way to convey that truth was in metaphor. In other words, it's because the message is so important that religions turn toward symbols, rituals, metaphors and allegory. The failure of people (particularly Christians) to understand this has caused infinite amounts of problems in sharing the Christian message and would create a huge unnecessary clash with the scientific rational mind.

Another time, I was blatantly encouraged to drop out of college. After my disillusioning experience at a Christian university, I was still going to Persian State University, and hanging on by a thread. I was never able to truly enjoy the experience as I was still nursing wounds from the fact that I would not have the collegiate experience I had desperately wanted and that my parents—particularly my mother—expected of me.

The New Creation Fellowship crew had the answer. They told me that, "Everything you need to know is in the Bible. Education just weakens your faith." Apparently, they had never heard of the intellectual giants Augustine, Aquinas, Calvin, Jonathan Edwards, or the fact that Oxford, Cambridge, Harvard, Yale and the University of Paris were all founded by Christians that believed the life of faith and knowledge were complimentary—not hostile to each other. Oxford's motto is still, "The Lord is my Light," the University of Paris began in medieval times out of Notre Dame Cathedral. Educated and knowledge-seeking monks and Christian religious orders surrounded Cambridge and Oxford—both Christian institutions. Yale was started in 1701 to train pastors because Harvard's Christian training was not up to their standards anymore.

Dismissing education and college so flippantly didn't seem right to me, but the Fellowship pastors explained to me that education was a bad thing overall. "People go to seminaries and they no longer believe in the Bible. It's a waste of your time. All you need is the Bible." While it's true that today some secular universities and many Christian institutions have a pretty strong bias against Christianity and even western civilization as a whole sometimes, this seemed pretty extreme and simplistic. But having decided that I wanted to be a Fellowship pastor, I listened intently as they told me about the unimportance of education.

I had been raised in a home, however, that deeply valued education. Both my sister and father had advanced degrees and my mother was a registered nurse who preached the importance of education. I wasn't so sure that the Fellowship pastors were right about education, but I also knew that I was miserable in college. In the end, I decided to drop out of college altogether.

I'll never forget the day I told my mother. She was back to battling cancer and one of the things that gave her great joy was my college education.

"I'm not going to college anymore," I told her flatly one day in our TV room.

"What?" She asked with a look of total shock.

"I already dropped out. I didn't enroll in third semester," I said smugly.

My mother was crestfallen. We had a screaming match followed by her weeping and telling me how much she had desired to see me get an education. It's a moment that haunts me to this day. I can still see her crying in the doorway. I can only hope that there are enough windows in heaven that she was able to see that I did indeed complete my college education and that learning became very important to me in the end. I would eventually go back to college, get an advanced degree, and get both invited and accepted into PhD programs, but Mom would see none of that; and my strongest memory is of me breaking her heart into a million pieces by telling her that I was finished with education. I can still hear her shaking voice like it happened an hour ago.

Despite the fact I had given up on my education, I still harbored doubts about what the Fellowship was teaching us. It seemed, for instance, that Randy the former cocaine addict turned junior pastor, was getting to do a lot of things I was not getting to do. While I continued to set up chairs and clean toilets, Randy was getting to lead the offering. Pretty soon, Randy was getting time behind the pulpit. Randy seemed to be turning into Gary's right-hand man. I understood that Gary and Randy had been friends long before I entered the picture, but I was under the assumption that now as pastors being mentored, Randy and I were equals. We had started at the same time, but Randy was getting promoted every month to higher, more important jobs. I wasn't jealous, just mystified.

It was my mother who pointed this out. She had resigned herself to the fact that I would not be going to college and that my life was now temporarily in the hands of the leaders of Calvary Temple. That must have been so hard on my parents.

"Why does Randy get promoted all the time, but you don't?" She asked one day.

"I don't know," I replied genuinely unsure of what was happening.

I began to ask myself the question, "What is Randy doing that I'm not doing?" I was raised in a Christian home and already showed some ability to teach and speak quite well. Everyone in the church seemed to trust me and I did all that I was told. Meanwhile, Randy was a new Christian that was just coming off of a serious drug addiction. How was he able to rise up the ranks so quickly?

Soon it became crystal clear. With Randy, every word out of his mouth was "Praise Jesus!" When theological questions came up, Randy never asked questions and swallowed everything whole. Randy, like Gary, was constantly "witnessing" to people on the street whether they wanted to hear him or not. Randy, in other words, was a lot like Gary and the indomitable Bill Block. This kind of aggressiveness in evangelism never suited my style. I preferred relational evangelism and pure friendship with no strings attached, but these things were not valued and indeed I began to believe that my preference for the quieter way of belief was a sign of my lack of faith. But there was one other key difference that stood out amongst all the others: Randy spoke in tongues.

The New Creation Fellowship churches taught that speaking in tongues is evidence that a person has received the Holy Spirit. Without tongues, one could not be sure that one had truly accepted Jesus Christ. This ran contrary to my Church of God teachings, but it is at the heart of Pentecostal belief. All of the leaders in the Fellowship had this gift and I figured that it must be one I needed to have as well.

There were times when the whole church was lined up in front of the pastor and he would be speaking in tongues. The yuppies, Allison and her father, and Lamar and his family, all found themselves up there speaking some unknown language. The pastors put their hands on us and in that moment expected us to start speaking a foreign tongue. "Just say the words, whatever comes to your head," they would tell us. Soon I found myself mimicking the sounds that I heard all around me. I knew I was faking it, but also wondered if this is the way you get the gift—by having faith.

Everyone seemed satisfied that they had received it, but I always walked away mystified. Why was I never slain in the Spirit? Why did I never feel anything? Why were my prayers unanswered? And most puzzling of all, why did everyone's foreign tongue sound exactly alike. I was familiar with the sounds of many languages and spoke two at the time. Why did these tongue languages always sound exactly the same? "Roto—shee-maaba—laa-kooo-looo-roto—shee-maaba! Yabba Dabba Doo!"

That was the sound that I heard over and over and it was the sound I mimicked. How come no one was speaking French or Spanish or Swahili or Bengali? Of course, it was possible that we were all speaking an ancient language like Aramaic, but I remained suspicious.[25]

There was now a growing group of us that had not gotten the gift of tongues. Allison, Kitty and I all were committed Christians who loved the church, and yet were not seeing the gift of tongues given to us by God. We were puzzled. "It will come," the church leadership told us, but as time went on, it was increasingly clear that this was not acceptable to them.

We thought we loved God. We worked hard for the church and we gave money, but we were not turning out like they wanted—like Randy. Even the yuppies were speaking in tongues now.

---

[25] I am not suggesting that I do not believe in the gift of *glossolalia* (speaking in tongues). I do believe the Spirit enables certain people to do that. I do not, however, believe that this is evidence of one's belief in Jesus Christ. A neurological study done at the University of Pennsylvania which involved taking images of the brains of people speaking in tongues revealed that their frontal lobes—the willful thinking part of the brain as well as the speech centers of the brain were quiet as they spoke in tongues. This seemed to suggest to the scientists that they were not forcing themselves to speak in tongues. Indeed, it was unclear what part of the brain was causing this to happen—if any. *The New York Times* article which reported the findings found in the journal *Psychiatric Research*, also mentioned studies that showed that people who speak in tongues rarely suffer from mental problems and are likely to be more stable than those that do not. http://www.nytimes.com/2006/11/07/health/07brain.html?em&ex=11630 48400&en=b763140e4ca628a9&ei=5087%0A

And we tithed. We were taught that "you can't out-give God" and that we should give as much money as possible. I didn't have much money, but I tried to give what I could. Randy's brother and his pregnant wife began attending and they too started to tithe upon becoming saved. Before long, this couple who lived in a trailer park gave every dime they had to Calvary Temple, giving with sincere love for Jesus but also the expectation that a big financial windfall was coming their way. I watched as the months progressed, the baby was born, and they found themselves totally broke. Not blessed by God?

Before long, I could sense that the leadership was beginning to have their doubts about me. One day while going door-to-door, we met two young middle school kids: "Mouth" and Ryder. Mouth was a short, drug using kid from a broken home who wore a black leather jacket and had a huge chip on his shoulder. We called those kinds of kids "stoners" back in my day. Ryder was his taller sidekick—a more genteel boy—who followed the highly verbal "Mouth" everywhere he went. They were a middle school Tom and Jerry, or perhaps a drug-using Pinky and the Brain. We invited them to church and much to my surprise, they showed up. Mouth, who truly was a smart-mouth and proud of it—came into church full of swagger and was as much of an intimidating presence as someone 5 foot 3 can possibly muster. Ryder just followed along.

They didn't seem to accept Jesus, but they sure stayed close to the church. I quickly befriended them and the two of them and their other young hoodlum friends took a liking to me. They started calling me "Pastor P." Unlike the others, I never pressed them to make a decision for Christ. I mainly talked to them, gave them rides home, and tried to befriend them. They seemed to like that, but I could tell that the Fellowship leaders did not.

One Sunday Mouth came in talking too loudly. Despite the fact that Gary was preaching, Mouth continued talking throughout the service. Eventually, Randy and a couple of others marched to the back of the conference room and threatened Mouth harshly. "Either be quiet or get out!" Mouth looked shocked and hurt, but quickly put his rebel mask on and left and never came back. Neither did Ryder. While keeping control of worship is important, even at my young age, I wondered why the church leaders couldn't see that Mouth was just a little kid in pain, probably rebelling to reassert himself after having allowed himself to become too vulnerable in our church.

One day as we were driving to yet another weeklong meeting of Fellowship churches, Pastor Gary turned around and looked at me sitting in the backseat.

"Your problem," he said, "is that you have a spirit of rebellion in you."

I was puzzled and didn't know how to respond.

"That's why you sympathize with Ryder and Mouth. It's because the spirit of rebellion that they have has now been transferred onto you."

I was cut to the quick. My hero, Three-Fingered Gary, had just told me that I was demon possessed. What did this mean? It meant that despite my hard efforts, Satan still had a hold of me. There were demons inside of me! I was evil! I was possessed!! It also meant I was disappointing my mentor. Words can't describe how scary and painful it was to be told by an admired pastor that you are an evil person that is against God. I was stunned. And I had another even more shocking thought, *what if Pastor Gary is wrong and they are just lacking in love?*

The Final Act

My mother's battle with cancer was not going well. Despite the fact that I believed in miraculous healings—and believed that they could happen at any time if a Christian would only believe—my mother was not getting better. I prayed and prayed and prayed some more. At night she would call for me when she felt herself slipping. She would tell my father Harry, "Go get Patrick! Have him pray for me!" Dad would come upstairs and wake me up in the middle of the night. "Mom's calling for you." Now, decades later, I realized she was suffering anxiety attacks, but I would rush down to her room and bind Satan in the name of Jesus trying to do what Bill Block and Three-Fingered Gary had done with others. It was amazing. As soon as I would show up, she would get calm and quickly fall asleep. I also resented it. I resented being woken up in the middle of the night, but on a deeper level, I resented that this was happening—that my Mom was dying. I could pray to make her anxiety go away, but the cancer never left.

Why was the healing not happening? What was wrong with my faith? Pastor Gary answered my question one day when he informed me that my mother had cancer because she wore a piece of Mayan jewelry around her neck. Since my mother and father had been missionaries in Central America and that was the best time of their life, my mother developed a fondness for pre-Columbian art. There was one piece in particular, a gold Mayan eagle that she always wore around her neck. Upon seeing that, Three-fingered Gary let me know in no uncertain terms that her cancer was being caused by "the golden idol around her neck."

"Mother, you have to take that necklace off!" I told her upon learning the news that she was getting cancer from her unwitting idolatry.

"Why?" She asked me.

"Because it's giving you cancer! It's an idol and God hates idols."

"I'm not taking it off," she replied emphatically.

"Why?" I asked wondering how she could not if she considered herself a Christian.

"Because my God is bigger than that! My God is bigger than this piece of metal."

I didn't quite understand that response, yet I did. She seemed to be saying that her God would never judge her or give her cancer simply because she liked a piece of jewelry. Her God would take her whole person and her whole heart into account. Her God would not be so legalistic as to dismiss all of her faith in Him and all of her works and then withhold his grace on the basis of something as trivial as wearing a Central American souvenir around her neck. I understood, but I still wondered why she wasn't being healed.

"Patrick," she said to me, "one day you'll outgrow Calvary Temple."

I acted as though I was offended when she said that, but the reality is that deep down I hoped she was right.

As time went on, I sensed I was not fitting in at church and was increasingly wondering if I would ever fit in. *Perhaps I am not a Christian, or not meant to be religious, or just not a good person capable of doing the right thing,* I thought to myself regularly. It seemed more and more clear I was disappointing my church leaders. One day, as we were witnessing on the street, I realized that it was a hopeless case.

On that particular day, Randy and I were paired together and we went to Tualatin's city park on a beautiful, hot, sunny day—where in happier, carefree days I had played basketball with Andy, Caleb, Pete, John and Erik; pretending to be the Hispanic Air Jordan: "Air Paco." At Calvary Temple, there was a staggering amount of unfunny or joyless moments in my life. I missed my high school friends and the way I felt when I was with them. So many were not religious, yet I had so much more in common with them than with Randy and everyone in my church. Why?

Randy hit the people in the city park like a bull in a china shop. I mainly stood beside him and carried the fliers. We went into a Pizza Hut during the lunch rush to confront people about their belief or lack of belief in Jesus, but the managers asked us to leave. I was relieved. I still didn't eat pizza, or hardly anything normal, although I had graduated to peanut butter and jelly sandwiches (but not with jam or seeds)! As we got kicked out of Pizza Hut, Randy was increasingly frustrated.

The park had a covered area where people could have picnics. Randy spotted a group that was sitting down preparing to eat a meal. "Let's go tell them about Jesus," he said. Every word out of his mouth was "Jesus this" and "Jesus that." I found it utterly nauseating. Further proof that I must really be a heathen headed straight for hell one day.

I realize now, decades later, that part of it was that I enjoy talking about other things than religion: music, science, sports, economics, movies, celebrity gossip, politics, history, etc. And over and over, I found myself with people who seemed to only be able to talk about Christianity, and occasionally sports. It wasn't really hating Jesus as much as it was that I was starved for some artistic and intellectual stimulation.

As we got to the covered area, it was clear that this was a group of mostly very small children and their mothers. It was the birthday party for a child of three years of age. They were all clearly having a good time. Randy was beginning to talk to one of the mothers and was asking if he could have a few minutes of their time to share Jesus Christ.

She seemed hesitant. I pulled him aside.

"Randy, this is a little kid's birthday party. Maybe we shouldn't do this here."

"Why?" he replied, "You don't think little kids need Jesus?"

"No, it's not that. I just think maybe it's better for them to just focus on their children right now."

Randy gave the woman a smile and walked away. He was furious, barked at me and said, "You come here now! Follow me!"

He took me away from the covered area and behind some bushes. "God, I hate working with you! I hate being partnered with you! I told Gary not to do that! Not to put me with you! You always bring me down! You never want to share Jesus! I ought to wring your neck. I ought to break your neck in two! I swear, I just want to.... I should just pound you!"

I was stunned.

"This is what I'm going to do," he continued. "I'm going to get in my truck and drive away. You're not coming with me. You can find your own way home. And I'm going to call Gary and tell him what you did!"

In a rage, he got in his car and shouted out the window at me. "I'm done with you!"

"Oh, and I want to tell you one other thing!" he said with disgust and a smirk. "Those people having a birthday party with their kids...they were Mormon! I hope you're proud of yourself, Patrick." He meant that thanks to me, all those Mormons would now be going to hell because I refused to interrupt the kids' birthday party. Their eternal future of fiery torment was on me.

With that final rebuke, Randy drove off. As with my mother, I understood but didn't understand. Yes, there was something very reticent within me in these situations. I didn't do evangelism with the "boldness" that the pastors so admired in each other. But did I really not care about the souls of children? Was I a lukewarm Christian intimidated by the world? Or was I steering us away from the children out of compassion for the mothers trying to have a birthday party for their small children. Was it all of the above?

The next day was Sunday and Randy didn't speak to me. Pastor Gary said nothing about the incident and Randy gave me the cold shoulder. About a week later, Pastor Gary called us out of morning prayers to ask us what happened.

Randy lit into me. "I was trying to tell people about Jesus and this little pip-squeak wouldn't let me! He's always bringing me down! I was trying to save some Mormons and he wouldn't help!"

Pastor Gary looked at me gesturing that it was my turn to share my take on things.

"I just didn't think it was appropriate to confront people at a children's birthday party. The kids wouldn't understand. I also didn't want them to get scared," I said very calmly.

Randy interjected yelling "Oh man, I just want to break your neck! I just want to shatter your skull. I just want to throw you down and break you in half! Let me at him! Let me at him!" He was ready to physically attack me.

I looked on with complete incredulousness. I had never had anyone threaten to rip me apart, and certainly not by a person training for a pastorate in front of their pastor. I felt vindicated that Randy had exposed himself in this way. I was sure that Pastor Gary would finally see Randy's true colors.

"Okay, that's enough," Gary said. "This is over." With that, he left.

I was absolutely gutted that Pastor Gary did nothing. He didn't come to my defense. He seemed to almost believe that Randy's behavior was reasonable. Was it favoritism? Did Gary feel the same way? How could he not defend me in that situation? Was my refusal to evangelize in that situation a greater sin than Randy's threatening to break me in half?

A few days later Gary forced Randy to call me. Randy apologized in a monotone voice in order to make sure that I knew that he didn't mean any of it.

My trust in Three-Fingered Gary evaporated, yet I loved him so. I had become attached to him in the way men do when they follow men they greatly admire on a mission with purpose. We were all stunned when a few weeks later it was announced during a service at the mother church that Pastor Gary would no longer be our pastor effective immediately. A new pastor, Pastor Rick would be taking his place. All of us wept uncontrollably. Pastor Gary was brought down to say goodbye to all of us and as I held on to him, I was shocked by my convulsions as I sobbed. We were never told why Pastor Gary was moved back to the mother church. But I'm pretty sure it's because our church wasn't able to grow past 50 people. Numbers were important in the Fellowship and we were actually shrinking and hovering around 20 or 30 each week.

The new pastor, Rick, was a man in his forties. I welcomed this older, wiser person as I thought that perhaps he and I would be able to operate on a deeper level than I could with Pastor Gary and Randy. But it was not to be. Rick was not much different than Gary, except that he was a slightly better preacher. I was never able to be the "on-fire Christian" that they wanted. I hated myself for it, but I couldn't do it. I couldn't sing the songs, pray the prayers, or show up in the mornings. I began to withdraw. I stopped smiling, stopped sharing, and I stopped caring.

Meanwhile, Mom was dying. She was now no longer working and was hooked up to an oxygen tank. Before long, she was bed-ridden and then Hospice was called in. Friends gathered and my mom began to phone as many people as she could to give them farewell messages of encouragement. It was amazing to watch her try to reach out to others in her darkest moment; to encourage them. She had special words for many people. People around the world were hearing from her—including some of my teenage friends.

Her lungs filled up with fluid and there was a hideous gurgling sound when she breathed. It was a miserable thing to watch. I found myself being the main caregiver in the family; although all sorts of people from the Tigard Church of God that I had left, were coming over to help out, make food, and comfort all of us. The people of this church I had abandoned were surrounding the bed when I lost it and clung to my mother as I sobbed. It was a bit embarrassing, but as the Prophet Bono of the band U2 once said, as he reflected on his father's final days in a hospital, "there's not much dignity in death, but dignity is over-rated."

As she got weaker and weaker, she still tried to make us laugh by throwing her pills in Dad's face: a last bit of physical comedy, which she was always so good at. She whispered to us to make sure the guests were drinking and eating and that we were being considerate hosts. She met with each one of us family members to say our final farewells. We each had a private time with her. I'll never share what she said to me, or what I said to her.

I had this profound insight watching her die: *There's something far worse than death: not living a life of meaning*. My mom's life was all about the giving of herself to others. Even as she lay dying, she was thinking of others. Dying to oneself is what can give our lives meaning and immortality.

"It's not God's fault I'm dying," She said to me. "It's just the result of a fallen world."

I was miserable in life, I was still eating crackers and candy bars, and going to a church my parents didn't really approve of. I had not accomplished anything yet and I had broken my mother's heart by dropping out of school. I was ashamed that this is what my mother would know of me. After all she had given me, I had not given anything back. I was doing a terrible job of paying off my debt to God.

"I promise I will make you proud," I cried as she lay in her bed wheezing the last time, she was coherent. "Somehow, I promise I will do something special in my life, Mom."

"You are my hero," I told her as I clung to her.

A couple of days later she stopped talking and died at 5 AM on January 24, 1991.

I awoke out of a deep sleep the moment she died. My great friend Mark Boring was over at my house—one of many that came to sleep over during these difficult final days. While he was sleeping, I woke up suddenly at 4:55 AM. I was wide awake, and I heard a voice say, "It's going to be okay." For five minutes I was filled with a strange peace and went into a bit of a trance. Then the door opened, and my dad had tears in his eyes. He said, "Mom doesn't have cancer anymore."

Fundamentally Wrong

It's amazing how the corpse of a loved one doesn't really look like them. It suddenly becomes so clear that our body is this hollow shell: that the essence of who we are is something greater than our skin and bones. The corpse almost makes a mockery of who the person was in this life.

I actually found myself enjoying planning the funeral with my former Pastor Gale. He exuded a sense of stability, maturity, and peace that had been missing amidst the constant warfare—spiritual and otherwise in Calvary Temple. The Tigard church people were there for all of us and we held my mother's funeral in the church that she loved.

I was told by Allison that nobody from Calvary Temple wanted to attend my mother's funeral. In their opinion, Mom had died because of the pre-Columbian idol dangling from her neck. It was either that or she had sin in her life. Cancer had won because Satan had won within her. The funeral was not a time for celebration but an abomination to them. I felt the sting of their rejection and also noticed how their behavior contrasted with that of the Church of God people in my life. For every poisonous church or religious community, there are always many more that are not that way. For every Pope Alexander VI who is trying to carve up the world for Christian imperialism, there are many more Christians like De las Casas and Wilberforce doing good and setting people free.

We did celebrate however, and through my mother's funeral at which I spoke, it became so clear to me that her God really was bigger than their God. Many of my high school buddies showed up.

At the last service of the Fellowship churches that I attended at the mother church, a guest preacher called me out from the audience. The entire time during the service I had felt so abandoned by God, so lonely, that I pleaded with God, "Please God, give me a prophecy tonight. Please, let me be the one that gets the prophetic word from you, so that everyone can see that I am okay and that you love me."

The service continued and nothing happened as I sat in my dejected loneliness. I so desperately wanted to be recognized as a good person.

And then suddenly in the middle of the sermon the Pastor stopped and began scanning the crowd.

"Is Patrick here? Is Patrick here? Where is Patrick?"

It was happening! I was thrilled! I raised my hand and the preacher looked at me and said, "God has given me a word tonight. God says, he sees that you have been tithing faithfully and God wants you to know that you will be blessed."

Everyone looked at me with affirming looks. It was always a special thing to get that prophetic word of truth—called out in front of everyone as a good person.

But the thing about this prophetic word was that unlike the last one, it was not true. I had not been tithing. I had long given it up. In every way I had withdrawn from the church and was simply going through the motions. Now in my demoralized state, I had asked God for a gift. I asked him to publicly affirm me through a prophecy. I got my wish, but the prophecy was wrong unlike the last time when the prophecy hit upon something that the preacher could not possibly have known. What did it mean? Why was one prophecy correct, and the other one—the one I wanted so desperately in my time of brokenness—wrong?

In my heart I felt like God was saying to me in that moment, "I am with you Patrick, even when my servants are not with me." Maybe there is a difference between religion and faith. Three-Fingered Gary, Bill Block and Randy, the former cocaine addict, might have worked for God, but they were not God. Neither could they ever love me like God. God was bigger than them. Faith is bigger than religion.

A week after my mother's memorial service, the new pastor, Rick, called me up. "This just isn't working is it? You're not participating, you don't seem to be into it. I can tell something is wrong. We all can."

"I just have questions sometimes," I said.

"Your problem is your attitude!" Pastor Rick yelled into the phone. He yelled a while longer and I said in a very calm voice, "This doesn't seem to be very mature. Is this mature behavior?" That infuriated him further. "You don't need to bother showing up in church anymore! You're bringing everyone down." he said. And with that, I was an ex-pastor-in-training kicked out of my church.

I didn't feel anything. After the loss of my mother, this pain seemed insignificant. If I felt anything, it was relief. I had no idea where I would go from there, but I knew I would no longer need to go to the Cascade Inn.

Of course, I survived, and time kept moving along. Eventually I put the whole thing out of my mind as I returned to Anderson University to finish what I started, went to graduate school, and ended up traveling around the world just as the guest preacher had prophesied. But unbeknownst to me, on a subconscious, and unconscious level, Calvary Temple had wounded me deeply.

Christian Fundamentalism's War on the Bible

I spent the next fifteen years living in perpetual condemnation, believing myself incapable of being an "on-fire" Christian. As I studied the history of fundamentalism and Pentecostalism in college, I was able to understand both the good and the bad of these traditions on an intellectual level. Many fundamentalists are good people, even great people. And they whole-heartedly believe that they are the true protectors of the Word of God, preventing it from getting corrupted by the world or a liberal church. But fundamentalism not only deviates from traditional orthodox Christianity theologically-speaking, but it elicits an unmerciful legalism that always purports to be based on indisputable fact and which robs Christianity of its grace and mystery.[26] Fundamentalism disdains questions or doubt, even though these are so present in the Biblical text itself,

---

[26] Evangelical scholar Mark Noll has written that fundamentalists and *some* evangelicals today often more resemble modern day Manicheans, Gnostics, and Docetists than they do anything that can be found in traditional orthodox Christianity. For a fantastic primer on the subject read Mark Noll's *The Scandal of the Evangelical Mind* which I believe should be required reading for any American Christian.

particularly the Psalms. Ironically, Pentecostal fundamentalism claims to be Bible-centered above all else, yet views everything through a post-enlightenment paradigm. The subtle complexity of Jewish thought in the text is completely ignored in favor of a rational, literal reading of Scripture, forever in pursuit of that which can be "proven." In trying to make the Bible smart, it is actually dumbed-down—reducing it to a poor man's Encyclopedia or Google search, devoid of nuance, depth, and literary greatness. Calvary Temple, like so many fundamentalist churches was great at telling people what sins would get them to hell, but not so good at loving people where they were at in life.

Despite the fact that with age I was able to understand that this really was a very narrow, limiting and ironically unbiblical way of viewing Christianity, I was not able to emotionally recover from the many feelings of failure that the Calvary Temple experience left me with. Even as I discovered a Christianity that was much more beautiful, grace-filled, and sophisticated than Bill Block's George S. Patton theology, I could not escape the feeling that I was a weak Christian unworthy of being in a church. That is what is so insidious about this kind of theology. It seems to lead to all Christians despite their varying ages, backgrounds, nationalities, education levels, personal history, and experiences to look and think exactly alike. And if you don't conform in exactly the right way—then the charge can be brought against you that you do not love the Bible—or God for that matter.

There was such an unholy pride in their faith and theology. Sinners were not creations of God, suffering from their distance to their Holy Father, they were hell-bound children of Satan. It didn't bother the Fellowship churches, for instance, to throw a Halloween Haunted House in which they acted out abortions and squirted fake blood on people in order to remind them that hell is where they would soon find themselves if they didn't repent. After all, these were sinners going to hell! They needed to be scared straight! And so, if I, as a Christian, was to ever doubt or struggle with my faith, or sin, it could only mean one thing: I was aligned with the dark side, pure and simple. Doubt wasn't part of the faith journey. It was always a mortal and immortal threat. All the evil of the dark side of The Force, without the cool light saber.

They did not have the Apostle Paul's humility who claimed to be the chief of all sinners and understood that it was grace, not the 100% perfect comprehension of the Bible, which brings us salvation.

Fundamentalism in Islam, Judaism, and Christianity was a defensive over-reaction by some sects to the threat of Darwin, Marx, Freud, and the Enlightenment. Al-Qaeda and other fundamentalists were not so much inspired by a true rendering of the *Quran* as they were of the ideas of men like Sayyid Qutb (1906-1966). Qutb, who had spent time in Colorado, found the United States to be a modern, decadent society. He loathed secularism, and anything not Islamic or under Islamic Law was detested. Haredi (ultra-Orthodox Jews) also reacted to the liberal thinking of the Enlightenment and the influence of secular studies. Fundamentalist groups in Islam, Christianity, and Judaism often isolate themselves from the rest of society, split up into many different sects, and claim to follow their scriptures literally better than any other group, denomination, or sect in their particular faith. They are always "the true believers," while others are heretical imposters.

This is one reason why there is so much confusion over the Christian Bible. Christian fundamentalists in particular, have been very loud about how the Bible can be taken literally, word for word and is free of any errors. They assume that the Bible is only worth something if it is 100% correct on all issues of history, science, and religion. This leads everyone else to ask questions like: Is the God of the Bible a nice, loving guy or an angry, totalitarian psychopath? Or is it even worth reading the Bible if you value science and do not believe the Earth was created in 6 days? And what about God's misogyny, ethnocentrisms, and ethnic violence in the Bible. Fundamentalists tend to tie themselves up into pretzels of illogic trying to explain the seeming contradictions and sections of Scripture that obviously can't be taken literally. It's an attempt to answer the challenge of secular thought in a tit-for-tat manner: "We have the answers for everything."

The reality is that ancient texts can have living truths and yet still be the products of ancient cultures, languages, history, and geography. Truly understanding the Bible, means doing a lot of preparatory work in understanding the culture, language, history, and geography of the Near East. It also means having a grasp of some old Greek, Aramaic, and Hebrew. It also means understanding that it is not one book, but many with an overriding macro-theme: redemption. Furthermore, you need to have an appreciation for allegory, metaphor, poetry, drama, ancient biography, and other literary forms since it is not one novel in one cohesive style. You then need to understand other ancient texts so that you can compare and contrast the Bible with other important documents of the time. If you do that, you start to see that the stories become very multi-dimensional and even more real and profound. The God portrayed is actually not distant, compared to other gods. The God portrayed elevates the status of women in a culture that demeaned them. The God portrayed turns his back on nationalism in favor of a multi-ethnic view. The God portrayed is creating for a purpose as opposed to creation being accidental. The irony is that secular Bible critics like Richard Dawkins or Christopher Hitchens view these Scriptures and stories in a similar way to religious fundamentalism: free of nuance and complexity. It's a pure, straight, non-analytical reading with the goal of proving others wrong.

Parts of the Bible remain a mystery to me. The tongues issue remains a mystery to me as do the slayings in the Spirit. I'm mystified by what happened when I received the accurate prophecy and why I received the inaccurate prophecy. Sometimes I don't know what Jesus' words mean and the Bible commentaries don't help. And I know I have very little comprehension of my own human heart which the Bible calls "deceitful above all things" (Jeremiah 17:9).

What I do know is that God loves diversity. We can see it in the different species of animals and the radically different topography of our Earth. We can also see it in our facial features and our various personalities which are so different. Our cultures are so diverse, and the incredibly diverse way that Christianity manifests itself in the world is a stunning thing to behold. God may call all of us to have a bold faith, but not all of us are called to be Three-Fingered Gary. I, for one, would like to keep all ten of my fingers. Diversity matters.

And with our great diverse brains and the varied questions that they raise, it is okay for someone to ask whether the snake in Genesis was really talking or if that is symbolic. For those of us that are shy, inarticulate, and lack confidence, there is merit in living a life of humility and being concerned for others without having to stand on the street and ask people for an instantaneous decision to life's greatest question—"Will you accept Christ?" An odd question that is more the product of American consumer culture than of historic Christian orthodoxy.

Neither does it seem that any religion worth its weight in gold would mean needing to fear that wearing the wrong piece of jewelry or taking comfort in an R rated film or joy from a secular love song will be taken as an affront to a God. If there is an ultimate source, as the world's religions and ancient philosophers suggest, that intelligence is clearly so grand that scientists cannot even begin to replicate the complexities found amongst the insects he created. It doesn't seem like appreciating complexity, intelligence and education should be bad either.

In the years that passed, I never ran into any of the main players from the church. I know that two of the yuppies changed churches shortly after I left. I had watched as the third yuppie, Brian—possibly the most impressive and sharpest of all—chose to become a pastor in training and quickly morphed into something totally different—a robotic fundamentalist not much different than Randy. He became what I could not. Allison got remarried and became an Anglican. That sounded like a very good thing to me. Lamar and his family left the city, and eventually the mother church left the supermarket. I never found out if they moved or just went out of business. There are no services at the Cascade Inn anymore.

More than a decade later when the internet became a part of our lives, I tried doing a web search. I discovered that Randy the angry former coke-addict that had threatened to break me in half now had his own church. Clearly, he had made it in the Fellowship. But there was nothing about Three-Fingered Gary. His last name was unique enough that through a web search I found someone who might be him. If that was him, he was now a carpenter living in Washington State. He was not on the Fellowship roll. Years later I still carry a deep love for this man. Such is the power of the men of God that we follow—even when they are fallible. I did learn a lot from him. I hope he remains a person of faith and did not get burnt out by the Fellowship system. He loved Jesus. Did the Fellowship love him? That is a big question.

The only Fellowship person I ever ran into was Ryder, Mouth's lanky sidekick—Jerry to his Tom, Pinky to his Brain. About five years later I pulled up to a gas station in my hometown Tigard and the young attendant filling up my tank looked at me through the window. I rolled it down.

"You are...you are...I know you!" he said.

"Do I know you?" I asked.

"Yeah, I went to your church. My name is Ryder."

Ryder was no longer a dopey, gangly 12-year-old. He was now a tall, strapping handsome young man of 18 with a crew cut.

"Ryder is that you? You've really grown up!" I exclaimed.

"I'm going into the Marines next week," he said.

I made some more casual chit chat as Ryder finished up filling my tank.

As I paid him, Ryder looked at me deeply and spoke:

"I just want you to know that you were the only person in that church that was ever nice to me. I just want to say, 'Thank You.'"

"You're welcome," I replied, grateful, stunned, and saddened at the same time.

It had been years—and Ryder had only been a part of our church for a few weeks—yet the pain of the rejection from that church had stayed with him too. Both of us had found the power of God at Calvary Temple, but we also found judgment and condemnation. As communities that are supposed to be in line with the will of God, churches have the power to bring great healing or they can cause people immeasurable amounts of pain. When we claim to represent Christ in our churches, we are making a very bold statement. One that we better be prepared to live up to in a mighty way.

And when we fail as Christian communities—and we will fail—the spirit of humility and repentance needs to be so deeply imbedded in our church culture that we all take our wounds to the cross together as opposed to wounding each other.

Perhaps I should have told Ryder that I too was carrying pain from Calvary Temple. Perhaps I should have apologized to him for the fact that churches are made up of human beings and are thus fallible institutions. Perhaps I should have asked him if he was a Christian. Perhaps I should have led him to the Lord right there by doing the "sinner's prayer" and making sure he "accepted Jesus as his Lord and Savior." But I didn't. All of that seemed shallow, self-serving, and institutional. Instead I hoped that God could be big enough to reach Ryder one day at the right time, the way he had reached me. Perhaps it was not up to me or Calvary Temple to save Ryder's soul but up to God himself. Perhaps God loves Ryder enough to one day bring him healing for those wounds. Perhaps he already did and we piously religious ones were in need of having our wounds healed so we wouldn't damage others. Perhaps God chases us, knows us, and accepts us in ways that are mysterious and can't be measured. Perhaps, it all hinges on grace and cannot be neatly explained.

Whatever the situation, Calvary Temple, I know, would not approve.

6

Looking to the East: How Religion Treats the Individual

After my supernatural encounter with God at the Cliffs of Moher, things took a sudden turn for the worse before they got better. But with my faith restored, I finally made my way to Asia to begin living there permanently. Asia introduced me to the religious ideas and concepts of the East like Buddhism, Taoism, and Confucianism.

Jesus was not a Republican, blond surfer dude from Malibu. Not a Democrat either. Neither was he a Tory or part of the Labour Party. Most people know this, I hope. Jesus was not only Jewish, he was from the Orient—from a society that has had a way of thinking that was far more in line with eastern religions than with the individualistic, consumer-minded, therapeutic-deism that counts for a lot of western Christianity today.

As Christianity spread west, it got infused with Greek thought, a ton of Ancient Roman legalism, symbols and structures, and then an Ellis Island boatload of American cultural trappings and preferences. Western Christianity got so Americanized that Jesus deserves his own honorary green card. The American cultural values of radical individualism, extremely dualistic thinking, apocalyptic thought intermingling with national triumphalism, as well as the obsession with wealth, marketing and consumerism formed a very dynamic, divisive, and overly individualistic strand of the Christian faith. It is a version that would be transported globally throughout the world via Christian evangelists, books and media, Bible Colleges, and missionary work. It would be a Christianity that was not only very western, but *very* American.

Consequently, understanding the eastern mind became an important piece of the puzzle for me as I tried to discover what went wrong at Calvary Temple. But it is also important for all of us to understand as we enter into an era where Asia, not Europe or America, will be the dominant region in the world. More and more westerners dabble or engage in ideas, faiths, and practices from the Far East and Southern Asia. Furthermore, so many of the world's people, including our neighbors adhere to Asian religions that it makes it something important to learn about. And for Christians, an understanding of the oriental mindset of Jesus' Jewish community, as well as remembering eastern Christianity is important as well.

After my mom died, we got some life insurance money. She had specifically asked that I get enough money that I could finally go see the world as I had always dreamed of doing. I was twenty when I visited Shinto shrines in Japan, Hindu temples in Singapore, Buddhist wats in Thailand, and Confucian halls in Hong Kong and China. I examined the rituals, ideas, and cultural effects of these eastern faiths. Many of those journeys around the world would make up the stories found in my first book *Passport of Faith*.

Asia was everything I had hoped it would be. I was infinitely fascinated, and the trip helped to somewhat numb the pain of losing my mother.

One day, I went to a Christian retreat center in Hong Kong that offered a beautiful view of the Shatin valley. The buildings were built in a traditional Chinese style and the grounds felt more like a Taoist temple than a Christian center. It was called Tao Fong Shan and was founded by a Norwegian missionary who went to share Christianity with Buddhists in Hunan Province, China in 1904. *Tao* means "the Way," *Fong* means "wind" and *Shan* means "mountain." I stood underneath a giant cross looking down on the suburb of Shatin. I thought of my mother, wishing that she could see that I had finally at least made it to China. Little did I know that I was literally looking down on the neighborhood which would one day be my home for ten years as well as the hospital where my beloved son Marco would one day be born twelve years later.

My final night in Hong Kong, I visited the beautiful harbor as the sun was setting and the lights of the skyscrapers were turning on in front of the stunning mountains. I re-affirmed my love for all things Asian (except the food) and promised myself that I would be back. To honor my mother, I had decided to take college seriously and returned to Anderson University in Indiana. I figured that I needed to learn how to finish the things I started, and I was done with Calvary Temple's ideas about education being bad.

After that Asia trip and a trip through every country in Central America as I made my way back for one of my regular visits to Costa Rica, I found myself back in school for three years trying to learn everything I could about China, Japan, and religion. All I needed to do was finish my degree and get that assignment to Asia from the mission agency.

But as I shared in Chapter 1, the dream fell apart quickly. China was not open and the job in Tokyo fell through. Lost and back to doing McJobs in Portland, I had headed to Ireland where I met Bartley on the train and had a pint of Guinness with God at the Cliffs of Moher. So, what happened after that day when I met God?

Back from Ireland

After God showed up that day on the Cliffs of Moher, I was on a true spiritual high. I was able to get back to Dublin thanks to Bartley driving me back in that borrowed car. I made my other appointments in the UK and returned home to Oregon inspired by my fantastical, touching, and deeply humbling encounter with God.

Upon returning back home to Oregon, life was not instantly perfect. Quite the opposite! I lost my girlfriend (who I would later marry), I lost my place to live, and I lost my job in the span of ten days. With no family living in the United States, there wasn't much financial back-up in my life. I was broke and there was no home to go to.

My great friend and former Anderson University college roommate Nate (also known as "Natron" or "Derbysquire") helped me survive this time of chaos and disorder. Trying to get back to Asia was the dream, but at the moment, trying to have a few dollars was the priority.

The only thing of value that I had left in the whole world was a red four-door Hyundai. It was an older car but was running fine. I definitely could not afford to have anything happen to that car as I would need it to find a job, to go to work, and to survive. Feeling vulnerable and fearing that something might happen to my Hyundai, I went back to the Bill Block Calvary Temple playbook and literally prayed over my car with my hands outstretched like a cheeseball televangelist reaching for the TV screen. I went full Robert Tilton, out of desperation. You never go full Robert Tilton! *"Please God! This is the only thing of value I have in the whole world! Shamalama Ramalanga Ding Dong. Please protect this car! Don't let anything happen! Surround this car with your heavenly angels, or the California Angels, or super powerful Turtle Wax! Anything!"*

It was 11 PM that night when I stood outside and prayed over my car. Exactly twelve hours later, my car was totaled at an intersection in Lake Grove, Oregon.

I don't even remember what happened. But it was clearly not going to lead to a big insurance payoff since it seemed to be my fault. The car was toast. As I walked around my destroyed car, I swear I heard a quiet voice say to me. *"Patrick, if you lost everything would you still believe?"*

Was this my imagination? Was this a test? Had I suffered a concussion? Or was this just a series of bad-luck coincidences? I definitely wasn't in the frame of mind to be making up that question in my head at that exact moment. My car was wrecked, the other car damaged, and people were stopping around the intersection to have a look. Regardless of the purpose of this question, it was a good one. An important one: *Would I still believe if I lost everything? Or was my faith dependent on good things happening to me?* This was the Job question I talked about in Chapter 4.

I immediately thought back to the experience I had on the Cliffs of Moher. I remembered all the doubts that had filled me every time something didn't go my way. But I also remembered the ending and what it meant to me. The Cliffs of Moher had taught me that I don't know my own journey. I can plan as hard as I want, try to steer it as much as possible, but ultimately, it is in God's hands. Even if you don't believe in God, it certainly is not in *your* hands. John Lennon was right about that!

Like so many people of faith, I had always assumed through childhood and youth that the reward for believing is that everything will go your way. Otherwise, why else do it? It's how you get your life to go well, and how you avoid hell. But that is an immature transactional faith. *"I'll believe in you God, but you will give me this."* Slowly but surely, I was beginning to learn the lesson that a life of faith requires actual faith and always involves doubt as well. We are not worshipping a magical genie that makes every wish come true. It is more about surrendering our own will daily, than it is about getting what we want. If we are honest about it, most of the time, we couldn't handle having all of our wishes come true. Like the proverbial lottery winner who becomes a multi-millionaire overnight and ends up having a much sadder life filled with regrets about having ever won, we mostly do not know ourselves and what we really need to make us happy. We will especially go out of our way to avoid any kind of challenge or pain that requires self-introspection and resiliency, yet those are the things that actually can lead to perspective, growth, and a deeper sense of satisfaction.

Surrender and facing the unknown is a process where we begin to learn a lot about ourselves—the good, the bad, and the ugly. And through that difficult but rewarding voyage, we learn a lot about God and his overall purpose for our life. Or if you are not religious, you at least learn that character is destiny and find out what you are made of.

The question still lingered as traffic was stopped and the old man whose car I hit, was yelling at me: his voice sounding like the adults in a Charlie Brown TV special. I was in another world as he prattled on.

"Yes," I replied under my breath. "Even if I lost everything, I would still believe."

A couple of weeks later, I received a phone call at 5 AM in the morning.

"Is this Patrick Nachtigall?" said an accented voice from obviously somewhere far away.

"Yes, this is he." I responded groggily from my sleeping bag on the floor. Natron and I didn't really have furniture, beds, or even closets. The true Ug Nachtigall bachelor life.

"This is Longman American English Academy in Pusan, South Korea. We need you to come over to Korea immediately to begin teaching English. We will send you a free airline ticket, we have a free apartment for you, and you will receive a good salary in cash every month. But we need you to come right now!"

It was May 1995, two months after the Cliffs of Moher.

Unbelievable! A school 5,000 miles away in Asia was offering me a job: $1,400 a month cash with all other expenses paid for. It was money I could save. I responded instantaneously:

"Yes, I will take the job!" I accepted right on the spot.

There was no hesitation. Asia was my dream, and I had pretty much lost everything. And there was the fact that I was totally broke. I had tried to apply for credit cards in the past and was always rejected because back in 1995, credit card companies didn't pass out cards to youth like crack cocaine. It was difficult to get one without a credit history, so I was always turned down, and getting turned down went on your non-existent credit history and then made it difficult to get one to establish or repair your credit history. It was a vicious cycle, but I kept occasionally trying.

But the next day in the mail after the call from South Korea, I received my first credit card ever. I now had a whopping credit limit of $500, which seemed like an enormous amount of money to me. That would be just enough to help me survive until I received my first envelope of cash from my Korean employer.

And so, I filled my two suitcases with the only things I possessed in the world. Clothes, some music, a Bible and Bible commentary, and as many books as I could fit into the two suitcases. My friends dropped me off at the Portland International Airport and I flew to L.A. where I boarded a Korean Air 747-400 to Seoul, continuing on to what would be my new home: Pusan, South Korea.[27] I was going to finally live in Asia! I wasn't going to be feeding lepers or building huts, but at least I wasn't going to be dropping napalm on them either. If a pint of Guinness with God was possible, then so was a shot of *Soju*. Now I'd meet God again on the other side of the world, at the cliffs in Pusan overlooking the sea from the other side of the Pacific. After a 17-year wait, the dream was finally beginning. I was moving to Asia!

The Eastern Religions

Eastern faiths serve a similar purpose as western faiths and philosophy: they try to explain the universe and our place and purpose in it. Of course, there are many different religions that arose out of the Asian continent, but Indian civilization and Chinese civilization are the most notable sources of today's eastern thought. Hinduism, Buddhism, and Taoism trace their heritage back to India and China even though they took on different forms in places like Tibet and Japan.

Man's place in the world, in general, is much smaller in eastern thought than in western thought. Western democracy, Islam, and Christianity have a strong role for man to play in the redemption and healing of the world. It's as if man is the central character on stage. You can see this clearly in Renaissance art which is filled with historical moments, self-portraits, and male and female bodies. Eastern art, on the other hand, often de-emphasizes human beings and focuses on nature. Many classic Chinese and Japanese paintings feature trees and mountains dominating the canvas with humans appearing incredibly small, almost

---

[27] Pusan has since Romanized its name differently and it is now spelled "Busan." In this book, I will continue to call it Pusan because, as you should realize by now, I have a weakness for nostalgia. I also refer to the United States as "the Colonies."

as an after-thought. The idea of a self-portrait only began to reach China and Japan at the end of the 19th century.

While man and woman are on a special mission in western enlightenment thought as well as in Christianity and Islam, in eastern religions, humans are a small part of something far bigger than themselves. The cosmos—of which we are a *very* small part—operates in a certain way that is far beyond us. Western secular thought and western religions are confident that man can conquer and change his world and destiny on a big stage. Eastern religion has far more modest goals: to understand one's limited place in the cosmos and to escape the cycle of suffering and death. There is far more cross-pollination between eastern and western religions than we realize, but these two very different worldviews still hold true.

In the East, there is not the strong need to divide religion from philosophy. The West tends to classify philosophy and material things as "real" and religious things as belief separated from "true knowledge." You can see this in all of our western debates about religion versus science. Awareness of our place within nature, of our limitations, and of our propensity to delude ourselves as human beings is an important form of truth. But for western secularists and religious people, the only things of value are beliefs that are rooted in rational thinking. This is even true of fundamentalist Christianity, as I saw at Calvary Temple. They try to prove that the Earth is only 6,000 years old because it is a "scientific fact" that must be proven.

As I mentioned in the last chapter, fundamentalism is very much in competition with the secular world to lay claim on rational, quantifiable truths. "Every word in our Bible is true and can be proven. The contradictions or errors are because scientific discovery has not caught up with the Bible," a fundamentalist pastor once told me. So for instance, if the Book of Joshua in the Bible says that God made the sun stand still in the sky, instead of viewing that as a poetic, artistic way of saying that "it was a very long day," we are supposed to take that to mean that God literally stopped the sun from revolving around the Earth. Of course, the slight problem with that interpretation is that the sun never revolves around the Earth. The Earth revolves around the Sun!

For some reason, when Jesus says, "I am the door," they don't literally believe him to be a physical door. And when he says, "sell all you have and give it to the poor," *that* doesn't tend to get taken literally either—especially by fundamentalist prosperity gospel preachers. Suddenly, the language in the Bible is just being symbolic, m-kay?

If fundamentalist Christians were truly committed to the primacy of spiritual truths, they would react more like Buddhists and Hindus who don't feel like science and spiritual truth have to be enemies or forced into an uncomfortable compatibility. Neither did historic Christianity.

In those months between college and my surprise trip to South Korea, I had spent a lot of time at the Way of the Pilgrim bookstore. It was located in NW Portland, just a block from my beloved Cinema 21, where my buddies and I liked to go see foreign films—including my favorite Chinese films by Chinese director Zhang Yimou.

This bookstore was a small Eastern Orthodox bookstore. There are three branches of Christianity: Roman Catholicism, Protestantism, and Eastern Orthodoxy. Eastern Orthodoxy considers itself the original church and traces its origins back to the Apostles. The problem is that the Roman Catholic Church claims that it is the original church and St. Peter was the first Pope. What happened is that after the era of Emperor Constantine when Christianity became powerful, wealthy, and political, this faith movement morphed into Christendom: a large collection of feudal kingdoms, duchies, principalities, and nations with imperial ambitions that made Christianity their officially mandated religion. During this Late Antiquity period, there was a dramatic split between the Christianity of the east and the Christianity of the west. Just like the "beans and cornbread" that Louis Jordan & the Tympany Five sang about in 1949, the eastern and western church "had a fight and fought all night." Orthodoxy and Catholicism got into a bit of a lover's spat from which they have never recovered. The year was 1054 and this historical heavyweight boxing match sponsored by Don King was known as "The Great Schism."

Roman Catholicism became the biggest branch in Christianity spreading all over the world. It, however, suffered another schism when Martin Luther and the theologians of the Protestant Reformation established the pope-less Protestant Church.

Islam has its branches too, including Sunni, Shi'a, and Sufiism. Buddhism has Mahayana, Theravada, Tibetan Esoteric Buddhism, and the Zen school of Buddhism. Jews are also divided between Orthodox, Reform, and Conservative. Within all of that, each religion has its own sub-sects and denominations, and even cults. Quite often there's one branch that takes things very literally, one that is very mystical and ritual-based, and one that is very practical and modern. It's surprisingly similar, until it gets incredibly complex. One thing is for sure, denominational division and branches are not simply a thing of Christianity. Cultures, prophets, history, theological discussions, heresies, and many other things lead to the great diversity in each faith. That's why making generalizations about any religion is extremely difficult. There are pacifist Muslims and there are militant Christian cults forming child-armies.

While the Roman Catholic Church expanded north and west and became the largest branch of Christianity, Eastern Orthodoxy was centered more in the region of Asia Minor, the Balkans, eastern Europe, and Russia. Protestantism is very rooted in the Bible and the individual, Roman Catholicism is heavily rooted in the role of the Church leadership (the Vatican), and Eastern Orthodoxy focuses more on ancient tradition.

Eastern Orthodox cathedrals are gorgeous and ornate. They are filled with paintings called "icons" which are referred to as "windows into heaven." Before people were widely literate, art was a way for people to see and understand Bible stories and commune with God. The smell of incense is important in Orthodoxy, as is the liturgy or mass. The first time I walked into an Eastern Orthodox church, when I was in my 30s, I was left completely speechless. I had been to Notre Dame in Paris and St. Peter's Basilica in Rome, the two most famous Roman Catholic churches. They were wonderful, of course, but the Cathedral of Christ the Savior in the heart of Moscow flattened me.

The icons, the images, the gold, the incense and the stern-looking robed priests seemed like something from a different world; and that is the point! You feel a sense of timelessness in cathedrals and an escape from the loud, material world. This cathedral in Russia was a far cry from Calvary Temple's supermarket whose altar was located where check-out counters once existed. What I didn't know when I visited in 2007 was that the Cathedral of Christ the Savior had been rebuilt in 2000, consequently it was in mint condition. It is still one of my favorite places in the world. Every time I go to Moscow, I walk from the Kremlin, along the Moscow River to my favorite church.

Eastern Orthodox cathedrals and services make Protestant churches look like spring break at Daytona Beach.

They are austere, calm, other-worldly. You almost forget you are on Planet Earth. Almost.

Something funny happened to me in Kazan Cathedral located in Red Square. The Kremlin is my favorite structure in the whole world. I don't feel that photos ever do justice to the beauty of the buildings and cathedrals that are in Russia's iconic center of religion and government. I walked into Kazan Cathedral with my wife and son. We were fortunate enough to be in this beautiful Orthodox cathedral when a choir was in front of the altar singing the mystical, medieval sounding hymns. All of the male choir members had long beards, dark robes and Rasputin-like looks. The combination of their reverent faces and the haunting music was other-worldly and inspiring. As I looked on in awe, I saw them all holding up their choir books. At that precise moment, the priest I was looking at accidently dropped his music book. What was tucked inside? An English copy of *Road & Track* magazine! The whole time he was singing in this other-worldly, haunting style, he was reading *Road & Track!*

It was very important for me to learn about Eastern Orthodoxy to get a more balanced view of Christianity. At the Way of the Pilgrim bookstore I learned about a whole side of Christianity that I had never been taught anything about. Much like the Asian religions, Eastern Orthodoxy embraced faith, mystery, and paradox. Just like the eastern religions, Orthodoxy thought the whole science versus faith issue was goofy, unnecessary, and totally pointless. Clearly, some things are so real they cannot be quantified or easily explained.

That doesn't mean they are not intellectual or don't tackle heavy subjects. Quite the opposite. Orthodoxy reveres brilliant-minded "Church Fathers" like Basil the Great, Gregory of Nyssa, Gregory of Nazianzus, John Chrysostom, Athanasius, Clement, Origen, and Irenaeus. This was the exact opposite of Calvary Temple and I felt genuinely ripped off that I had never been taught any of this in church or in university. There was this whole rich, historic, and important heritage that was completely ignored. For most evangelicals, Christianity doesn't really start until their particular denomination was invented in the 19th century. They give a passing high-five to Calvin, Wesley, and of course, Martin Luther. But I never learned about this rich intellectual heritage, or this more mystic, eastern Christianity that had some beautiful ideas about divinity, the cosmos, and Christ's place within all of that.

I discovered the *starets* that were Russian monks that had ascetic experiences and often gained amazing special insight and gifts of healing and prophecy. They were like Indian Gurus, but they were from Christian Russia's history. The most interesting was Seraphim of Sarov (1759-1833) who spent 30 years living in total isolation in a cottage and a tiny cell in a monastery. His feet were so swollen he couldn't really walk. At one point he had spent 1,000 nights in a row standing on a rock in his cell. But when his cell door opened, he was able to heal the sick, give people answers to questions before they even asked them and perform other miracles. People from all over Russia came to meet with him, sometimes more than a thousand per day.

Since then, I have been inside many Eastern Orthodox cathedrals in Russia, Romania, Ukraine, Bulgaria, Greece, Egypt (Coptic), and many other places. They are often immersed into one particular ethnic group such as Greek, Russian, or Ukrainian. While your average evangelical church might even have a gift-bag for the first-time visitor, Orthodox churches are often not very amenable to visitors. Nevertheless, because both secular and religious people in the west judge religions and Christianity by western ideas of religion, it's a shame that people are not exposed more to some of the healthy challenges that eastern religions offer, such as de-emphasizing radical individualism, and intellectual conceit that acts as though we don't have scientific and academic limitations.

After the World Cup in Russia, the Japanese football team, after they lost, cleaned their locker rooms. It made global news around the world, since it was such an impressive, selfless and thoughtful gesture. Eastern religions, including the eastern version of Christianity are often very wise to de-emphasize the extreme self-centered nature of western individualism and can bring us back to a greater awareness of the importance of nature and creation— which we are increasingly devalued in our environmentally challenged modern world.

Welcome to East Asia

I arrived in Pusan from the Colonies on a rainy night in May of 1995. The first thing that happened was the guy picking me up scolded me. There was no, "Hi Patrick." or "How was the flight?"

Instead it was just, "Why are you late??" I would learn very quickly that underneath the reputation for politeness, East Asian cultures are often very direct and immediately tell you when you have messed up. I was late because I had missed my connecting flight in Seoul due to a short connection time. He took me to a *Yeogwan,* a modest, Korean-style inn with pillows filled with wheat-husks and mats. "Tomorrow I will take you to your school," said the driver. I was so exhausted, I fell on the bed and slept in my clothes.

The next morning, my alarm went off and I got in the shower. It was at that moment that the female innkeeper walked in. She was yelling at me in Korean and carrying a breakfast of soup, kelp, and kimchi. I gathered that she wanted me to eat the food immediately and pointed at a table and kept yelling. I was in a delicate state—*en flagrante*—but she didn't care. My stunning legs apparently did not impress. For her, there was food delivered and it was time to eat *now!* That's the East Asian directness.

I would encounter the East Asian directness hundreds of times living in Asia. Usually with comments like: "You are fat!" "You gained weight!" "You look like a Saipan man with your ugly moustache, that's not good!" Anything done incorrectly or in a non-conformist fashion is quickly pointed out. This is the legacy of Confucianism, a philosophy that is very clear about how society should be ordered and what is right and wrong. Everyone has their place and there are no exceptions. If I did the wrong thing, or dressed the wrong way, or had a shoelace untied, I would either get scolded or laughed at. Just a shoelace untied could provide hours of laughter, "Look! The dumb westerner can't tie his shoes and one shoe is tied and the other is not. Ha Ha Ha!" In the West, someone might just say "Hey dude, your shoelace is untied." In the East, it was a source of great merriment and shame.

East Asian societies are shame-based cultures, while western societies are guilt-based cultures. In the West, when we do something wrong, we feel guilty as an individual for that bad behavior.

"I stole my mother's wedding ring to sell it for crystal meth. That was bad!" I might say as a western guilt-based person.

But in many eastern cultures, it is shame-based. "I stole a Honda and drove it into a pole. Therefore, I am a shameful, worthless human being because of this action, and I have brought shame and dishonor to my whole family as well as to future generations of our family."

Even in our different responses to a bad action, easterners view it in a more holistic way. This is why so many East Asian students feel such an incredible pressure to succeed academically. Because if they don't, they are letting down many people besides themselves. When I dropped out of college, I didn't think about how it would hurt my mother. Neither did I think, *I have brought shame to my Mom, my Dad, Grandfather Nachtigall, and even old Ug Nachtigall. I've disgraced everyone.* No. I just did it because that's what I selfishly wanted as an individual. The needs of the larger group and the cosmos are carried around daily more in the East than in the West.

"You are lucky," one of the English teacher agents told me. "You are being assigned to the best *hogwan!*" *Hogwans* were little institutes or academies for educational purposes. Longman American English Academy in Pusan was brand new and headed up by two men: Mr. Kim and Mr. Lee. The operational manager was a 27-year-old Korean woman who went by the name "Michelle." She was very rich, dressed up every day to be a total glamour-puss, was always looking in the mirror, and was quite bossy. I would end up getting scolded by her many times which led me to call her "Yoko" behind her back. She would eventually make my job pretty miserable. But in the beginning, I was one of four American teachers helping to launch this school, along with four female Korean teachers ranging in age from 23 to 40 years of age. "Ellen" was friendly because she wanted to practice her English with me, not because she liked me. As with so many South Korean women who tend to feel that they must look glamourous and have all possible defects, no matter how small, repaired, Ellen had a surgery to make her Asian eyes look more western by adding a fold to her eyelids.

"Sue" was 23 years old and a sweetheart. "Helen" was the maternal teacher figure who was about 40, and "Connie" was a Korean who had picked up an Australian accent in Sydney. Then there was 26-year-old Ms. Ju who looked like a supermodel and never said a word to us foreigners. She was very mysterious and looked like she could be an assassin in Quentin Tarantino's *Kill Bill Volume 1*. And last, there was "Minnie," a single woman in her late 30s whose disdain for foreigners could never be hidden. She was assigned to be my flat-mate and a spy of sorts for Mr. Kim and Mr. Lee. Joining me and that Korean crew was Roar, a 22 year old from Maine who was raised by hippies in San Francisco and whose mother had just died of cancer, and Jeannie, an amazon Bette Midler-type of a woman whose direct, blunt style would go down very badly in East Asia. It's okay for them to be blunt, but not us. Her friend was Shannon, a young lady with a very large tattoo of a serpent on her breast that went up past her cleavage and up her neck. This was before the world was heavily tattooed. Back in 1995, these women stood out to an extreme degree in the U.S., let alone in a Korean town like Pusan. I had a feeling that those two would have a difficult time surviving in rigid South Korea. They only made it about three months before they packed up and went back to New Mexico. I liked them.

My first day, I was taken up to the 10th floor of a building in Pusan and shown the school which occupied the floor. I was instructed that I must bring a gift from America for Mr. Kim—preferably a Scotch. I got him a photo book of Oregon instead, with a photo of my beloved Ecola State Park. I bowed and presented it with two hands as you should always do in East Asia. After I was introduced to everyone, Michelle/Yoko said, "Okay, you start today. You have three classes from 3 PM to 6 PM."

I had just arrived! I was expecting a couple of days of downtime! At least I hoped to get some training. But I was being thrown to the wolves, or in this case, a classroom full of four and five-year-old Korean kids who spoke no English. They gave me a book to teach from, a box with pens and markers, and showed me to the class. Inside were some very cute Korean children. Within minutes the room was like *Apocalypse Now*. I was overrun and being jumped on by these little munchkins and the whole class was out of control. I was literally on all fours with children hanging off of me. My life as a teacher was off to a rough start. *No American in the Vietnam War had it this bad,* I thought to myself as the kids covered me on the floor. It was worse than the Tet Offensive. I was completely overrun.

That evening, Roar and Minnie took me to my new home, an apartment in the gorgeous suburb of Shin Mandeok. It was a short bus ride through the Mandeok Tunnel into our suburb nestled into a tight little valley with sharp, green mountains on three sides of us and Korea's longest river, the Nakdong on the west side. The apartment was in a tall series of concrete towers and ours was on the 4th floor.

With the Longman *hogwon* just starting out, I ended up never working more than six hours a day. For several months, I worked roughly four hours a day. I spent the rest of my time fanatically reading everything I could get my hands on about geo-politics, China, religion, and East Asia in general. I visited Buddhist temples, checked out books from the U.S. Consulate library, and saw movies in very smelly movie theatres where the snack of choice was dried squid instead of popcorn. It was not unusual for our boss Mr. Kim to take us all to *Noraebang* (Karaoke). I was particularly gifted at Karaoke, able to do my impressions of Michael Jackson, George Michael, Prince, and even Michael Bolton. The Asians went crazy for Karaoke and even crazier for a westerner that could do impressions of famous singers. Michelle/Yoko, however, was very jealous of the attention that I was getting and would sit in the corner and glare at me as I moonwalked. She wanted the stage to herself as she belted out the latest K-pop hits which were unbelievably catchy and 25 years later are still in my head.

Roar was an atheist, Minnie was a Buddhist, and I was a Christian. We spent hours discussing religion. Roar's atheism was based on western, rational thought. Logic and science led him to conclude that there was no God. Minnie's Buddhism was rooted in the fact that she was born into a Buddhist family. Even though about 33% of South Koreans are Christians, Minnie didn't understand Christian thought. She mostly felt my questions were strange. Like many East Asians, she didn't think about what religion she was, or what theology she subscribed to. There were certain rituals at certain times of year that she needed to perform, and that was it. This is very much the case for many East Asians that are Buddhist or Shinto. There is not that western sense of "this is the religion I choose, and this is why." Being Buddhist is like being born with brown eyes. It just is.

I did not try to convert Roar to Christianity. But living in South Korea made him begin to wonder about the limits of western, materialistic, rational thinking. In time, he moved away from his original philosophical ideas and embraced eastern ways. Roar would go on to live in South Korea for many years, learn the language and accept the power of many eastern ideas. He would eventually spend five years becoming a master of *Danjeon* breathing. Traditionally, *Danjeon* breathing was about opening up oneself to consciousness, but Roar found that *Danjeon* in the *Suseonjae* style offered physical healing that western medicines and science could not. Today he travels the world teaching the methods and benefits of Danjeon breathing.

Puck You, I Eat Food Now!

Americans were not popular in South Korea in the mid-1990s. That is an understatement, actually. Despite the

United States fighting in Korea and helping to save half of the peninsula from Kim Il Sung and all of his demon spawn, protests against the U.S. were regular occurrences in Pusan and elsewhere. It may be due to the U.S. having so many military bases in South Korea, or because of the western influence of American culture. Both Koreas are actually quite nationalistic in general. There were very few of us Americans anywhere in this city of two million people. If you ever passed an American on the street, it was a total shock, and you'd do a double-take and stop in the middle of the sidewalk. "What are you doing here?" You would inevitably ask. We were very isolated. Neither did we see any other ethnic groups or foreigners.

South Korea is the most homogenous nation in the world. Particularly in the 1990s, outside of the massive city of Seoul, Koreans were not used to seeing any kind of foreigner. Not only did they hate Americans, but they definitely did not like dark-skinned people. Since I have tan-skin and at that time a ridiculous moustache (Korean men never did), I was viewed as a dirty "Saipan man." Saipan was an island far in the Pacific where the Koreans would travel on vacation. They were fond of the island but not the darker-skinned people.

Racism was not really an ethical, moral matter in South Korea. Like the Chinese, the Koreans viewed themselves as the center of the world (China's name in Chinese *Chung Kuo* literally means "Middle Kingdom), and the only race of people that were legitimate and that mattered on Planet Earth. Confucian influence made these definitions of status concrete and non-negotiable. Koreans were superior. Period.

This meant that when I walked down the street, entire buses of people would point out the windows at me. When I rode on a bus, people would change seats or stand far away from me as if I was a leper. Children would often walk by, point and giggle at the foreigner. And it was not uncommon to have Korean teenagers flip me off and say, "puck you" (because they couldn't pronounce the "F").

Being told to puck off all the time got very tiring. I started to feel like maybe I could somewhat relate to African Americans riding at the back of the bus and drinking from separate drinking fountains. I was a spectacle and pointed at with disdain constantly. All the hatred aimed in our direction made all of us westerners pretty frustrated and angry with the South Koreans. Inevitably, you want to retaliate and say bad things, or create stereotypes that can justify your hatred in return. I did both things at times, to be honest. I also spent a lot of time disappearing into my headphones listening to Pink Floyd's *The Division Bell*, A-ha's *Memorial Beach,* and Tears for Fears' *Raoul and the Kings of Spain*. Not all Koreans were like that of course, but the vast majority looked at us with disdain or total indifference. This was before the internet and before globalization took off; there was just very little interaction with foreigners for Koreans who lived outside of Seoul. But there were some Korean people in my neighborhood who made me feel welcome.

Nobody was more welcoming to me than the Han family. I met them in my first couple of weeks living in Shin Mandeok. Across the street from my apartment tower was a little restaurant called "The Pizza Club." It was a small space with room for only four to six tables. Most people came into the restaurant and ordered a pizza to take away. One day I decided to try it out. A very elegant 29-year-old woman with a huge smile made my pizza in front of me, put it into a box, and put a ribbon around the box. Her smile was so different than what I was used to in Korea. I became a regular and I eventually became great friends with Kyeong Sook and her husband Mr. Han. They had two small children who I played with regularly. I fell deeply in love with the Hans, and they became my surrogate family. I spent so much time at The

Pizza Club that every once in a while, I helped out as if I was an employee. There were some other pizza places in our neighborhood that I liked better, so I would often order from there and run home trying to hide the box lest one of the Han family saw me with a rival pizza.

Yes, I ate pizza. I also ate meat and many other fattening things. My extreme eating phobia was gone! How did it happen? How could I go from thinking all foods look like disgusting insects that are going to make me throw-up until I die, to eating ribs at rat holes like Sizzler? What happened?

It was love. When I went back to college, I met the girl that would one day become my wife. I was asked to be a chaperone at a party for young missionary kids. Since I was once the kid of a missionary, I went. I arrived first and before long, walking down the street, was a girl named Jamie who reminded me of the actress Elisabeth Shue from *The Karate Kid*. I was smitten as she walked down the street in khaki shorts, a yellow shirt, and a bandana in her hair just like Elisabeth Shue wore in the television show *Call to Glory*—on ABC. I immediately put on the caveman moves and went in for the kill. Ug Nachtigall would have been proud. Even though I looked like a 1980s *Miami Vice* pimp wearing enough cologne to kill a colony of bees, Jamie let me get near her.

Jamie was also the child and grandchild of missionaries— just like me. She was raised in Cairo, Egypt and was now attending Anderson University. Sadly, we met not long after my mother died of cancer and just as her father was dying of cancer in his 40s. I found myself reliving the whole thing again as Jamie and I walked through his death in our seventh month of dating. We would eventually lose both my dad, Harry, and her mom, Sharon, in very sudden circumstances, leaving our son without any grandparents and us without parents.

Jamie was well-traveled, very globally minded and super smart. On my advice, she spent a summer working with extremely disabled people in Hong Kong and also worked at Mother Teresa's Home for the Destitute and Dying while Mother Teresa was still living and working there. Nevertheless, she had no desire to ever be a missionary. My year away from her in South Korea was a time for both of us to think about whether we really wanted to get married. We knew it was going to involve so much travel, dislocation, and inevitably, the ugly politics of church life.

At one point, while we were dating, Jamie decided that she wanted to take me to a special fancy dinner on a very special date.

Oh no!! This is not happening! I thought to myself. *A fancy dinner?* Unless it was 10 courses of chocolate mousse, I was in serious trouble. I had been turning down all her offers to go out to dinner or have dinner with her parents or eat anything that wasn't pizza—which I had finally conquered at the age of 20 right after my mother died. She would have been so proud! Actually, she would have fainted! Alas, my mother never lived long enough to see me eat a slice of pepperoni pizza.

I finally confessed and told Jamie the whole embarrassing, humiliating story. "I'm a twenty-year-old male who is afraid of a piece of rice but wants to live in China for the rest of my life."

She didn't laugh. She didn't make fun of me. She didn't even act like it was weird. She was really mature about it. But much to my surprise, it didn't change her mind. She wanted me to get over it. *Crap!*

I tried to keep putting it off, but eventually Jamie got mad and challenged me. "I enjoy eating and food is a part of life. I want to be able to do this."

I was furious, scared, humiliated and in need of a miracle.

I called my sister Marcel, who had known me and my situation ever since that day in the orphanage when she picked me up, with my belly extended by malnutrition.

"I'm dating this girl I really like, but she...she....she wants me to eat food! How dare she!"

My sister felt sorry for me and offered sympathy and moral support.

Nevertheless, I liked Jamie a lot and wanted to do this. I was calling my sister from a pay phone at a commercial shopping center in Anderson, Indiana. There was a McDonald's across the parking lot.

"Marcel, if I go to McDonald's, is there some food I could try? Is there something super easy I could try? What's the simplest thing I could eat?"

My sister thought about it for a bit. Then she said, "Why don't you get a hamburger with no onions, no pickles, no ketchup, and no mustard. Just a plain hamburger."

I thought about it. In desperation, I agreed. "Okay. I'll do it."

We hung up and I drove my car through the drive thru. Up until that point I had only eaten McDonald's animal crackers, McDonald's chocolate chip cookies (when I got over my phobia of cookie dough), and french fries (which came almost 10 years later.)

I ordered one plain hamburger and drove to the middle of the parking lot. It was nighttime and I wanted to be far away from everyone when I threw up to death. I believed this was how I would go out. *So, this is how they will find me*, I thought. *The car door open, my body lifeless and limp, vomit and one tiny bite taken out of a hamburger on the ground, with the car facing a Payless. I hope they cover my grave in environmentally friendly kitty litter to make my humiliation complete.*

I prepared for the end. I was ready to meet my maker.

I took the most miniature bite of a hamburger ever taken in the history of humanity. All I got was bread, which was surprisingly not bad, even though the size of the bite was roughly the same size as a tick.

It was time. I took a big enough bite to get meat (although most readers will dispute that what is in a McDonald's hamburger is meat).

I chewed, and I swallowed.

"OH MY GOD!!"

"THIS IS THE MOST DELICIOUS FOOD EVER IN THE HISTORY OF THE WORLD!!!!!!!!!!!!!!!!!!!!!!!!!!!"

I was in love again! McDonald's!!! *Now I get it! Now I get why there are so many around the world! Over 75 billion sold!*

A few days later, I called my sister again.

"Hey Marcel. What other food can I try? Is there something else I might like?"

She thought about it again. "Hmm...Why don't you try going to Taco Bell. Get a burrito. Don't look inside. Just take a bite. There's a wrapping around it."

I drove to Taco Bell. I found an empty parking lot for maximum privacy.

I took a bite of a chicken burrito.

"OH MY GOD!!"

"THIS IS THE MOST DELICIOUS FOOD EVER IN THE HISTORY OF THE WORLD!!!!!!!!!!!!!!!!!!!!!!!!!!!"

Very shortly after that, I graduated to Wendy's, Arby's, Little Caesars, Burger King, Popeye's and after a twenty-year absence, I made my triumphant return to KFC.

Then I hit the all-time gold mine!

THE OLIVE GARDEN!

I was off to the races. I made that date with Jamie at the romantic restaurant and remember the carrot soup and chicken like it was yesterday. It went down fine. I didn't clear my plate, but I didn't throw up all over my date. And I survived!

Glorious moments of bliss and religious experiences followed at T.G.I. Friday's, Applebee's, Ruby Tuesdays, The Outback Steakhouse, Red Lobster, Friendly's, Fuddruckers, IHOP, Denny's, and Hooters (just kidding, Jamie).

I would eventually gain 25 pounds that would make me overweight and take me quite a few years to lose. I still don't like vegetables and find fruit super boring and not filling, but I had discovered a lot of food. I still refuse to even say the c-word, let alone eat it (that's a food that you find a lot in the fields of Kansas). I won't even spell it out because I hate it so much. I can write popcorn and peppercorn or Cornell University or the name of the black intellectual Cornel West, but I refuse to write or say the c-word. It's a hold-over from my traumatic days of staring at the plate my parents put in front of me.

Of course, all of the food was incredibly unhealthy, something I knew nothing about because it was a non-issue. I didn't think about carbohydrates or excess sugar or salt. I had been skinny my whole life and I assumed that all food was healthy except chocolate bars—unless they were those evil Breakfast Bars. I seriously didn't think that all this food that everyone was eating could be unhealthy, fattening, or even deadly. Years later when I would live in Europe, it became obvious on trips back to the United States how dangerous and over-processed and chemically infused American food is. Of course, now that I had finally learned to eat normal food, the world decided to rebel against this kind of food and even meat! *D'oh!*

Thanks to Jamie's pressure and support, now I could go to Asia, eat rice, and hang out at The Pizza Club with my Korean friends and eat with them. It was great, until one day

Kyeong Sook decided to give me a free pizza covered with the c-word on it.

Panty-Boy Comes to the Rescue

Kyeong Sook and I talked about Christianity and Buddhism a lot. But it was her sister-in-law Duk Pun with whom I spent hours discussing life and religion. It was during one of our discussions that I had a major moment of enlightenment about the difference between east and west. Duk Pun said to me: "I don't have a hard time believing in the historical claims of Christianity. I believe Jesus could have been divine, I believe that he could have lived, and that he could have been resurrected from the dead. What I have difficulty believing is that my life has any meaning, and that God knows me."[28]

As a non-westerner, Duk Pun had no problem believing in the supernatural claims of Christianity. It was clear to her that the world was spiritual and that there was more than the material realm. But Buddhism's reduction of the importance and role of an individual led her to believe she had nothing to offer anyone. It was impossible for her to imagine a loving God who cared about her and had a purpose for her life. The other side of eastern religion is that it can de-emphasize life to the point of meaninglessness for some.

Christianity does elevate the human being to a special place in the universe. It emphasizes that God wants an actual intimate relationship with us as human beings. He is not distant, neutral, or promoting meaninglessness. Neither is he an illusion. This emphasis on the importance of human life led to the insistence of global human rights and even secular humanism, which has so much confidence in man's rational and scientific abilities. Clearly, there is power in the

---

[28] *Passport of Faith: A Christian's Encounter with World Religions. P.130.*

idea of human beings having a purpose and a particular place within the cosmos. Growing up without that, Duk Pun had a more fatalistic view of the world—which is common in eastern thought. Some elements of fatalism are not necessarily bad. There is much that we cannot control, and our limitations will make themselves known in this life. But living without purpose, hope, and meaning is lonely, frightening, and demoralizing.

Could there be a balance between western religion's lifting up of the individual and eastern religion's healthy humility about our need to see ourselves as part of something bigger than ourselves? The Han family ended up converting to Christianity and emigrating to the United States after I moved away. I do not know what happened to Duk Pun and whether she converted or remained a Buddhist. I do know that her friendship was a priceless treasure for me. Not once, in all of our debates, did she ever tell me to "puck off!"

Buddhism teaches that a lot of our suffering comes from our ego and our desires. Long before Freud, Siddhartha Gautama of the Sakyas was teaching that our conscious and sub-conscious often get us into trouble. We have no real self. That is an illusion. The sooner we figure this out, the more quickly we can escape from suffering.

I can't help but feel that human beings are important and that there is a purpose for each life. But both Christianity and Buddhism teach that we have a great capacity for creating pain in the world because of our selfishness and self-protective nature. That has certainly been the case in my life. And my story about Panty-Boy is all about our desire to protect ourselves and how we can hurt other individuals—when they are just as important and meaningful as us.

At the *Hogwon*, I became the most popular teacher because of my use of comedy and wackiness in all my lessons. The kids would arrive screaming "Patrick, Patrick!" which felt good. Michelle/Yoko, however, made it clear that I was a lousy teacher. Although we could never have screamed or confronted Mr. Kim or Michelle/Yoko because that would cause a major loss of face and they had the superior status, they could do it to us. Michelle/Yoko absolutely reamed me out in front of everyone one particular day when she had used the camera in the classroom to spy on my class. It was demoralizing and I realized that my time living in Asia on this stint would be shorter than I had hoped. I was a lousy English teacher. My classes were like a Robin Williams comedy routine: entertaining, but not a great way to learn English.

One particular low moment that exposed my lack of teaching skills and lack of character occurred when an overweight 6th grade boy named "Jeffrey" was acting out in one of my classes. He was a loud kid who was often joking around, but also got teased frequently. There were hardly any overweight people in Korea, and as I said, East Asians are very candid about differences they find to be unacceptable.

I had created a superhero character called Panty-Boy that I would draw on the blackboard for laughs (can you believe they thought I was a bad teacher?). I had a theme song that accompanied it as well. Panty-Boy had the body of a human being with a cape, but his head was the shape of men's underwear. Any kind of bathroom or undergarment humor was sure to get a laugh from kids even in a different, foreign culture. I had learned some Korean, but working with kids meant that I was more likely to be able to say in Korean, "I can see your underwear," instead of something useful like, "the bathroom is upstairs on the right."

As Jeffrey continued acting out and talking while I was trying to teach, I got upset and lost my temper, "Jeffrey! You are a panty-boy!" The whole class stopped and then broke out in laughter pointing at Jeffrey. "Jeffrey is a panty-boy!"

they all chanted in unison. He was embarrassed, shamed, and got very quiet. I had regained control of the classroom. All was fine, I thought.

That night at 9 PM, our class ended when the bell rang. I went to my desk, put away my stuff, and conversed with the teachers for a bit. I then went down the stairs to go outside and catch my bus home. As I got down to the street level, I saw a big group of kids in a circle all laughing and pointing. They were all chanting "Jeffrey is a panty-boy! Jeffrey is a panty-boy." Jeffrey looked like a bull trapped in a bull ring, going around in circles, threatening to lash out with his backpack as a weapon as the kids continued to ridicule him. It looked like something out of *Lord of the Flies.*

I yelled at the kids to break it up and go home. They broke their circle and started to head their separate ways still laughing at Jeffrey, the panty-boy. I watched as Jeffrey walked away wounded, alone, and with his head down. I felt like the biggest "mother-pucker," in history. In my effort to get control of the classroom, I lashed out at Jeffrey, creating a moment that might haunt him the rest of his life. I was disgusted with myself. I knew what it was like to be a nerd or an outcast, and now I had created a very embarrassing situation for Jeffrey. Of course, a nickname like *"panty-boy"* was going to stick with a bunch of elementary school boys who were sure to bring it up forever.

I started to follow Jeffrey as he walked home alone in the dark. He walked through dark, lonely alleyways, across bridges, crossing canals, with food stalls giving off their smells in the Pusan night. I was walking about 20 feet behind him. I was trying to figure out how to make things right. I eventually caught up to him and said, "Hey Jeffrey, can I take you to McDonald's?"

He got excited and we walked a few more blocks to one of the few McDonald's that existed. This was before globalization had made everything look alike with all of us around the world using the same brands, communicating effortlessly across the internet, and eating in the same restaurants. McDonald's was a special, unusual treat. I let Jeffrey order whatever he wanted. He ordered *a lot*. And I apologized to him. He was all smiles. I was still utterly disgusted with myself.

I cannot help but think that individuals matter. That there is something inherently very valuable about every human being. Jeffrey is not just another aspect of the cosmos, but a special sentient being that deserves the very best. And the pain in the world is real and caused by people like me in moments like this. The clear belief in Christianity, that there is a particularly good way that things are supposed to be, but that our selfishness disrupts this, makes a lot of sense to me. It requires not escape, but second, third, and fourth chances. In other words, it means needing to receive grace and dispensing it. I don't think it was an illusion that I wounded Jeffrey and that the answer for both of us was to detach. I feel like I violated something sacred, a priceless individual with a purpose in this world. That was not okay.

My time in South Korea came to an end in 1996. It had been a fascinating experience. I encountered racism for the second time in my life (the first was, ironically, at my Christian university) and I had explored eastern religions and philosophies, I had made some wonderful friends, including one of my American colleagues, Dan Kelley, who would not only be one of my best friends for life, but would keep me sane and laughing during difficult times both in South Korea and years later in Hong Kong.

On my final day, I went to the roof of our tall apartment complex and looked out over the Shin-Mandeok valley one more time, just as I had at Tao Fung Shan in Shatin, Hong Kong—a very similar looking, beautiful valley. I was ready to leave teaching English, but I was not ready to say goodbye to Asia. Once again, I spoke these words aloud on that rooftop, "Asia. I will be back." I still felt I had much more to do.

7

God and Wham! At Yale: How Religion Engages with the Academic World

After I returned from South Korea, Jamie and I got married in 1997. It was then time to finish my education before making my next attempt at being a missionary to China. We drove a Ryder truck more than 3,000 miles from Portland, Oregon to New Haven, Connecticut.

There is such a massive difference between the American west coast, the Midwest, and the northeast. San Francisco and Portland felt so laid back when I lived there. They were liberal places, socially progressive, geographically stunning, and filled with weird, colorful people that loved nature and granola bars. Overwhelmingly, people were not very religious, particularly in Portland and Seattle. Vancouver, British Columbia—one of my favorite cities—is the most secular city in North America. Stereotypes become stereotypes because they are rooted in some truth.

The American Midwest was flat, with pragmatic people that were more socially conservative and far more likely to be religious. Churches could be found on every street corner and giant mega-churches with thousands of people were not uncommon. People were friendly and polite and the waitresses at restaurants were very likely to be full of smiles and call you 'hon' as they serve you super-fattening, unhealthy but mind-blowingly delicious sweet tea.

New England, on the other hand, like the Northwest, is also very secular. There are hardly any evangelical churches, and most churches that exist are probably rooted in traditional mainline denominations, like the United Methodists, or are Roman Catholic or Eastern Orthodox. Education is highly prized in New England. In addition to Harvard, Yale, Dartmouth, and Brown, there are the so called "Little Ivies" like Amherst, Williams, Bates, and Bowdoin. These are colleges that are incredibly difficult to get into and are very well-known on the East Coast, but not so much in the Midwest and West Coast. Then there are other excellent nationally well-known schools like MIT, Wellesley, Northeastern, and many other world-class institutions ranked in the Top 50 worldwide. Interestingly, the deep respect for top-notch education was the result of religious Congregationalists, Unitarians, and Puritans that had been greatly influenced by Cambridge and Oxford Universities. John Harvard was a clergyman that had attended Cambridge, for instance. The idea that religion, particularly Christianity was closely linked to science and the life of the mind was very strong in New England. But as the United States expanded westward in the 19th century, American Christians in the Midwest became far more hostile to education.

Some of this was due to less educated settlers and immigrants living in the Midwest, but some of it was also due to the fact that as Christians got nervous about Charles Darwin, a divide opened up between New England's more "liberal" and "secular" tendencies and the more "Bible-based," Christianity of the Midwest and what eventually became "the Bible Belt." Consequently, there are very few evangelical churches in New England unless they are African

American or from immigrant groups. But that form of Christianity has not permeated the New England culture the way evangelicalism has saturated the Central and Southern United States.

New England and the East Coast cities of New York City, Philadelphia, and Boston have an in-your-face, working-class attitude that's palpable: "How 'bout I breaka your face?" These cities have a much more aggressive, street-vibe than Los Angeles, San Francisco or Portland. And they certainly have an overall more aggressive vibe than Indianapolis, Des Moines, and Oklahoma City. ·

As I mentioned before, Oxford, Cambridge, the University of Paris and other renowned European universities were started and filled with people of religious belief. The same was true in the Islamic world, which was often scientifically more advanced and innovative than the West. Not everyone was a turbaned, Osama Bin Laden hiding in a cave with porn tapes. Two of the greatest and oldest universities in the world were established in Cairo and Fez, Morocco. The latter one was founded by a woman; Fatima al-Fihri. These Islamic and Christian universities focused on logic, arithmetic, medicine, geography, and were very rigorous. Some of the smartest thinkers in Islam, Christianity, and Judaism lived in the so-called "dark ages," another reminder that people in ancient days were not total meatheads. That link to intellectualism remained in the early colonies and the northeast of the United States where many of the Christian denominations were deeply rooted in higher education.

Once I was accepted to graduate school, I needed to fly out to New England to find a place for me and my new bride, Jamie, to live. Now I had a classy wife to provide for, and living in a pigsty bedroom subsisting only on chocolate milk and mac and cheese, sleeping on a sleeping bag in a dingy apartment, and basically living like my ancestor Ug

Nachtigall was going to have to change. We had gotten married in July 1997 and my high school buddies were my groomsmen. Mike was my best man, and Alan and Greg stood beside me. Natron played acoustic guitar, and Mark, who had been with me the night my mother died, played the trumpet. My Tigard High School friendships and the people of the Tigard Church of God were great treasures in my life.

Yale University is located in New Haven, Connecticut which is only about 60 miles north of New York City. The way I drove, I could make it to Manhattan in 55 minutes. It was now 1997, and I flew into Newark, New Jersey which immediately looked like a crime-infested city where you might get killed—because that is what it was. Murder rates were particularly high in the 1990s. Immediately, as soon as I picked up my rental car, the New York City and New Haven areas looked like something out of Martin Scorsese's mob movie Goodfellas. I drove past "Paulie's Garage," "Paulie's Pizza," "Paulie's Motor Inn," and "Paulie's Trattoria." It was a hot spring day and people were hanging out of their cars, blasting rap music, and L.L. Cool J's "Doin' It" was playing on my rental car radio. The whole environment seemed saturated with sex, testosterone, and the threat of violence. The New York City skyline was lit up and the Twin Towers were still rising above everything. As the radio played, other than L.L., it was a collection of horrible '90s tunes—a decade I decided to musically ignore completely.

Unlike a lot of other Ivy League schools, Yale University is located in a very urban, working-class city. That actually helps Yalies to be more down-to-earth and in touch with the less fortunate parts of society than the other Ivies which are cloistered in elite areas. The campus itself is gorgeous, filled as it is with neo-Gothic architecture, beautiful lawns, Hogwarts-looking cafeterias and stunning Colonial buildings. Originally located not far away in the town of

Branford, Yale was started in 1701 and named after a merchant named Elihu Yale. In the 1990s, New Haven was still struggling with very high-crime rates. As I drove around New Haven, I was clearly stunned by the campus architecture, but as I looked for places to live, I became worried. The housing options were nothing like in the Pacific Northwest which had apartment complexes everywhere in nice, safe neighborhoods. Even a lot of low-income apartments in the Pacific Northwest were located in nice, safe, environments. Not so in New Haven. There was far less of a Middle Class visible anywhere, including in the housing situation.

In New Haven, there were barely any apartment complexes at all. And the division between a good neighborhood and a bad one was extremely stark. A neighborhood in Wallingford, Orange or nearby Fairfield County might have billionaires, multi-millionaires and movie and television stars everywhere, but across the way in the next neighborhood, it might look like the worst inner-city imaginable. Sometimes one side of the street was safe with expensive homes, and the other side of the street was dangerous and run-down. On occasion, after a class in the Graduate School of Arts and Sciences building just across from the gorgeous Yale Law School, I would meet Jamie at KFC. Fried chicken and I had made up after a split of more than 30 years, and now I loved it, as I packed on the weight. It was only a 5-minute walk or less to KFC, but it was like walking from Oxford, England to the heart of the Bronx. The demographics and the street changed 100% in that very short walk. Those cheaper, dangerous neighborhoods are some of the ones that I was looking at, and I began to wonder, *where am I going to put my wife without endangering her life daily?* Jamie grew up in Cairo, Egypt so she was used to chaos, poverty, and was not easily jarred. But as a newly married man, I didn't really want to force my wife to live in the 'hood while I went to the Ivy Tower every day.

As I visited ratty buildings and houses looking for a place to live, I was starting to get really worried. Time was running out and I really needed to secure a place for us to live before we ended up living in "Paulie's Apartment Complex," sleeping with the fish or something like that.

I was staying at a very cheap motel run by an Indian immigrant, and the room and carpet definitely looked like somebody had been "whacked" by the mob there a few hours earlier. You could practically see the police's chalk outline. This was bad. So, I turned to prayer and got down on my knees right on that nasty carpet where no doubt bloodstains still lingered.

Dear God, I really need to find a place for Jamie and me to live. I believe we are supposed to be here, but I need help. We need a place to live. You've got to come through. I'm running out of time. More emergency prayers from Patrick.

There was a new thing that had been invented called "the internet." Jamie and I had spent thousands of dollars talking over the phone when I was living in South Korea. Of course, the month after I left South Korea, email became standard and you could now write to each other instantaneously for pennies. D'oh! It did allow me to look for churches in the New Haven area, however. I found no evangelical churches, which suited me just fine after my Calvary Temple experience. I was not interested in getting spiritually beat-up and condemned any more than I already had been. I wanted to be somewhere that valued the life of the mind.

One of the few churches that even had a website at the time was a United Methodist Church in North Haven. The UMC is one of those Christian denominations that did value the life of the mind more than movements like the ones that Calvary Temple belonged to. I reached out to a guy named

Steve who was the manager of the website. Steve contacted me and invited me over to his house for a barbeque. He was very nice, told me about life in New Haven and when we finished, he said, "Hey! There's someone I would like you to meet."

"Who?" I asked.

"It's our pastor, Kermit."

Images of Kermit the Frog with a priestly collar went through my mind. *People actually name their kids Kermit?* I thought to myself. *Is his wife's name Miss Piggy?*

Steve continued: "Kermit is amazing! He would very much like to meet you. I told him about you. He is a Yale graduate and he absolutely loves missionaries."

"Okay," I said, not knowing what to expect. I hoped I wouldn't laugh when he said his name. I've never been the most mature person.

Steve drove me over to his United Methodist Church and walked me into the office. I was not prepared for what I was about to experience.

As we walked into the room, there was an old, gray haired man with thick bottle-glasses and an enormous smile on his face. A former college football player in his youth, he still had a tall, sturdy frame and was as strong as an ox with an iron-grip despite a shaky right hand. He was wearing sky-blue athletic shorts, a sporty golf shirt, and leaning back in his chair with his feet up on his desk, like a naughty kid, a quarter his age, might do. A ray of light or unharnessed energy radiated from him.

Steve stepped back, as if he knew he was introducing me to a force of nature and just needed to get out of the way and let me experience the power of Kermit.

"Patty me-boy," he said.

"Patrick," I corrected him. I had always been known as "Patricio" or "Pat" and in college I decided to start going by

Patrick because Simon LeBon of Duran Duran had a two-syllable name, so I wanted one too. I know. I'm pathetic.

"Patrick?" Kermit said.

"Yes, it's Patrick," I gently corrected him again. I was serious about my two-syllable name.

"Okay, Pat."

He never called me Patrick again for the rest of his life.

"So, you are here to go to Yale, and you want to be a missionary."

"Yes."

"I love missionaries! I was a missionary. Pat, I oversaw missions for the United Methodist Church in the Belgian Congo. I was based in Brussels. I love Brussels, Pat. I miss Brussels. Brussels was great. It's very dark there throughout the year. But those were the best times of my life. I loved it! I like bike-riding. I lead bike tours across Europe. Do you like biking? I've got to introduce you to my wife Susi. She's amazing! She would love you, Pat. Do you mind if I call you Pat? Pat, I hear you need a place to live and haven't found one. Steve's a great guy, Pat. A great member of our church, Pat.

But here's the thing, Pat. I'm actually done at this church. You see, in the United Methodist Church we don't stay at a church for years and years. They move us around after a few years, Pat. So, my time is done here, Pat. In fact, I'm cleaning out my desk, Pat. I'm 70 years old and I am now supposed to retire! Can you believe that? I'm nowhere near retirement, Pat. I have a lot more left to do!

Well, here's the thing, Pat. I'm friends with the District Superintendent, nice guy, Australian. We had a talk, Pat. There's this church in East Haven called St. Andrew's United Methodist Church. They want to close it permanently. They are down to five people, but those people don't want to close the church, Pat. I don't think we should give up on this church. They have a parsonage, it's a big old house that's 120 years old. It's totally empty! Susi and I don't need it. We have our own house in New Haven, and we are living there with our dog Willoughby. Great dog, Willoughby.

So how about this, Pat? What if you become my assistant? Help me keep this church alive. We'll work together and I'll give you little jobs to do. Actually, just taking care of that parsonage would be a great help, Pat. It's not good that it's empty and nobody is living in it in that neighborhood. We'll give you the whole house for $250 a month rent. It's a five-minute drive to campus across the Q bridge, Pat. Go take a look at it tomorrow and tell me what you think, but I'd love to have you, Pat."

And that was Kermit. I was stunned. Provided that the house was okay, my prayer had been answered, just in the nick of time. I was also "in love." Kermit had charmed me, as he charmed absolutely everyone. Every once in a while, you meet someone with an irresistible personality. Kerm was so charming he could convince Satan to give up a life of evil and commit his evil self to rescuing puppies and singing John Denver songs for the rest of eternity. Kerm and his wife would end up being two of the most important people in my life after my mom and dad.

The next day I met Ralph and Carolyn. They both had super thick southern Massachusetts working-class accents. Along with a big, tall Dan Marino look and sound-alike and an elderly couple, Howard and Shirley, they were the only ones keeping this 120-year-old church open. Carolyn sounded just like Edith Bunker from the TV show *All in the Family* and Ralph sounded like a mellow, sardonically humorous Archie. They gave me a tour of the 120-year-old house on Forbes Avenue. I videotaped it for Jamie so that I could show her. Although it was old, it had a large kitchen, a dining room, and an upstairs with a great study nook. It also had a big room that could be my China library. I had amassed a huge collection of books on China by this time. There were also two other bedrooms. Being a man used to sleeping on the floor and eating mac and cheese each day, it looked great to me. I took the video back to Jamie, we took the deal, and I said to her, "You're going to love this guy, Kermit."

The Anti-Calvary Temple

Now that we are far, far into this book, this would be a good time to explain what a missionary is. The wait was intentional. As a child, in Costa Rica and San Francisco, I didn't really know what a missionary was—but I wanted to be one. I knew you tried to help people, worked for a religious organization, and that was about it.

The truth is that "missionary" is an outdated word with a lot of baggage. It's very vague and gives people images of a white guy in a pith helmet going to Africa to shove his Christian Bible down the throats of natives he looks down on. While things like that happened throughout history, it's the exception. Today, missionaries can be doctors, nurses, teachers, pilots, linguists, Bible translators, development experts, businesspeople, agricultural experts, social justice workers, English teachers, and pastors. There are many ways to try and impact the world. Usually you are working for a Christian organization and trying to make a positive change in one of those areas. You might be working in the fight against sexual slavery or caring for children that live in the sewers of Bucharest, Romania, or bringing education to girls in a remote jungle. It can be truly transformational stuff that makes the world a better place." With such a negative colonial history, the word "missionary" carries a lot of negative connotations and is frankly unnecessary and overly vague.

Because I wanted to get involved in some kind of social work and bring aid to China's poor, it was important for me to learn all about China's culture, government, economy, social problems, and history. I had studied some of this on my own and as an undergraduate in college, but now it was time to go far deeper. For this reason, I went to graduate school where I could learn all about Chinese history, anthropology, and religion. The perfect place to do that was at Yale University where the foremost historian on Modern China taught. Dr. Jonathan D. Spence. The Cambridge and Yale educated Spence, was a true giant in the field of history and the author of numerous books on China, including the definitive textbook on Modern China. He was handsome and looked and sounded just like the older Sean Connery. He was the biggest faculty star on campus and his undergraduate course on China was one of the most popular classes offered at Yale. At the Graduate School level, the classes were small seminars of 12 to 24 people, which was much better. I loved showing up to class early and sitting next to him—acting like a total rock groupie. The Pamela Des Barres of the academic world. Spence gave his lectures, shaken, not stirred.

With the 14 million volumes in the 42 libraries that make up the Yale library system along with all the expertise on China, one could do an entire Ph.D. dissertation on China without having to even go to China. It was a particularly wonderful place for China scholars filled with special Chinese collections scattered throughout the university. It was especially perfect for anyone examining how religion had developed and changed in the Communist era.

Dr. Lamin Sanneh was also a historian at Yale, who was tenured at Harvard off of the strength of his first classic book *West African Christianity* and then tenured at Yale due to his groundbreaking book *Translating the Message: The Missionary Impact on Culture*. Born a Muslim into royalty in the West African country of the Gambia, he was educated in Africa, Europe, and the Middle East, and had taught on four continents.

He was a world-renowned scholar on Islam, advising the Vatican on its Christian-Muslim relations efforts and wrote several books on Islam. But he was also an expert on "World Christianity" (an academic field which takes a special look at the very fast-growing non-western, polycentric, non-Colonial Christianity that emerges from places like China and Africa as opposed to from the well-established Christian traditions and theologies of western civilization and Orthodox civilization). Both Sanneh's lectures and his writings were notoriously difficult. A brilliant man, every sentence was incredibly precise, academic, and often pretty obtuse. Even the average scholar of history or religion could struggle in his lectures or with his writings. Although English was not his native language, like the great Russian writer Vladimir Nabokov, his use of the English language as a non-native English speaker far surpassed 99.99% of all English-speakers, even at a place like Yale.

Part of his groundbreaking research was on the subject of missionaries, something he was well-acquainted with coming from Islamic Africa where both Muslim and Christian missionaries had tried to spread their faith for centuries. Dr. Sanneh argued brilliantly that the idea that western missionaries had gone to places like Africa and simply imposed western Christianity on the locals was both offensive and inaccurate. This was the standard belief in the academic world: poor Africans had Christianity shoved down their throat by white missionaries and their tribal religions destroyed. Slavery and colonization followed. Sanneh turned that argument on its head. Aside from the fact that Africans were not idiots without the ability to critically think, there was also the fact that Christian missionaries always translated the Bible into the local language of the Africans. Consequently, the white, Christian colonialists, had disempowered themselves. Furthermore, Africans had more agency than was recognized, including in fighting the slave trade. Why? Because within the Bible, there is a strong critique against imperialism as well as the idea that any one nation or language or culture possesses God's truth.

This is a really important idea. What he was saying is that every other religion has a sacred language and sacred scriptures in a particular language (Hebrew for Judaism, Tibetan for Esoteric Buddhism, Arabic for Islam etc.), but Christianity stands alone amongst world religions in that it's not rooted in any one particular ethnicity, country, or civilization. There are, for example, Christian communities speaking in over 3,000 languages around the world. Meanwhile, Jesus spoke Aramaic which is almost entirely a dead language. *"Christianity is the only religion that spread primarily in a language not of its founder,"* he would often say in class. It's not American, it's not Greek, it's not Jewish, it's not Roman, and it's not Spanish. That is why the Bible is translated into every language imaginable, because no one culture or even language has the authority to be the gatekeeper of God's Word. *"More people pray and worship in more languages in Christianity than in any other religion,"* Sanneh would say in his gentle voice. And Christians had created more dictionaries and preserved more disappearing languages than any other force in history. Many tribal languages around the world would be dead if it weren't for Christian missionaries. Even at this minute, ancient tribal languages are being saved by Christians.

What that means is that every tribe, every people that receives Christianity has direct access to God and are equals with everyone else under God. This is far different than the capricious gods of the Greeks, or the unknowable gods of much of East Asia, or the purely transactional, angry gods of many tribal religions. So westernized Christianity was not really able to conquer the African mind. Once the Africans received it, they made it their own, and this happened in China and everywhere else. It's a powerful argument with huge repercussions which goes against the traditional narrative that Christianity robs people of their culture. What Sanneh was saying is that it actually robs the missionary of the ability to have a monopoly on truth.

Today, Christianity is consistently the fastest growing religion in the world when it is measured by how quickly it is being accepted by new ethnic groups as opposed to measuring the birth rate.[29]

There are more Christians in Africa than in the United States or Europe: 400 million. China is on track to be the nation with the biggest population of evangelical Christians in the world. Although the Anglican Church is from England, there are far more Church of England members in Nigeria than there are in all of the U.K. Christianity is no longer "western," if it ever was. The vast majority of Christians in the world are not European or North American. Neither is the average Christian wealthy or someone with white skin. This is something even few western Christians realize. And a lot of Chinese and African Christians do not trace their Christianity to white missionaries, Calvin, Luther or any other European thinkers. They are the product of prophets from their own continent. Ethiopia has had Christianity far longer than Europe. Western Christians and western atheists and agnostics have often made the mistake of thinking

---

[29] Islam is currently the fastest growing religion in the world due to people being born into the faith and categorized as Muslim, as opposed to conversion. But contrary to popular belief, birth-rates in Islamic nations are starting to slow.

Christianity comes from Oral Roberts University in Oklahoma.

Dr. Sanneh became my academic advisor and my professor in four different classes. Despite his extreme intelligence and highly academic way of presenting materials, Dr. Sanneh was a very gentle man, with a soothing soft voice. He loved football and was known to celebrate a goal by dancing around. He always walked on campus with a big, peaceful smile on his face. I would visit his office, ask him a question, and he would launch into a fascinating 45-minute answer.

Since I was there to study the expansion of Christianity in China since 1979 (when China began to open up to the West and experiment with special economic zones that practiced free-market capitalism), I clearly shared about my plans to try and work with Christian communities in China.

"I'm envious of you!" he would always say. "China is where the action is going to be." Sanneh knew that, ironically, while western academics were believing the era of religion to be over, the Marxist Chinese were examining the history of western civilization and were deciding that Christianity was the major factor in the rise of the West, and the key to the success of the United States. China was allowing students to come to universities in the West and they were becoming Christians, including many that had become leaders in the Tiananmen Square Democracy Movement of 1989. They were convinced that Christianity provided a force for social harmony and civil society that was missing in China in the post-Mao Zedong era. Once again, the absence of religion ended up with secularized religion. When his ideas led to massive famine and anarchy, China was lost and in desperate need of change. That change started to begin with Isaac Stern's visit to musical students in China—the one that was documented and which I saw with

Ricky and his mother back in the late 1970s. The one that had inspired me to be a missionary to China.

It wasn't just Dr. Sanneh. Dr. Richard Wood who was an expert for the Clinton Administration on Japan privately tutored me on Modern Japanese history from the Meji Restoration and its impact on Japanese religion. Most remarkable of all, professors like Jonathan Spence, anthropologists and historians, were extremely excited about my desire to focus on the role of Christianity during the process of modernization in the People's Republic of China. In other words: How was the growth of Christianity since 1979 helping China change over to a more democratic, capitalistic, prosperous society with a stronger social contract? At the time, this was a very cutting-edge subject. None of these professors were Christian and they were not even aware of how fast Christianity was growing in China and around the world. So much of this was happening under the radar. Yet never once did they think studying religion or Christianity was stupid. Quite the opposite! Their feeling was more like, *we need to know about this. We have completely underestimated how important religion is to political, economic, and cultural developments.*

The students were the same way. They were extremely curious about my subject and took it very seriously. There was no hostility toward religion or toward Christianity at all. Everyone at Yale was highly motivated to study very hard, and they were all infinitely curious about every subject. They craved extra homework and 1,000-page reading assignments per class. But it was not competitive, and nobody felt threatened in the least. In other words, they were not snobby, and they viewed religion as just as valuable as the sciences. "This is fantastic! I've never heard any of this!" one Israeli student said in front of Spence's class after I presented on the rapid spread of Christianity in China in our Modern China seminar. "I've seen these evangelical Christians all over Singapore, but didn't know what this was about," said Marcus, a brilliant Chinese kid from Singapore. "You rocked this!" said Ping An, an African/Chinese student.

"Why is this happening?" a student asked. Dr. Spence, the brilliant China expert began to speak, but sitting right next to him, I hushed him down.

"Let me take this..." I said as I literally waved him off. A look of shock crossed his face. But I was in a zone like an NBA player who gets the "hot-hand" and sinks a bunch of 3-pointers in a row. "Let me do my thang."

Don't think that I was always hitting 3-pointers like Michael Jordan against the Portland Trail Blazers in the 1992 NBA Finals. One time I accidently turned in an essay to Dr. Spence that was an error-filled rough draft—and it was about one of his own books!!! That was a disaster.

The main library at Yale is the Sterling Memorial. It's 16 stories high and is in the shape of a gothic cathedral. As you walk in, you are in the nave and instead of an altar, there is the circulation desk, card catalogues (in the old days) in the aisles, stained glass surrounding the building, and at the front is the Alma Mater mural; an Early Renaissance-style mural that looks like it is portraying the Virgin Mary or something from the Bible. But it doesn't. It's a "Cathedral of Learning." It's honoring knowledge and the educational institution itself. In a way, you could almost say it makes fun of religion in a cheeky, sacrilegious kind of way. I was always amused by that. But I felt at home here. I always did my reading on the 16th floor so that I could have a view of the cross-campus grounds and watch the New England leaves change color in the fall and the snow fall in the winter. The study carousel was incredibly uncomfortable which prevented me from falling asleep while reading. The rest of the time I preferred the Austin-Powers looking Cross-

Campus Library (now the elegant and classy Bass Library), and the Day Missions Library at the Colonial Virginia-looking Yale University Divinity School which had a phenomenal collection of anything to do with Christianity and China.

Jamie, who has always been exceptionally brilliant and able to master absolutely any job anyone ever gives her, became the Membership Coordinator of the Yale University Art Gallery and Yale Center for British Art, the two massive art museums at the university. They loved her, of course. She's a highly gifted manager. Jamie attended wine and cheese art soirees and took extremely wealthy Yale donors and alumni on bus tours of art museums in Midtown Manhattan, Harlem, Boston, Amherst, and many other places. They were often wealthy, little old ladies with too much time on their hands. The whole experience for both of us lived up to every stereotype imaginable. The highlight of my day was meeting up with her at Yorkside Pizza next door to the Graduate School or some other greasy spoon near campus.

We were both so happy to be far away from the anti-intellectualism of a lot of evangelical Christianity. It was like being released from prison for both of us. Here, people loved learning and were addicted to it. The pastors at Calvary Temple had told me that college would be terrible, that I would lose my faith, and that the Bible could teach me everything that I needed to know. Questions were not allowed. Secular places were supposed to be evil, and hostile to religion, especially Christianity. But that wasn't happening in graduate school. It was the exact opposite. Everyone we knew in New Haven was incredibly open-minded and respectful, and even Pastor Kerm was a Yale graduate!

These academic people weren't the close-minded ones. It was the fundamentalist pastors at Calvary Temple that were hostile and prejudiced. Even one prominent Church of God leader wrote me a nasty, completely unsolicited letter out of the blue: "You must think you know everything if you are choosing to go to Yale instead of Anderson School of Theology." That was a painful letter to receive. I cried. It's no wonder that many intellectually curious young people leave the evangelical church.

The Power of Kerm and Susi

The wounds of the Calvary Temple experience were deep. They had made me feel demon-possessed, like a total fraud, and like someone who was totally evil for liking secular music, secular books, and for challenging their theology. I still felt totally unworthy of being called a Christian, of being a missionary, and knew some people might think being at Yale was some kind of betrayal. All these professors, the vast majority of them not religious, were healing me and giving me hope. And people like Dr. Sanneh and Dr. Wood were Christians showing me that you could take the life of the mind seriously at the highest level and still be a credible academic and a credible Christian. They were very brilliant and very spiritual at the same time.

But nobody healed me more than Kerm and Susi. Kerm was always full of energy and affirming comments. His wife Susi, no academic slouch herself and a graduate of Bates College, was always loving and so nurturing to Jamie and me. "Where are the John Wesley puppets, Kerm?" were the first words I ever heard her speak. *They teach children about John Wesley? They care about Christian history before 1900? Who are these people?* I wondered. Just as with Kerm, I fell in love with Susi at first sight. When my first book came out in 2006, I acknowledged them by giving them a shout-out at the beginning. When I called her to check up on her a few weeks later, she answered and said, "Patrick, I'm sitting in my chair in the living room reading your book, right at this moment!" That was Kerm and Susi. They were our constant cheerleaders. They thought everything we did was great, and everything about us was wonderful. That was not true, of course, but sometimes in your life, you need someone to come along beside you and just cheer. After seeing how Kerm and Susi showed me unconditional love and support, I decided I would do that for others for the rest of my life: to actively find those who are feeling beaten up and need someone to believe in them again. I hope I've done that for many people.

Kerm was a mentor who was never threatened and hoped that you would succeed and go much farther than him. That is also something I took from him. Don't be one of those leaders who is obsessed with your own rise. Invest in the next generation immediately and hope that they go far beyond you. I've always taken that to heart as well. Nothing annoys me more than leaders that bottleneck and refuse to get out of the way to let other people rise. It's such a colossal waste of talent and potential, and it happens so often in the church. People build their little empires with themselves on top and never want to make way for the next generation. Hey man, Jesus took off after three years!

And Kerm and Susi loved intellectual discussions. The world of science and secularism was not scary. No subject, no theological question was off-limits, and that was incredibly healing also. Kerm was tireless, and Susi would tease him mercilessly. They had a bit of a comedy shtick as Kerm would get into all sorts of things and Susi would say, "Kerm, what are you doing now?" They made us laugh all the time. They not only became the mentors I needed, and the grandparents I never really had, they also became the parents I never had again after my mother died in 1991. My father had returned to Costa Rica, remarried and I never really saw him again very often—except for brief biannual trips to Costa Rica with Jamie and Marco.

Check Your Brain at the Door

Why do so many people think religion is intellectually vacant and that you have to check your brain at the door to believe in God? And how did the pastors at Calvary Temple get to a place where they thought all education was bad and not able to engage the university and the sciences?

A lot of it is the fault of Christians, particularly in the United States. Three-Fingered Gary and Pastor Bill Block are very much the products of a form of Christianity that spread like wildfire in America. They are descendants of famous preachers like Billy Sunday (1863-1935), who prided themselves on not being educated or trained. "I don't know any more about theology than a jack-rabbit knows about ping-pong—but I'm on my way to glory."[30] He believed the vast majority of educated people were damned to hell. "Thousands of college graduates are going as fast as they can straight to hell. If I had a million dollars, I'd give $999,999 to the church and $1 to education."[31] Nice.

In Heaven, he expected to see a mansion with a 'For Rent' sign which was supposed to belong to a professor of Union Theological Seminary in New York who went to hell instead.[32] Stay classy, Billy.

It doesn't get clearer than that. God good. Education bad.

The story of how Christianity got so threatened by the academic world is a long one, and a similar thing happened

---

[30] McLoughlin, William. *Billy Sunday Was His Real Name.* University of Chicago Press, 1955. P. 123.
[31] Ibid, 138.
[32] Weisberger, Bernard A. *They Gathered at the River: The Story of the Great Revivalists and Their Impact upon Religion in America.* Quadrangle, 1958. P. 258.

in Islam and Judaism. All three religions gave birth to fundamentalist movements at the end of the 19th century and beginning of the 20th century that fueled a radical rejection of science. Enormous books have been written on the subject, and this book is already longer than Tolstoy's *War and Peace*. There are lots of excellent books on this subject.

What I will say, is that the rise of Charles Darwin, Karl Marx, and Sigmund Freud as well as philosopher Friedrich Nietzsche, frightened many Christians. In the fields of science, economics, psychiatry, and philosophy there was now an alternative worldview that claimed to omit God completely. The ideas of these men entered into the universities, including religious ones like Harvard and Yale, so the response from many Christians was the creation of a lot of private Bible Colleges and/or a complete rejection of higher education.

Darwin, Sir Isaac Newton, and Albert Einstein were not as hostile toward religion or the idea of a God who is the source of all things as many scientists and Christians believe. But fundamentalists and other Christians reverted to viewing the Bible in an, ironically, scientific, literalist way, which meant that if science was right, the whole Bible and all Christian beliefs would fall like a house of cards.

Of course, this was not true. But many Christians still believe that to this day and think the words I'm writing now are directly from the pit of hell. Actually, I'm in Germany right now and it's quite lovely.

As I will discuss in the next chapter of this book, I believe that we are now entering into an age where it will be absolutely necessary for religion, philosophy, and science to work together more closely than ever due to certain technological advances and global challenges we are facing.

The Little Church That Could

The parsonage on Forbes Avenue was filthy. The neighborhood was extremely working class, filled with plenty of accented Italian American Paulies and Paulie Jrs. We lived right next door to a mafia-owned biker bar that was the noisiest place on planet Earth from 8 PM to 2 AM every single day of the year. Functional, quiet mufflers were a non-thing in New Haven. Our street was a main industrial road filled with loud trucks that shook the house all day and night. Car alarms went off all day long. There was one that went off without fail every night at around midnight that drove us both insane. Across the street from the church was the Paper Moon Lingerie store. And the house was so dirty, it took Jamie three days of scrubbing everything to make it livable. Of course, I hadn't noticed this when I took the initial tour. All I cared is that it had a roof.

While life during the day was in an Ivy League cocoon, we actually loved the fact that we lived out in the real world, with gangsters, new immigrants, drunken Phil knocking on our door asking for money, and Kerm showing up daily with a new down-and-out soul he had met on the streets.

Our church had five people, but with Kerm and Susi, the church began to grow very quickly. We had regular dinners open to the neighborhood with talent shows. Most people did stand-up comedy routines or told jokes that were very naughty. I got up and did a Woody Allen routine as the "Hispanic Woody Allen." Kerm loved that. The church raised money by collecting their beer cans at the front of the church. And Kerm preached awesome, intellectual sermons that were completely different from anything I had ever heard. Susi could play the organ. Occasionally, a "professional musician" named Willis showed up and sang in church accompanied by his bagpipes. His voice was so hilariously bad and the sound of the bagpipes so terrible in our empty church building that it was the only time I saw the smile wiped off Kerm's face. It was torture for him, and Jamie and I couldn't contain our laughter.

Despite being a small church, Kerm treated it like it was a big church. And people began to believe in it. They started to show up. For Christmas, Kerm had us do a Christmas tableau. *What's a tableau,* I wondered?

Kerm told me what was going to happen: "You are going to be dressed up as Joseph, and Jamie will be Mary. Ralph and the men from the church will be the kings and we will have a baby doll in a manger. We will stand on the street corner of Forbes Avenue in front of the church and people will see us as they drive by."

What? It was like 20 degrees below with light snow. What was the point of this? In our neighborhood, we might get mugged, or whacked by a guy named Guido.

But Kerm was the boss and we were getting cheap rent. Jamie and I took up our positions and stood there posing and freezing to death as trucks, gangsters, and police cars drove by. We did nothing. We were just frozen into position and also literally frozen.

I was having Calvary Temple/Tualatin Park flashbacks. But nothing bad happened. People honked, waved and said in their thick New England accents: "Bless youz people!"

Sixty-year-old Ralph was dressed as one of the Kings that brought gifts for the infant Jesus. At one point, he looked down at his gift for Baby Jesus and pointed at the lingerie shop, "Look!" he said. "I got a gift for Baby Jesus from the Paper Moon!"

This was not an ordinary G rated church. I was home!

Then there was the time that it was announced that we were going to have an Easter play acting out the crucifixion and resurrection.

"Pat, you are going to be Jesus."

I thought the long-haired, working-class, Dan Marino look-alike in our congregation should do it. His name was Jamie and he played saxophone in a band. He looked like a quarterback Jesus. Perfect!

"You don't want a Hispanic Jesus. Maybe someone else should do it," I suggested, hoping to get out of it.

"No, Pat. You were an actor in high school, you should do this."

Low rent. I did it.

We went into rehearsals. Kerm took this play—that would probably be seen by forty people if we were lucky—*extremely seriously*. It was like Broadway for him. He wanted it to be perfect.

Even though it was the story of Jesus of Nazareth, you couldn't keep New Haven out of it—so it was more like Jesus from the 'hood. Jamie, the Dan Marino tough guy, played Judas and he betrayed me, but definitely not with a kiss.

In that very emotional moment when Jesus and Judas face off and Judas walks off to turn Jesus over to the Jewish high priests for arrest and punishment, Jamie-Marino said in his thick Sopranos-like accent:

"Hey! I just ratted out Jesus!"

But I had the worst of it. In rehearsals I learned that I would be crucified.

"Where do I get crucified, Kerm? Where's the cross?"

"Oh, there is no cross, Pat. You are just going to stand in the middle of the stage like you are on a cross and say your lines," Kerm responded.

What? There's no cross at all? This was going to be embarrassing. Miming a crucifixion.

"But I do have this for you, Pat! Here's the crown of thorns you will be wearing."

And with that, Kerm handed me an actual crown of thorns! It was painful and I was supposed to wear this real crown of thorns but be on an imaginary cross!!!

"Why does the crown of thorns have to be real, but not the cross?"

"Go with it, Pat. It will be great! The audience will love it!"

When show time arrived, I did my part and was crucified emotionally and literally. As I prepared to die on the imaginary cross wearing a real crown of thorns on my head, I delivered my lines with as much dramatic effect as possible:

"Father, forgive them for they know not what they do!"

I deliberately paused, since I'm—you know, acting out *a crucifixion!*

Kerm whispered at me extremely loudly so the whole audience could hear:

"It's your line, Pat!"

I shot him a look. Of course, I knew it was my line, I was just pausing! I'm on a cross for God's sake—literally, and literally!

"My God, My God! Why hast thou forsaken me?" I cried under the weight of the crown of thorns acting out the intense suffering and abandonment of Jesus in his darkest moment.

Another dramatic pause.

Kerm unhelpfully interjects: "It's your line, Pat! I'm thirsty! I'm thirsty!"

Okay, how can it be that Kerm wants a super perfect, and professional show with a real crown of thorns, but when I give a dramatic pause on the cross, he ruins the entire show by feeding me my lines loudly in front of everyone! *Really? This was happening?*

It was hopeless. Time to speed it up. I finished my final lines as Jesus and died.

"I'm thirsty. Itisfinished-Fatherintoyourhands Icommitmyspirit." Head down. Crucifixion done.

Death is Always Nearby

I died on that cross. Of embarrassment. But I also almost died a mile away after that. I've nearly died four times: once as a child, once when I crashed my car on a freeway outside of Portland when I was in high school, and once in Hong Kong when I had emergency surgery when my appendix completely disintegrated and nearly poisoned me to death.

The "Q Bridge" was a bridge that spanned the Quinnipiac River and separated East Haven from New Haven. Every weekday, I drove the five-minute commute on the freeway and across the bridge to school. But it was always extremely dangerous. Connecticut drivers were the fastest drivers I have ever seen anywhere other than the German autobahn. In order to go from the school to our house, I had to enter onto the freeway, immediately cross four lanes to get onto the Q Bridge and not head to New York City. As soon as you were on the bridge, two lanes coming from New York entered onto the bridge. Then the bridge began making a "C" curve so that you couldn't see what was up ahead, but I needed to immediately merge and get three lanes over in order to take the first East Haven exit. Because of the insane amount of traffic and the extremely fast driving, it was always a very tricky, dangerous move. It's still the craziest, most dangerous stretch of road I've ever seen.

One afternoon, I got onto I-95, crossed the lanes of the Q Bridge and ended up in the right lane just before the blind-spot. As I got to the middle of the bridge in the far-right lane, probably going 75 mph, I saw a car completely stopped up ahead. The car was parked in the middle of the Q bridge! There was absolutely no way to move into the left lane as usual, so I slammed on the breaks as hard as possible. My car screeched to a halt. The bumper of my car literally must have been one inch away from the parked car, right there in the middle of the bridge.

I felt a moment of relief, and it was just like in a movie.

I looked in my rearview mirror and a giant semi-truck was headed straight for me—also a victim of the blind-spot. I was now completely stopped with no room to move and trapped in the lane. Neither could the truck enter into a left lane. I had enough time to think to myself, *this is how it ends*. The semi-truck slammed on its brakes and came to a stop about a foot or less away from my rear bumper. Cars honked, brakes were slammed, and there was lots of swerving on the freeway as people yelled—it should have been a massive disaster with multiple deaths. And I definitely should have been killed. But I wasn't. When I eventually pulled out into the speeding traffic, I looked into the car that had been parked and nearly killed me and there was a man just sitting there looking straight ahead. Trying to commit suicide? Frozen after a car problem? It was impossible to know. The Q Bridge (Pearl Harbor Memorial Bridge) has since been remodeled and improved. I could have died right then and there. Why didn't I? Luck? Destiny? God's will? Regardless, we live on borrowed time and literally every day, every moment could be our last.

As graduation inched closer, it was time to decide how we would go to Asia. Would we take some kind of teaching job with a religious organization? Try a more overt social-service route? Go with a mission agency from some Protestant denomination or return to our native Church of God where both our parents and grandparents on both sides had served? We were leaning toward not going with the Church of God. Frankly, we had enjoyed the New England atmosphere and the anonymity it afforded so much that we wanted to stay in this kind of environment, perhaps working with the United

Methodists. That was what Kerm was pushing us toward. "We need you guys!"

Missionary kids and pastor's kids pick up a lot of baggage as they grow up watching their parents work in churches or on mission-fields. Inevitably, you see the darker side of things and pastors and missionaries are often in the firing lines. Then there's the institutional politics, and the feeling of being watched constantly. We were leaning against going to the mission agency where Jamie's wonderful mother, Sharon, was now one of the key leaders. Would that be a good idea to work with family in this kind of setting? As much as we adored Sharon and trusted her more than anyone in the world, we didn't want to cause problems. But we were being offered the opportunity to go into China, connect with underground and above ground Christian communities, and do whatever kind of work we wanted to do. For the first time since Church of God missionaries were kicked out of China when the Communists took over in 1949, there was a plan to re-engage with the Middle Kingdom.

I went to a Thai Restaurant in downtown New Haven and met up with Dr. Jonathan Bonk. He was head of the Overseas Ministries Study Center across from the Yale Divinity School which was a hub of Christian scholarship. OMSC was also a place where scholars come to study at Yale and utilize the research facilities, as well as the place where the respected International Bulletin of Mission Research is produced. I often would drop by his office on return visits to New Haven to hear about the latest academic research. I explained to Dr. Bonk our family history, our current situation, and our dreams for China at this critical juncture in that nation's history.

Dr. Bonk always reminded me of Robert Redford. He had that handsome, serious, experienced look. I listened intently and he surprised me. "I think you guys should go with the Church of God."

"Really? Why?"

"You guys are going to need the freedom to dream up new things, create, and innovate. You're going to need a looser structure that lets you follow your ideas of how to do things. I think that's the only place that is going to give you that kind of freedom."

And that decided it. We followed Dr. Bonk's advice. We would become the third generation on both sides of our families to become missionaries with the Church of God. Gulp.

Our time in New England had been so healing and rewarding. Jamie and I had explored every corner of every state in New England, the Atlantic Coast of Canada, and had fallen in love with New York City and Boston. Everyone had been so wonderful to us and we had learned so much in so many different ways. And I finally felt a sense of closure regarding the Calvary Temple experience, although those feelings of condemnation still wash over me from time to time. It's not easy to get over being accused of being demon-possessed. Ask Linda Blair.

Saying farewell to Kerm and Susi was going to be difficult. They had become the family—the parents I needed at that key moment in my life. We packed up another Ryder truck and planned to leave at 5 AM so that we could drive the big truck through Manhattan before rush hour got too bad.

"I'll be there," said Kerm.

"But it's so early. You don't have to do that," I replied.

But that final morning, Kerm was there, standing on Forbes Avenue with his dog Willoughby. We gave him our final hugs and thanked him profusely. The big smile was there.

I got in the driver's seat of the big yellow truck. We both looked out the side-mirror one last time to see Kerm behind the truck and by the parsonage. Big tears were streaking down his face.

I was heart-broken having to say "goodbye."

Years later, when our son Marco was born, we took him to meet Kerm and Susi. We still have a video of little Marco walking around Kerm and Susi as they gently listen and talk to him as he jabbers away.

A couple of years later, when I called to check up on them, Susi told me, "I'm worried about Kerm. He's forgetting lots of things." It was the start of Alzheimer's.

Eventually, Kerm would lose his ability to really be at home and moved to an assisted living center in Fair Haven. We lost Susi while we were on a short visit to the USA. A giant snowstorm brought everything to a standstill in New York State and we weren't able to make the drive across the state to the funeral in Connecticut.

Occasionally over the next decade after we left New Haven, I would be on the East Coast and would always make it a point to drive up and visit. After Susi passed away, I went up and visited Kerm.

There he was, in a crowded room filled with older, sick people and a loud television blaring, as nurses ran around. He was in a wheelchair with a big smile on his face and those big glasses.

"Hi Kerm. Do you remember me?"

"Yes." He didn't.

"How are you doing? I've missed you. I'm so glad I got to know you. I love you so much." I said.

"Yes. Boy, we sure had some good times."

Does he recognize me, I wondered? *He's talking about good times.*

"Have you seen my Susi? You have to meet my Susi. She should be here by now."

He couldn't remember that she had passed away or that I knew her.

"I'm sure we'll see her. You look so good, Kerm."

"Boy, we sure had some good times. Those were good times."

"Yes, Kerm. Those were good times."

It was torture to finally end the conversation and get back on the road knowing I might never see him again.

Kerm died shortly after that visit.

"Yes, Kerm. Those were good times."

8

Leprosy and McDonald's in China: How Religion Inspires Us to Do Good

After 21 years of waiting, I finally moved to China. I was a missionary, trying to help people, and seeing first-hand the rise of the Chinese nation after centuries of humiliation, as well as why religion matters to modern societies. I was also introduced to chocolate soy milk.

The walk to the leper colony was a long one. It weaved through giant limestone mountains, through great open spaces, rice fields, and Chinese villages so small that only a handful of people lived in the ancient Chinese red and grey brick houses. This was rural Guangxi, a province of almost 50 million people, famous for the stunning city of Guilin which sits all around karst formations of limestone that stick out like stone humps around the Li River and the city itself. The journey to the lepers began by either taking a long train or short plane ride from Guangzhou, before taking a bus out into rural China, then a rented mini-bus to go on remote roads hardly anyone had ever seen, and then finally a long half-day walk to an extremely remote village populated with people that were outcasts: ex-communicated from society because they had the disease of leprosy. This was like a journey going back in time a few centuries.

Jesus cared for lepers, hung out with them, and healed them. I should point out that you can believe in Jesus and be a good person without having to find actual lepers to hang out with. That's not a requirement for being a Christian. I was taking all of this far too literally. My old church probably thought I was roasting in hell. But actually, I was roasting in hot, and muggy China. The extreme humidity in Hong Kong and China would give me a ten-year long rash.

This was one of two leper colonies Jamie, Marco, and I began to visit on a regular basis. When Marco was in school, I would go alone or occasionally take church friends, or visitors from other countries, if they wanted to experience it.

Overall, our job was to build up a network of partners that would support social service projects, support Christians serving in official registered churches (Three-Selves Patriotic Movement), and also support illegal Chinese underground churches (*jiating*). These two very different groups had historically been at odds with each other as one side received official government recognition for towing the party-line within their churches, and the other one was persecuted for practicing religion outside of the purview of Beijing's Religious Affairs Bureau. I happened to arrive at a unique moment in China when the underground church and the registered churches were, at least in some places, cooperating in unprecedented ways. The officially registered churches were enjoying more freedom from government intervention and were busy constructing new church buildings across the country. Meanwhile, the underground church was exploding in numbers and the atheistic government was starting to acknowledge the importance of religion. The persecution varied from province to province and valley to valley throughout China, so one always had to be very careful. Some areas were quite free and open, while others could be very dangerous and closed. You were in the hands of the local authorities. But overall, things were more open than they had ever been since 1949 or would be in the future.

As the Chinese government studied the West, their scholars came to the conclusion that religion was an important part of social stability and civil society. The government began to allow religious people to practice more openly and it was even made legal to be a Christian and be in the Communist Party. The subject that I had been studying in graduate school was now being studied at the highest levels of the Chinese government throughout the coming decade. Religion was deemed to have an important role if China was to continue its rise. So, while university professors in the West were teaching Marxism, actual Marxists in China were studying religion! As Dick Deadeye said in H.M.S Pinafore: "It's a queer world!"

As for leprosy, it had been pretty much eradicated by modern medicine. Cases still break out on occasion. It's a disease that can damage nerves, skin, eyes, and lead to people losing their hands, feet, or other body parts. Before hanging out with active lepers, I made sure to have my gorgeous legs insured by Lloyds of London. They were valued at $3.95. In Biblical times and throughout history, the contagious nature of leprosy and the disfigurement frightened people, so lepers were shunned from society and put in remote places as had happened in this colony in rural Guangxi that I was visiting. Some of these lepers had active cases, but most did not. Had I picked up leprosy, as a westerner with access to modern medicine, I would have been able to avoid having my body parts drop off—especially those vital ones. But these lepers grew up in extreme poverty in a country with very few resources or interest in helping people like them. They were truly outcasts.

Typically, China had little concern for the sick, disabled, and deformed who were called "*canfei ren*" which literally means disabled garbage people. One of my friends was born with a slightly bent finger. This made her "damaged goods" and was a source of embarrassment and shame for her. She said it would inevitably hurt her marriage prospects. Standards for perfection are high in Confucian societies whether it's in regard to school grades, one's profession, or one's beauty. And as I experienced in South Korea, people in China are very blunt about what is wrong with you and will point it out to your face, "You look fat, Patrick! You gained weight since I last saw you, and your haircut looks bad. It is not handsome. You look dirty." This kind of blunt commentary from good friends was totally normal in South Korea and China. It did wonders for one's self-esteem. If that's the way it is for the average person, you can imagine how terrible it was for the lepers or disabled.

China Abandons Religion

The period between the 8th century and 3rd century BCE is known as the Axial Age. It was a time when major civilizations around the world were forming very sophisticated philosophical and religious ideas, particularly in response to growing wealth and inequality. Zoroastrianism and Judaism were giant moves away from local, tribal gods to a belief in one God (monotheism); a route both Christianity and Islam would follow. The Indian civilization produced Hinduism, Buddhism, and Jainism which also sought to transcend the limitations of the religions of the time. It is important for modern people to remember that these developments were not a war to replace reason and scientific thinking but were meant to be complimentary in a universe that also demanded vehicles for transcending them. Buddhist *nirvana* was higher than the gods and beyond the limitations of rational thinking which was accurately viewed as occupying a limited quadrant of human experience and the universe.

In China, the Axial Age produced Taoism, the philosophy of Confucianism, and Buddhism which was brought by Buddhist missionaries from India and arrived in China shortly after the time of Christ. While some reading this may think that I, as a missionary, was corrupting China by taking western Christianity to China (a foreign religion) there is evidence that Christianity and Buddhism arrived in China at the same time, around 50 years after the death of Jesus Christ. Christian Chinese rock carvings have been found that date back to AD 86. In other words, Christianity is just as old in Asia as it is in Europe. The disciple of Jesus named Thomas went to Kerala, India around AD 52 and established a Christian community still known today as the St. Thomas Christians (*Malankara Nasrani*). Christianity even established itself in Africa and Central Asia, before it centered itself in western Europe for a long time. Unlike other religions, Christianity inherently always resisted having a fixed geographical hub.

Confucianism, Taoism, Buddhism, and Christianity were all present in China when Mao Zedong took over China in 1949. The socialist People's Republic of China began to wage a war against religion within the decade. American missionaries from my denomination were forced to flee as all foreign influences were removed. During the Cultural Revolution, gangs of youth were sanctioned by Mao to tear down Buddhist temples, Christian churches, Confucian ancestral halls, and Taoist temples. Tremendous works of art were mindlessly destroyed and millions of religious people, including priests, nuns, pastors and other believers were killed, jailed or persecuted.

The atheistic People's Republic of China replaced religions with the religion-like cult of Mao and Communist ideology. That did not work out so well. Mao's poetry was considerably better than his economic policy. His Great Leap

Forward turned out to be a tremendous leap backward and his Cultural Revolution that followed destroyed what little glue that was holding Chinese society together. Then came a period of moral anarchy where kids turned on parents, students killed (and even cannibalized) teachers to prove their devotion to the Party, and everyone was forced to worship Mao. China turned into one big re-enactment of *Lord of the Flies* with a cast of 400 million.

Mao Zedong Thought led China into the economic backwaters and now this once advanced civilization was so poor some people were eating rocks or tree bark and drinking horse urine to survive. The country had always been prone to famines but now nearly all the people were living under the poverty line. Mao died in 1976 and China's era of reform began in 1978-1979 and they started opening up to western ideas.

The Chinese are naturally entrepreneurial and highly motivated, so when capitalism began to be practiced, China's economic growth was stunning. Its economy grew roughly 9% each year for about three decades. Most economies are lucky to grow 1% or 2%. It happened so quickly; the world wasn't even fully paying attention initially.

When we told our friends about our impending move to China in 2000, most people still thought that China was an extremely poor country where everyone was starving to death or only had rice to eat daily. China's "economic miracle" was not yet global news. People around the world also assumed that everyone in China was a communist. By the time we arrived, however, the truth was a little more complicated. China was still a very poor country with one billion people living in poverty, but it was moving from agriculture to manufacturing and from being a rural country to primarily an urban one. It was de-centralizing and even experimenting with democracy at the village level. Special cities and regions designated as "Special Economic Zones," like Shanghai, Beijing, Dalian, and Shenzhen were starting to build skyscrapers, starting private businesses, and connecting to the outside world. Foreign countries were opening up factories in China and taking advantage of China's hard-working, low-wage labor. Most of China, especially the interior, was not reaping the benefits of this new openness yet. But the country wasn't as socialist or famine ridden as Americans thought in the late 1990s.

I love Americans, but they are such drama queens! Within a mere four years after moving to China, I would discover that Americans were now under the impression that China was a world power that was going to completely dominate the United States economically and militarily. From one extreme to another within four years. It was amazing how quickly Americans' image of China changed. China was not a super-power at the time or even close. Nearly a billion people were being left behind as the socialist safety-net dried up and people's wages were too low to keep them out of poverty. Issues of corruption, shadow banking, extreme pollution, poor education, left-behind villages, lack of females due to the "one-child policy," and an aging population were enormous problems and are still obstacles that China will have to surmount to get to the next level of economic development. They may become the largest economy in size soon, but not in complexity and sophistication. China is currently getting stuck in something called "the Middle-Income Trap." The days of easy, rapid growth are most likely finished. And they are still far away from being able to truly compete with the United States as an advanced economy. Today, they are ranked about 65th in GDP per person according to the International Monetary Fund, just below Mexico.[33] Viva Mexico! Viva Taco Bell!

Nevertheless, China was a far cry from the country I visited in 1991 after my Mom died. At that time, the border guards looked extremely menacing as I gave them my passport. They were stern male soldiers in full uniform frowning and growling, not the bored Chinese twenty-something kid that might stamp your passport today. I was not allowed to go out on my own, although I did sneak out of my hotel in Foshan when the minders were not looking. Otherwise, I was monitored constantly by Chinese government-appointed minders who spewed Communist propaganda and anti-western thought during their tours. "China is a paradise; the West is a land of crime and poverty." Everyone in China dressed in the same drab clothes, and no one ever smiled. You never saw couples holding hands or having a romantic moment. Back in 1991, China still looked more like today's North Korea than the images we have from today's China. Now arriving 10 years later, the country was on the brink of an even greater major transformation and I was going to get to see it first-hand.

That first trip to China in 1991 was also memorable because I didn't eat anything the entire time. We were taken to large banquet halls and served ten course meals of Chinese food meant to impress foreigners. These were feasts the average person couldn't afford, of course. We were being offered the very best, but due to my ridiculous phobia of food, I ate nothing. I survived my time in China by eating a candy bar a day and ordering a milkshake—which fortunately these tourist hotels occasionally had. There were no McDonald's or KFCs or anything remotely recognizable in those days. Everyone marveled at these exquisite dishes of Chinese

[33] Americans under-estimate how wealthy and developed Mexico is, and over-estimate how rich China is.

delicacies as they came out and I couldn't eat a single thing. Not even a sip of the various soups they presented. It was humiliating and deeply frustrating. I remember telling my father, "Dad, I would give up 20 years of my life to be able to eat like a normal person." That made him very sad. He didn't realize the extent of my frustration and humiliation over the years. He didn't realize that not eating was eating me up inside. *How was I ever going to be a missionary in China or anywhere?* I wondered.

With the Chinese now enjoying upward mobility, a moral vacuum emerged. It became a Darwinian every-man-for-himself society where there was no common understanding of how to act toward one another. There was no more need to look out for one's "comrade" or fear about what would happen if you didn't. Individualism ran rampant. The communist socialist safety-net was taken away from people and there were no more government handouts or communist comrades to care for them. During this time of transition, one of the few groups that made an effort to reach out to the poor, the destitute, and the abandoned were Christians.

So, what made Christianity so different in China? As Christianity exploded in the 1980s and 1990s, it offered China a moral compass for the nation. Christianity taught that there was more to life than materialism and that we have the obligation to care for all of our neighbors—not just some. The Christian notion of *agape*—the deepest kind of love—which means *"loving your neighbor as yourself and seeking their highest good instead of your own,"* was a revelation to millions of Chinese. The Chinese were impressed that the Christians did not care whether you were rich or poor, healthy or a leper, pretty or ugly—all were equal and had the right to be loved. This broke through a lot of the hierarchies and fatalism found in Buddhism, Confucianism, and Taoism. And the fellowship between humans was based on love and a transcendent, absolute source, not a temporal, ever-changing Communist ideology obligated by the State. That was a big deal!

Along with *agape*, there was the fact that Christianity puts the concept of grace at the forefront. Grace: meaning that you are not the sum-total of your faults, your failures, your sins, your weaknesses, your birth-order, your appearance, your wealth, or your *karma*. The Christian idea of grace meant that everyone was equal and precious in the eyes of God and that every fault we have is rendered unimportant by the grace of God exemplified in Jesus Christ. Jesus made it clear that his *"Kingdom is not of this world,"*[34] meaning that his way of viewing things was more expansive and rooted in transcendent love and grace than the forms of measurement in our societies. Jesus doesn't care if you were a murderer, a sex-trafficker, a Wall Street criminal, Charlie Sheen or even an American politician, everyone has full value in his eyes. For Jesus, eradicating sin was more about all of us finding a water that would keep us from getting thirsty and having a burden lifted off our back than it was about judgment and legalism. That was a powerful and liberating message for the Chinese at a time when it seemed like there was no moral framework about how people are to behave toward one another. There were also many people who carried extreme guilt about the crimes they had committed on innocent people during the Cultural Revolution. You don't get over cannibalizing your math teacher that easily. I sure didn't.

Now my long wait was finally over! It was the beginning of the 21st century, the world had not ended in 2000 like Prince predicted, and after a 22-year wait, I was finally in China. And baby, I was "ready to roar!" I was getting to be a part of how this message of grace was inspiring the disabled,

---

[34] John 18:36 in the New Testament of the Holy Bible.

the diseased, the poor, and the left-behind. Together with Chinese Christians, I could practice *agape* love and try to help this country through the most important transition of its history by caring for her people. And the best part of all was that now, 10 years later, I was no longer afraid of rice! In fact, I loved it! Thank you, Jamie! And *arroz con pollo*!

The lepers would have loved a Gordita Crunch, but there was no Taco Bell in China. Instead, we would take up medicine, bandages, fruits, warm clothes, and money to the lepers. We also supplied the Chinese Christians with things they needed, like a Reference Bible or other things that were hard for them to find. Sometimes it was outdoor gear. There was an extreme shortage of Chinese Bibles even though the Chinese government was now allowing Bibles to be printed. Both the lepers and the Chinese Christians would usually be overjoyed to see us. For the lepers, this was especially true since no one in the world ever cared about them. The government had no time for them, nor did society. The only people that made any effort to even acknowledge their existence were the Christians. And the Christians not only acknowledged them, but brought them food, supplies, and even more impressive—love and genuine friendship.

Leprosy, like your toddler, can make you really tired and exhausted. So many times, they were just lying in their beds in their decrepit little homes. They didn't always smell too good either. Nothing like the boys' locker room at Twality Junior High, but still, pretty bad. The lepers were kind. And it wasn't uncommon for them to be in tears because they were so moved by being visited. Nothing was better however, than touching the lepers. Human touch is so fundamental to us that babies can literally die or be brain damaged by not being held and touched. Touch was not something the lepers experienced very much. China is not a touchy culture in general, but when you are a leper, it's completely out of the question. I'm at the other extreme. I'm Latin and I love hugging and will hug everybody! The lepers didn't know what to do with me. One visit with me was probably more touching than they had received in five decades! I'm surprised they didn't file a restraining order against me.

Walking through the mountains of Guangxi, Meihui[35], a thirty-nine-year-old Christian woman sang Christian hymns that would bounce off the walls of the sheer mountain cliffs and make an echo. The songs were not Christian hymns from Europe or the United States. They were Christian songs completely written and composed in China by Chinese Christians that had lived in hiding during the communist era. There were literally thousands of these songs. One Chinese woman was said to have written more than 800. Of course, this being me, I preferred to pass the many hours listening to Radiohead's *Kid A* and *Amnesiac*, which made for a depressing and haunting soundtrack to go along with the many run down, decrepit, left-behind towns and villages that exuded a unique gloominess.[36] It would have been funny to make Meihui sing a Radiohead song, telling her it was a famous hymn in English, maybe the song "Creep."

I did enjoy Meihui's singing. It was certainly more uplifting than Radiohead and furthermore, this was the non-western Christianity that Dr. Sanneh had talked about and for which he had expressed envy that I would be getting to experience first-hand. They were free from western, European, and American Christian influence, tradition, and theology. And I was not there to supplant them or bring an Americanized version of Christianity, but to support them as

---

[35] Name changed for security reasons.
[36] Radiohead, No Doubt, and Snoop Doggy Dogg were about the only 1990s musical artists I was willing to listen to. All three of them are great for visiting leper colonies in remote China.

they spread that *agape* love. We didn't need to plant some denominational flag. We just needed to love people.

One day, we came across a group of senior citizens, in a tiny, little village on top of a mountain. They still dressed in the kind of outfits Mao Zedong wore. They huddled around a tree at the top of a hill far from everything. My Chinese Christian friend Meihui said to me, "Okay, Patrick. Explain to them Christianity. They've never heard anything about it."

After all my years of study, of living around the church, of thinking, analyzing and processing my experiences with religion, I found myself at a loss for words. These were Chinese people that had grown up under imposed atheism and whose ancestors as far back as you could go were probably Taoist and Buddhists with a worldview that was far removed from the Christianity we practiced in the West. Perhaps years ago, they had ancestors that were Christians. But that would have been long ago. Some of them may have even been born in the Qing Dynasty. Those like Meihui were still a minority. Christians like her had credibility in the eyes of the Chinese because these underground Christians had paid for their faith with blood—persecuted and tortured by the Chinese government for daring to believe a "western" faith. Except that it wasn't a western faith and it was in the process of expanding from the East again, across Central Asia to secular Europe. Many Chinese like Meihui were moving all over the world: To Africa, Central Asia, Europe, Latin America, and becoming missionaries themselves.

Yes, I was fully aware of the irony that many Chinese were now missionaries to Europe and to my home country, while I was trying to be a missionary to their country. But our two very different experiences were in fact very complimentary and could make for a powerful combination when done the right way. The synergy of partnership could make us both stronger.

Usually, I am not lacking something to say, but as I stared at these old Chinese peasants, I felt unsure of how to even begin. I eventually gave some kind of lame speech that was incoherent even to me. They had blank looks on their faces. I didn't do a good job, but somehow, I could tell it didn't matter. Meihui and the others singing those Chinese songs were going to do this better than I ever could. I knew things about logistic, networks, and supplies that could help Meihui, but she would always be the better missionary and that was fine with me. I would always be better at '80s karaoke, and that is truly what matters most.

In Love with Fragrant Harbor

When Jamie and I arrived in Hong Kong, we moved into a tiny 580 square foot apartment that still managed to have three rooms, a kitchen, a living room, and two bathrooms. Each room was perfect—for a Ken and Barbie doll. We initially lived on the 20th floor and our second apartment would be on the 39th floor in a complex with 35,000 people. Marco would play in his rice box (instead of a sandbox) out on the balcony, high above the streets. This was normal life. Living in a small, crowded city of seven million people alters your psychology quite a bit. We became accustomed to massive crowds, tight quarters, living without a car, and moving at the speed of sound on super-fast elevators, fast escalators, subways, buses, minibuses, ferries, taxis, trams, and trolleys. We scanned our "Octopus" cards instead of using cash and got spoiled by ordering food and having it arrive two or three minutes after we ordered. Hong Kongers are incredibly hard-working, and life is more fast paced than in New York City. When we prepared to move away after a decade of accelerated life, we were warned that moving away from Hong Kong's extreme high-speed culture would be like coming off of cocaine. It was! And I should know!

Our apartment sat on top of a mall connected to six other shopping centers and attached by covered walkways that protected us from the very high humidity outside. It was like Biosphere meets Blade Runner. Jamie and I studied Cantonese at Chinese University and met fellow students from all around the world. We met lots of accomplished Christian people that were doctors, lawyers, investment bankers, and they had definitely combined their Christianity and their intelligence and education into fascinating career paths. I even got to regularly attend the Christian Businessmen's Luncheon at the prestigious Hong Kong Club downtown. These businessmen were extremely high net-worth individuals that owned companies, were the presidents of banks, or were deeply ensconced in the investment community. These were highly successful Christians, and they were all very humble. That was impressive. I was invited to speak once, and I seriously gave a lecture entitled "What Austin Powers Can Teach Us About Male Sexuality." It was a huge hit! "Yeah, baby!"

Our local church was no less successful. The Hong Kong Church of God was a congregation of young people. How young? Our beloved church secretary Grace was 19 years old. The average age of the congregation was 21 years of age. And the "old elders" that made up the church board were between 26 and 30. Pastor Edmund was 28 years old. Despite being young, this church put every other church I had been in, to shame. It was an incredibly well-oiled machine filled with weekly activities, community outreach, special events, and regular cell group meetings. They pulled off massive events with ease, they had enough musicians to have four back-up musicians (at least) for every instrument. If this group of kids had been a Church of God in my home state of Oregon, they would have been the 4th largest financial giving church in the State—despite the church being filled with teenagers and twenty-something kids. With so many young people, the church was extremely energetic and fun. Jamie and I felt like old grandparents there, but we loved it. The young people embraced us as the "stale cookies" that we were, and we loved them as if they were our own children or little brothers and sisters. We were never able to give them as much as they gave us. They remain our beloved family to this day. We helped (we hope) guide them through issues of life and faith, and they helped guide us through life in the fragrant harbor. They all had adopted English names and the names were often funny and creative. For example, there was: Apple, Chicken, Kinky, Snowy and Lobby (named after a hotel lobby).

Hong Kong means "fragrant harbor," and this undeveloped, sub-tropical collection of islands and peninsula connected to Mainland China was settled as a trading outpost during a period of time when China was being exploited by western powers. Hong Kong was ceded to the United Kingdom in 1842 under the Treaty of Nanking. Then in 1898, a 99-year lease was signed that promised to revert Hong Kong to Chinese rule in July of 1997. All of that time under British rule meant that Hong Kong developed its own unique culture. It had the industriousness and traditions of Chinese culture, but it created highly efficient, transparent institutions that propelled it to being one of the world's wealthiest and most successful territories. Hong Kong was the perfect combination of East and West. While China spent those 99 years remaining in third world poverty as it experimented with socialism, Hong Kong prospered and developed sophisticated, global citizens. When we moved there it was easy to tell who was from Hong Kong and who was from China. The Mainland Chinese didn't dress as well, had "bad" manners, and definitely didn't have the sophistication or ethical standards of Hong Kong people. They might even get on an escalator the wrong way or get stuck and confused at automated machines. Sadly, 1997 finally rolled around and just ten days before Jamie and I got married, Hong Kong became a Special Administrative Region (S.A.R.) of China. Living in Hong Kong a couple of years later, there were not many outward signs that China was now in control. But China's heavy-handed tactics grew each year culminating in the protests for democracy in 2019.

There were lots of remnants of British rule in Hong Kong and that included the pop music. We listened to a new band called Coldplay that had their first single out called "Don't Panic." I will always associate that song with our first days in Hong Kong when we still had no furniture and slept on the floor. Radiohead and Interpol were always playing in my headphones as was Johnny Cash's *American IV: The Man Comes Around*. I became obsessed with a U.K. band called Doves whose music guided me through the darkest times of the next decade. While obviously not a Christian band, their music has a lot of spiritual resonance. Nobody had prepared me for how stressful being a missionary would be. It would surprise people to know that it is one of the most stressful occupations you can choose. They don't teach you that in church! On the Holmes/Rae stress scale, the average person scores 100. A person under so much stress that they start to get stress-induced medical ailments scores a 300. The average missionary on the average day scores a 600 and up to 800 in the first year. Why? The list is long but includes: constant fundraising, cultural adjustments in every area from the language you speak to the currency you use, high rates of depression, high rates of physical illness, guilt over what the children have to give up, guilt and shame for leaving your family behind, an increasing emotional distance from good friends in your home country as they find you completely non-relatable or envy your "exotic" life, exposure to stress dealing with a foreign school system with your children, the over-spiritualized nature of the work, the 24/7 nature of the work and working closely with your spouse 24 hours a day in the same job, constant fear of not having your immigration status renewed and being forced to leave your new country/home, constant fear of not having your rental contract renewed, political and armed conflict, church conflict, team conflict, very low salaries, outbreaks of disease, and exposure to some of the world's darkest and worst social problems. Those are just some of the things that make it stressful and we encountered all of those. The truth is that many times it was the non-Christian music of Doves that got me through the darkest times. Sometimes to survive religion, I needed distance from religion.

We also got introduced to the music of Robbie Williams who was part of a UK boy band called Take That. Robbie, a funny cheeky character, was never able to break into the US market and remains a household name mainly in Europe, Latin America and Asia where he fills stadiums. I sang one of his songs at church talent show. A song called "Better Man" which is about someone trying to be a better person. For once, I sang the song straight and without comedic effect. The lyrics meant a lot to me:

...*as my soul heals the shame*
I will grow through this pain
Lord I am doing all I can
To be a better man.[37]

"Bonnie Tyler Needs a Hero:" Why Do We Do Good Things?

What a hero I am! Bonnie Tyler would love me! After all, I left behind a life of comfort in the United States to help

[37] "Better Man" on the album *Sing When You are Winning*. EMI. 2001. Songwriters: Guy Chambers and Robbie Williams.

some of the poorest, most outcast people in the world in one of the most remote places, right? Some people were extremely impressed by what I was doing. But I knew better than to think I had achieved some kind of sainthood. I knew that I would still hurt, maim, or kill anyone for the last chocolate milk on the shelf—including my own child! How confusing to do something extraordinarily unusual in order to help suffering people, yet still know that you are not really pure, holy, or a particularly good person.

Once YouTube came online in 2007, I would watch many videos of Christians debating people of other religions and secular thinkers. This was especially true when I grew frustrated with the injustices of the world and the darker side of life that I was exposed to as I traveled around the world. Over and over, I felt the non-religious people did far better in these debates than the religious people. The most intriguing debaters were the atheists dabbling in evolutionary psychology. This controversial but very trendy field started getting public recognition due to atheist and western Buddhist thinkers like Sam Harris, Richard Dawkins, Yuval Noah Harari, and Robert Wright. They all argue that all of our human behaviors are motivated by the fact that we are a hunter-gatherer species. So, for example, they would argue that any parts that make up "Patrick" are only designed for finding food, reproducing (yeah baby!), fighting, or fleeing from danger. Some would go further and argue that Darwin teaches us that we all have been born with a "selfish-gene" that makes us obsessed with our own survival. The argument continues that when we are trying to help others, it actually advances our own selfish interests and increases our chance of survival in some way. Consequently, we are not truly able to genuinely be selfless or good. In fact, we are quite obsessed with being accepted by some group, praised regularly, and hope to never be in a bad place ourselves—lest it hinder our own survival.

I respect all of these thinkers and have read most everything they have written. Some of that really rings true to me. For most of human history, we *were* hunter-gatherers, living in tribes competing with other tribes, or barely surviving day to day in agrarian societies. We were not suburban soccer moms living in a 5,000 square foot McMansion in Kansas City attending the local evangelical megachurch. It is only very recently, (and for much of the world only in the last 50 to 100 years), that we have been able to live lives that are so leisurely that we are free from making life and death decisions daily. With my eating habits, my deathly fear of ladybugs, and my inability to bench-press 30 pounds, I would not have lasted five minutes in the days of hunter gatherers like Ug Nachtigall. Old Ug would be ashamed of what a wuss I am. For most of human history, life has mostly been difficult and about day to day survival.

Even the very rich of a century ago, lived in squalor compared to us today. And the Palace of Versailles outside of Paris, which was known as Louis XIV's pleasure palace—an oasis of luxury and materialistic decadence amidst the greater poverty of 17th century France, was a total pit. Today, when you visit you see stunning ballrooms, immaculate bedrooms, and grand staircases. But in the days of the Sun King, it was a palace filled with a few thousand people and no bathrooms. People used chamber pots, the walls, the stairwells, and even the church floor! Louis himself only bathed twice a year! Enjoy your next tour of Versailles now. It's the world's most celebrated latrine.

The idea that we are hardwired for our own survival and are prone to selfishness is hard to argue against. Quite a lot in my Christian faith says the same thing about human intentions, and contrary to popular belief, the Bible is mostly filled with stories of people behaving *very badly* toward each other and toward God—often in the name of religion. The Bible says, *"The heart is deceitful above all things,"*[38] and in the New Testament, the group most concerned with being religious, following the rules, being "Godly," and righteous were the ones Jesus identified as hypocrites that were totally blind to their self-serving ways. So, it seems that even when we are doing good, we can also be acting selfishly. Are we just all jerk-faces deep down?

In my case, look at how many ways I benefitted from helping lepers: 1) I got to live out my dream of living and working in China, 2) it gave me a life of adventure, 3) quite a few people have praised me for being "good," 4) it even provides a great story for this book that you are reading now which is destined to go down as the greatest piece of scientific literature since Jackie Collins' *Hollywood Wives*. That's not to say that I wasn't really trying to help people. But can I honestly say that I had no self-serving intentions at all consciously or at least sub-consciously when I did those acts of charity and displayed such altruism with the lepers? Hardcore Darwinian, secular materialists would say "no." At some level, no matter how nice I was, I was ultimately somehow doing some of this, if not all of it, to benefit myself.

Okay, so I'm a selfish jerk-face and was just in it for myself. But what about you? Are you also simply motivated by selfishness without the capacity for a beautiful moment of pure sincere selflessness for another person? Let's imagine that moment when you first put your newborn baby in the car seat on the way home from the hospital (or for those of you that have not had children yet, imagine that moment when you turned on your new iPhone).

[38] This is in the Old Testament book of Jeremiah, 17: 9.

When you held on extremely tightly as you pushed your newborn in their stroller and buckled them in the car seat, was it just because you were concerned with passing on your genes to the next generation? When you worked overtime so that your child could go to Disneyland, were you just being selfish? When you de-iced the car for your spouse that cold winter morning, were you just backhandedly serving your own needs? When you donated $500 to the Muscular Dystrophy Telethon, were you just thinking about your own survival? And when you spent $400 dollars to sit through a Korean boy band concert with your 11-year-old daughter, were you acting selfishly then? No, you took one for the team!

Okay, so maybe the evolutionary psychologists are right, and you are not a hero either. But what about those heroic firemen on 9/11 that ran into collapsing skyscrapers leaving their family, their homes, and their safety behind? Or those videos we see of people climbing onto subway tracks with only seconds to decide to take action, but who jump down in front of the train to rescue a human being that has fallen onto the tracks? Or once again, the parent that sits through *Barney on Ice*? Believe it or not, some have argued that in cases like that, it is our selfish gene "misfiring." So, a supreme act of heroism is an evolutionary deformity? The more cases like this you examine, the more you see that the selfless actor is doing things that can't possibly benefit their own survival or even the survival of a larger group they are a part of, if that is how you want to reason it out. Who would go to a Wiggles concert for selfish reasons?

But we are increasingly being taught by people that value science over the "fiction" of religion that regardless of whether there is a selfish gene or not; your love for your baby, and my love for my child are just rooted in a selfish desire for survival—to pass on our genes. I can buy the part about me somehow being selfish in helping the lepers, but I'm not sure

I can go there when I think of the heroic actions of the 9/11 firefighters. After all, if they were just acting out of their own group or nation's biological self-interest, how dare we think they are any better than the Saudi Arabian 9/11 hijackers? Were they not also claiming the same thing? It seems to me that even though we can be pretty nasty and problematic as human beings; we also have occasional moments of glorious selflessness. A moment where we transcend our selfishness.

Brother, Can You Spare a Soul?

Most of us feel as though we have a soul, a "heart" that houses our deepest feelings, or a conscious (self). And we have moments in life when that soul seems to get touched to its very core—our essential being. It might be when Marvin Gaye hits a particular note in the song "What's Going On?" or that moment when Anne and Gilbert finally admit their feelings in *Anne of Green Gables*. It might be the first time your child looked at you and said, *"I wub you, mama,"* or that glorious Hawaiian sunset that you saw on your honeymoon, or when you made it to the summit of that mountain you climbed. It may be the first time you saw *Fast Times at Ridgemont High,* like it was for me. The point is that we all experience a feeling of being touched to our very core by an external source. Maybe if you are a musician, you feel it every time you play the piano or pick up the guitar. It might have been that moment when the entire stadium at the U2 concert sang in unison "Where the Streets Have No Name."

But as some scientists and psychologists continue to try to define humanity's reality without religion, spirituality, or the supernatural, we are being told that we are sapiens without a soul or a spirit. That means your cute little child is just a bunch of chemicals thrown together. They are a collection of organic compounds and so are you. The good feeling when you cuddle them is just oxytocin. My question to you is this: are you really sure you want to go into debt $80,000 to send your little organic compound to college?

It gets worse. We are supposedly just algorithms, so we really are not that different from your beloved iPhone. Both make calculations and then carry-out an action. When your phone hears you need new shoes, it pulls up Nike ads on Facebook. When you see your child is hungry, your impulses kick in and you open up the mac and cheese and feed them. What made you do that? The evolutionary biologist and evolutionary psychologist are suggesting it is just an algorithm taking effect because you are programmed to make sure your little Organic Compound Jr. grows up to go to college, because that will increase *your* chances of survival. (Maybe we should just name our children Organic Compound Nachtigall #1 or Organic Compound Nachtigall #2. It would remind us that we are all just algorithms and chemicals and that emotions and feelings are just the impulses that help us selfishly take care of our own selves.)

If thinking of your child as if they were an iPhone seems cold and difficult to swallow, that's because something within us believes that our children are more than just soulless algorithms with arms and legs. When our children experience tragedy, pain, or even a skinned knee, it definitely seems like they are more than just organic compounds. We feel these incredible sympathy pains when they get hurt and a strong desire to make it better. If they are just organic compounds, why do we consider it a tragedy if they fall, get sick, or die at an early age? The logic is they simply didn't win the Darwinian survival of the fittest competition that our chemical selves are in daily. It's probably better that they died. Less competition for resources for the rest of us. Life and existence are just the *Survivor* reality TV show.

Sorry, that doesn't resonate with me. It doesn't just seem cold and meaningless, it flies against our own experience, feelings, and I would say—even our own reason and logic.

To believe that, you have to believe that these organic compounds inside of us have somehow made the decision that life is good and that they are actively seeking to survive in the brutal game of life. Then these squiggly microscopic things make this moral/right vs. wrong decision in our body in order to program us for survival. That doesn't make sense since these compounds have no moral or ethical foundation to decide that life is valuable or desirable. We don't have a soul, but they do, perhaps? If so, we are going to have to build really small churches for these microscopic spiritual atoms and genes.

Are we all primates like Michael Jackson's chimp Bubbles that are really closer to an iPhone than a creature with a soul? I doubt it. Issues of beauty, order, complexity, the need for a beginning, for causation, and for some form of objective morality have a way of being vital to our understanding of everything. When I visited the lepers, I did take risks. I could have gotten leprosy, gotten in trouble with the Chinese authorities, lost my passport, gone to jail, or have been persecuted. I doubt I was completely selfless or even a majority selfless. My Chinese Christian friends, however, took even greater risks. Did we take those risks just for other organic compounds? I am not arguing, as some Christians do, against evolution appearing in nature. I am arguing against evolution being the sum total of the human and cosmic experience rather than an essential part of it. The soul is where we are touched by the transcendent: The soul itself is in a process of evolution. It is where we rise above simply being a collection of chemicals, a soulless iPhone made of flesh and blood.

No De La Soul, But Can We At Least Tell Right From Wrong?

As these great thinkers—and they are great thinkers—argue that we don't have a soul and are just a collection of self-serving algorithms, I started to think that believing that would be very freeing in some ways. That also means we don't have a conscience (the ability to tell right from wrong). Think about it! No more constantly worrying about pleasing God. No more obsessing about mistakes I have made in my life. I had no choice after all! No more feeling guilt about the family of four I ran over on that desert stretch of Arizona highway just outside of Phoenix after a meth deal gone wrong. I could be free of constantly worrying about how I was doing on the morality scale. Some Christians might argue, "You can be free of all of that with Jesus, my child," but then they go back to their judgment and comparison based on your displays of outward piety. Many religious people, including some former Christians, have switched over to this "no conscience" view and feel a burden lifting off of them. It's as if all of these religious and moral expectations were just creating unnecessary psychological damage and neuroticism. I guess I don't owe my dad an apology for wrecking his new car when I was 16! Awesome!

The new belief being adopted is not only that we have no soul, but we don't even have free will because we are just a collection of compounds that create impulses in order to survive. And when we fall in love, that is just our oxytocin acting up. When they say that a particular couple in love have "good chemistry," they mean it literally! That's all it is!

But the closer I look, the less plausible it seems. Flawed laboratory tests like Benjamin Libet's University of California San Diego study in 1983 are being widely applauded because they supposedly prove that we have no free will. In that experiment, brain activity in the motor region was activated and controlled finger movements prior to the subject's conscious intention to move their finger. Tests like these supposedly show our inability to decide our own thoughts and actions. It seems like another strike against the idea of the soul, the spirit, free will and religion. Those that believe this even believe that one day we will outlaw jails, and no one will be able to be labeled a criminal. All actions we humans take are outside of our control. Even Hitler is innocent. But the problem that remains is that unconscious intention is conceptually beyond scientific enquiry and involves dynamic interaction between conscious and unconscious brain activity formed throughout our entire lives. The reason many of the secular debaters won the YouTube debate against the Christians and other religious people is because they avoided completely what *they themselves* cannot prove or articulate, and focused on what the Christians, Muslims, or Jews could not prove or articulate. The burden of proof was always on the religious person and not on the meaningless, organic compound.

There are at least five conscious states: a thought, a belief, a desire, a sensation, and an act of will. Religions have long been aware of this. Neuroscience is great at examining the relationship between brain states and conscious states, but it doesn't tell us what a specific state of consciousness is and what kind of properties characterize it.[39] In fact, studying the mind isn't like studying physics or chemistry where measurements can be free of excessive biases. This is something that many scientists like Richard Dawkins seem to miss and miss badly. Neurology is dependent on narratives created from collected data and filtered through personal perceptions. That makes causal explanations about the mind impossible. Biases do play a big part in

[39] Moreland, J.P., *Scientism and Secularism*. Wheaton: Crossway, p. 87.

neuroscience and are processed within the individual researcher's brain: a brain which is supposedly guided by involuntary brain mechanisms generating an illusory sense of a personal, independent, unbiased person. See the problem there?

Here's the deal: the questions addressed by the studying of the philosophy of the mind and religion are very different than those examined in the sciences, yet they are vital in attempting to understand our full humanity. Philosophy and religion are the only rational knowledge by which we can judge science and nature. Science, philosophy, and religion need each other, and this will be even more the case in our "cyborg" future where we are experimenting more and more with artificial intelligence and robotics. Science will not explain what thoughts, beliefs, and feelings are, or be able to judge their meaning or goodness. Nor can it address the nature of the self and its value to the universe.

Somehow, we need to explain why we feel the strong sense that there is a right and wrong. Why we make the choice to get a bunch of rock stars into a room together to sing a cheeseball song to help famine victims in Africa. And we have to be honest that we all act like we believe we have a soul, and not just when we listen to James Brown sing "Sex Machine." Sam Harris, the very articulate and thoughtful atheist, admitted on the *Inside the Hive* podcast that "consciousness is something that we still can't explain, and we don't know what it is."[40]

It may seem like I am picking on atheists, evolutionary biologists and psychologists as well as the most prominent spokespeople like Dawkins and others. In some ways, it's quite the opposite. The questions and discoveries that scientists and atheists raise are important and onto

[40] Inside the Hive Podcast with Nick Bilton. "Sam Harris Explains Why There is No Free Will". October 25, 2019.

something. They are part of the same ultimate quest to understand the deep, existential questions: "What are we as human beings?" "Why we are here?" And "What are McDonald's beef patties made of?" Thanks to them we are learning a lot about how the brain works and how brain chemistry affects us in myriad ways. But anyone who studies neuroscience knows we know little about the brain and even less about consciousness. These great thinkers are very incisive about pointing out the dangers and downsides of religion, and quite often I agree with them. They also remind us that we are affected by chemistry, environment, and society. We also know that damage to the brain can affect morality. They also accurately point out that many animals exhibit a lot of human behavior that is exactly like ours and does serve to ensure their survival. Darwin was no idiot. Nor was he evil. He was actually a very kind, gentle, and humble man raised in a religious home. Furthermore, there are many philosophers and religious people that are subscribing to the belief that we are not moral actors but organisms that respond to situations and stimulation. These are helpful debates, but as I've considered it, it seems to me that it is still a case of throwing out your cute baby's soul with the bathwater. The YouTube debates were helpful, fun, clarifying, but not convincing.

According to the way a lot of secular reasoning is playing out, the lepers were evolutionary losers, and I was a loser for taking the risk to help them. This kind of "scientific" belief system (and it is a belief system) actually leads to some pretty frightening conclusions. One of my best days as a teenager was when my mom forced me to volunteer at the Special Olympics. I didn't want to go and felt awkward about it. I thought it would be sad, hard to connect with the disabled, and very awkward. After all, it's a tragic situation, right? I ended up having a tremendous time. I had no idea how fun and full of joy people with Down Syndrome can be. They are so loving, and they love to laugh, and make you smile as they offer unconditional love and friendship. My wife Jamie is particularly gifted working with people with Down Syndrome, and she did so professionally in both Seattle and Portland. I further learned about their non-traditional gifts. What does this scientific belief system mean for them and on what moral grounds can we condemn the Nazis for experimenting scientifically on the mentally disabled?

How the Scientific, Rational Mind Can Lose Its Way

Science is wonderful and incredibly important. As I mentioned, my father was a man of science and a Christian. The fear-based anti-intellectualism and strong prejudice against science that can be found in some religious communities today is tragic and stupid. There are things that religious people can critique (like problems with the scientific peer review process), without painting all of science as untrustworthy and hostile. We all depend tremendously on science and its accurate measurements and mechanics— like every time we religious people fly in an airplane. Science throughout history has a pattern of being helpful, educational, groundbreaking, and also of overreaching significantly. This overreach tendency is one I think we will see often in the 2010s -2050s. We are ushering in an age where we will need to be skeptical at times about the utopia and trustworthiness that technology and science promise as they literally seek to alter our humanity and societies in unprecedented ways.

I believe that what is happening is that science and technology continue to discover more things about us that we can then analyze. That's great! These new facts about our brain chemistry, our bodies reaction to oxytocin, or our subconscious reactions to certain smells and colors make scientists feel like they have identified all the key components that make us human and predict our behavior. They discover, for instance, that we are more likely to be charitable to a homeless person if our nostrils are filled with a good smell like flowers instead of a bad smell like garbage. Or that monkeys bully each other and have nerds and outcasts too—just like humans. Or they discover that you are more likely to view a man with a beard as virile, but also less trustworthy. From all these data points being discovered in the laboratory, some scientists then say: *"We have quantified what it is to be a human being. Humans are a collection of chemicals and impulses that arise out of an algorithm which factors in all these data points. You may not be aware of it, but you gave that homeless person $5 because you were standing next to a Mrs. Field's Cookies shop instead of a garbage dump. And ultimately you were being selfish. We get you!"*

But this data-point driven scientific triumph over religion and philosophy seems shallow to me. It's analogous to the way that Google and Facebook think they know us. They have amassed so many data points about us that they know which ads we want to see, they overheard that we are shopping for New Kids on the Block on vinyl, they know we like cat videos, they know how we vote, and in the future they will know when we are running out of toothpaste and deliver that toothpaste to our door before we can even order it. That's the "internet-of-everything"/ "data is the new oil" world that we have entered. But no matter how many data points Facebook and Google collect, they will still not truly know you. Your spouse probably still doesn't truly know you. You are far too mysterious for their scientific and technological algorithms. They may get some things right and maybe a lot of things right about you. But they are not going to know that you decided to skip your yoga class on Friday because you heard there was a fire at a homeless shelter and you decided on the spur of the moment that you would go down and see how you could help. They will not predict that volunteering at the Special Olympics is going to be a life-changing experience for you because of one particular athlete with Down Syndrome.

That mysterious you is what this book is about and that is what spirituality is about.

A Challenge for Science

So are the scientists and evolutionary psychologists, right? Actually, the scientific movement of reducing us all to impulses reacting to the commands of a "selfish gene" is already being discredited. For one thing, genes are not static units of code as was thought but are more multilinear and affected by an organism's proteins and complex cellular processes. Gene-editing is challenging more simplistic views of genes and is raising even more moral and ethical questions that science alone can't answer. Should people born with birth defects be eradicated because it would be a better world? Are we absolutely sure that the boy with Down Syndrome adds no value to this world and that "perfect people" will give us the kind of beauty that many flawed geniuses have given us throughout history? Is it ethical to create designer gene-splicing, but risk deformity in our child in our effort to make them perfect, beautiful and smart embryos?

Furthermore, the idea that our body, with all of its cognitive faculties, is wired only for survival means that the universe is ultimately amoral and not rooted in truth. If that's the case, the scientist is not a neutral person in pursuit of objective facts; they are an organism that is committed to their own selfish survival no matter what the cost. The "pursuit of scientific truth" becomes just an illusion for personal advancement. Can our sensory and cognitive faculties be trusted to be objectively scientific if they are dedicated to only one purpose---our own survival?

Science, which pursues real knowledge or reality, is dependent on being able to find objective truth (religion and philosophy being untrustworthy and subjective). But science cannot prove that it has truth, because that would require that science have an objective possession of truth in order to prove it to be true. This is why science and religion/philosophy go around and around in circles. Because science cannot tell us how things ought to be. Science cannot justify the laws of logic or mathematics because they are *a priori fields* while science is an *a posteriori* field concerned with laws and theories open to empirical observations. *A priori* means that these are areas that are known by direct rational intuition without appealing to sense experience to justify them.[41] In other words, science is not good at telling me whether I was being nice helping the lepers or being selfish. Nor is it good at giving me a reason as to why I should bother.

For me, what makes more sense is that, like so many religions teach, there is a source that created life. Even when someone like Stephen Hawking argues that quantum physics establishes that the universe began in a vacuum, that vacuum is still *something* that requires space and energy. Where did those come from? That ain't no vacuum![42] Logically there seems to be a beginning, a source, and a reason for being. And it exists in a universe of good and bad. As the Buddhists recognized, we all want pleasure and happiness. That's because we have concrete knowledge and experience that good is better than bad. In other words, we were intelligently

---

[41] Moreland, J.P., *Scientism and Secularism*. Wheaton: Crossway, p. 77-78.
[42] Ibid, 115.

designed for good and for life, which includes wanting to survive.

And it's not because a tiny critter or gene in your body said you need to survive, or you need to intervene for the sake of society and civilization. Rather, you were born valuing other human beings, thinking life is precious, and feeling a moral (let's even say spiritual) imperative to act, whether you are an atheist, agnostic, or whatever.

Yuval Noah Harari is an example of another acclaimed thinker who views us all as chemicals in a world where religion is mostly useless as it has outlived its utilitarian purposes. The future as he describes it is pretty bleak and he is definitely known to be a pessimist. That's the logical conclusion of his worldview, in my opinion. Nevertheless, he says, *"I personally never cease to wonder about the mystery of existence."*[43] Indeed! And there is a reason we wonder about that mystery. We were created to wonder in order to discover our true identity and purpose.

Asps, Scorpions, and Algorithms

I spent roughly 10 years living in Hong Kong and working both in that city and in Mainland China. It turned out to be an absolutely perfect time to be in China. China from 2001 to 2014 really opened itself up to the world and became a different country. The Pearl River Delta where we spent so much time became the manufacturing base for the world, and China joined the World Trade Organization.

I watched friends join the newly established middle class, wearing NBA Jerseys, downloading movies from Hollywood, and each year dressing more fashionably. When I first began traveling around China after moving there, the people were

---

[43] Harari, Yuval Noah. *21 Lessons for the 21ˢᵗ Century*. London: Jonathan Cape, P. 2018.

all wearing cheap knock-off brands that were poor quality and hilariously named: There were "Bitch" shoes (I wanted a pair so bad), "Uncle Martian" instead of Under Armour, Sunbucks Coffee, Wu Mart, Pizza Huh, Borio Cookies (they were gross), Johns Daphne Tenderness Whiskey (Jack Daniels), and Knie Shoes with a swoosh! I liked to buy cheap Erke shoes with a semi-Nike swoosh. On my most recent 2019 visit to China however, the stores were Gucci, Bulgari, Louis Vuitton, Tesla, and the Chinese are now the biggest consumers of luxury brands in the world.

The new middle class changed the landscape right before my eyes. Rice patties were built over and in their place are enormous suburbs, cities, as well as the world's largest malls and tallest skyscrapers. No more one state airline. Multiple different Chinese airlines flew me around and the Chinese became global tourists. They built the world's largest dam which was the height of the Seattle Space Needle and almost 8,000 feet wide (and which at one point had a third of all Caterpillar equipment in the world on its construction site). They built the world's largest high-speed train network, created a booming stock-market, moved their people toward digital payment, hosted the 2008 Summer Olympics and won the right to host the Winter Olympics in 2022. They also became the second largest economy in the world in size, if not complexity. They became global leaders in solar power and alternative energy and created a Silicon Valley-like tech hub in Shenzhen just a few miles from our home in Hong Kong. They launched global companies like Huawei and Alibaba Group and Weibo that became a Chinese version of Amazon and Facebook.

The changes were so rapid and so extreme through that period of time, that literally every time I went into China, there were new buildings, new factories, new train-lines and new airports and train stations. One day in 2003, Ken, a friend living in Mainland China, and I were headed to the university near the Hunan border. It was a 30-minute ride down an old, dusty road in a little old white minibus. I turned to Ken and said, "China is changing so fast that in ten years, this will be a highway, we will be in a new bus, and it will take ten minutes." That was my bold prediction. I returned seven months later and there was a brand-new road, a brand-new bus, and it took ten minutes to get to the university. But that's nothing for China! When I got to the university, I met up with one of the students I had befriended, who went by the English name of "Orange." He had a big surprise for me.

"Since you've been gone (7 months), the university has tripled the number of students and the size of the campus has tripled also." He then warned me, "Be careful though, the quality is not great and sometimes large pieces of the concrete ceiling fall down on you." The construction was fast, but shoddy. It was not uncommon to see a new house or building in 2001 look old and run-down by 2010. Our new world often abandons quality for speed.

But Orange was right! It was astonishing! More than half the campus was brand spanking new! If this story seems like it can't possibly be true, keep in mind that China recently used more cement in two years than the United States used in 50 years. And Chinese college kids, like Orange, were the best. They would swarm around you to practice English and the conversations were great. They were so curious, friendly, and fun.

Those were heady and exciting days. The Chinese still weren't accustomed to foreigners in most places, so I would often stick out. It wasn't uncommon to be followed by a group of people as if I was a rock star. People wanted photos of Marco, wanted to touch his hair, and passed him around the train when he was an infant. Strangers would say "Hello," in the hopes of striking up a friendship. It wasn't uncommon to be in a Chinese town and have some young person try to befriend you and then spend the next few hours with you. They were so anxious to practice English and get to know a foreigner. Unlike in South Korea, I was never told to "puck off!"

I was even able to eat Chinese food beyond just rice. That did not mean that I partook of delicacies like chicken feet, orangutan lips, or ox penis (not without a first date!). But I found plenty to like and became addicted to green tea. But I did have a new eating challenge on certain occasions. When the Chinese eat, they often eat at a round table and eat communally. Everyone shares from the dishes on the table. They also tend to eat all sorts of animal parts, eat everything off the bone, and spit out the gristle and inedible parts. Those often end up on the tablecloth right in front of your face and have the potential to launch major pandemics. I remember one time in Yunnan Province struggling to get a meal down as the Chinese man next to me put his gristle next to my plate, spit pieces out on the floor next to my chair, and hurled a snot rocket close to my Erke shoes. It's amazing that I was once afraid I would throw up to death if I ate a chocolate chip cookie, but somehow now I could manage to make it through a Chinese meal of Snot Won ton.

I didn't always feel like visiting the lepers. The walks were long, the heat was brutal and muggy in the summer, and I'm more of an introvert than people often realize. There was one particular day when I was walking through the fields and was deeply annoyed by the heat, the walk, and I was feeling like a bad person because I was not in the mood to visit the lepers. My organic compounds began to talk to God, and I complained: "I'm tired. I'm tired of doing this. I'm tired of trying to be Jesus!"

And I heard God respond in that moment and say to me, "Oh, Patrick, Patrick, Patrick. You're not Jesus. You're the leper!"

What? What does that mean? Then I figured it out.

I'm the leper? I'm the leper? I'm the leper!!!

It was an amazing moment of enlightenment! I suddenly truly realized there was no pressure to be good. There was no debt to God that I needed to pay back. There was no *karma* that I needed to erase. The sad truth is that even on my best day, I would never really be like Jesus. In fact, there's not much difference between the lepers and me. They are sick and so am I. They are deformed and so am I. They stink and so do I. I'm selfish, self-absorbed, imperfect, and sometimes morally diseased. But God wasn't expecting me to be Jesus, rather Jesus offers grace and hope to people like me. It was the beginning of a massive weight being lifted off of my shoulders. I serve the lepers because I am one. And in that process, I began to find out who I am supposed to be. Losing life meant gaining it. Like the cycles of nature, we observe in this created world, death often makes room for new life. Crucifixion leads to resurrection. I'm not the hero of the story and I don't need to be.

It was a powerful experience. But was it all in my mind? The human desire to look for patterns? I have consistently found that so often the spiritual experiences I have led me to do and think the opposite of what I naturally would be inclined to do. It is something from outside defining me that can see reality in a wholistic way that my conscious and sub-conscious mind cannot. Quantify that moment with your algorithms, Google!

Life and the world have a way of corrupting us. Even though we originate from a source that is good and we all long for good, things are not right. China, as a nation, really began to experience this in the decade after I moved away from Hong Kong. The modern world of wealth and algorithms has taken a toll on China's soul—like it is taking a toll on ours as well. China, just like me, spent a lot of time thinking about how great it can sometimes be to distance yourself from your history and tradition. Perhaps a better, more secular world awaited if only these old, ancient religious beliefs and traditions were put in the trash bin where they belong.

As China got wealthier, the amount of corruption went through the roof. Crony capitalism began to dominate China and things like going to college had more to do with "who you know and who you pay," as my friend Orange put it, instead of on merit. He finished college, became a Christian, and moved to Japan. The pollution got so bad in China that cancer rates and pulmonary issues became a massive problem. Almost all of the top ten most polluted cities in the world were in China during that time and each day breathing in most cities was like smoking a few packs of cigarettes per day. The bad air from factories in China was being measured as far away as Boston. My health took a steep dive while living in China. I developed chronic ailments all the time. So did Jamie.

Many scams arose in China with people losing all their money, and entire suburbs and skyscrapers were empty; built to artificially stimulate the economy and provide opportunities to skim from the construction costs. The Chinese young people who were so open, excited, and naïve became increasingly jaded, cynical materialists with a nationalist bent.

Then in 2014, Xi Jinping became the President of China. He would eventually declare himself president for life and borrow cult of personality ideas from Mao Zedong. China rapidly moved to a surveillance state model, using its newfound expertise in technology to begin the process of installing 600 million cameras that will monitor everything the Chinese people do. They saw the way people in the West were increasingly being controlled and defined by the algorithms of Google and Facebook and saw an opportunity.

A social credit system was introduced that is like something out of the science fiction Netflix show *Black Mirror*. Even the amount of toilet paper dispensed at public restrooms would be controlled under the new system. "The Great Firewall" was built to restrict internet access. Muslim Uyghur minorities were captured and put into prison camps and a very open persecution of Buddhists, Taoists, and Christians began again. Churches were bulldozed, pastors were arrested, and Christianity was prohibited. China has a historic pattern of being closed, opening up to the world, and closing itself again. I happened to spend my ten years there when it was at its most open. In 2019, when our family returned to visit Beijing, it was palpable that this was now a surveillance state suspicious of the world. Will this approach work and will it bring happiness?

The material world has a way of disappointing and not filling our needs the way we think it will. We humans want good, but often mess it up. It isn't just Christianity that points that out. The Buddhist sage Shinran wrote:

> *I am false and untrue*
> *And without the least purity of mind*
> *We men in our outward forms*
> *Display wisdom, goodness and purity.*
> *Since greed, anger, evil and deceit are frequent;*
> *We are filled with naught but flattery.*
> *With our evil natures hard to subdue*

Our minds are like asps and scorpions. [44]

That's why a strictly materialistic worldview, one free of religion or spirituality, without divine revelation, free of mystery, and without an ultimate source for determining what is good and bad is dangerous. Religion certainly has the capacity to be dangerous. But having no input into the non-quantifiable but very real parts of our lives is even more dangerous. Our desire for love, truth, goodness, and meaning come from somewhere else far outside of ourselves and in my view, we must pursue that source. That is the spiritual life.

Help Me, Help You!

Hopefully, you've done something nice for someone recently. Maybe you decided to watch your friend's child so that she and her husband could go out on a much-needed date to Long John Silvers. Maybe you made some kombucha for the elderly lady that lives in your neighborhood all alone. Maybe you struck a deal with the Cali drug cartel and offered to give them a discount on 63kg of heroin and 92kg of cocaine. That's what I did yesterday! Why? Because we need to look out for each other. The world's religions have always had a strong command to care for others. Every faith tradition has a call to help humanity. Sometimes it is to obey the will of God, or to create good *karma*, or to avoid being cursed. As I mentioned at the beginning of the book, all humans are born with a sense that they are being watched, and that somehow moral behavior is recorded. That includes atheists. Religions name that feeling and give a reason for it. But people do not simply do what is right to avoid punishment and survive as Darwin suggested. They do it because the process of giving selflessly produces good in the

[44] Shinshu Shogyo Zensho II (Kyoto 1953), 527. Cited in Alfred Bloom's *Shinran's Gospel of Pure Grace*. Tucson 1965, p. 29.

world and feels righter and truer than doing wrong. Obviously, there are the occasional psychopaths, but societies tend to create norms that prevent their kind of anarchical world order.

Jesus was a master of paradox. And his most famous speech was pretty anti-Darwin's survival-of-the-fittest. He basically said:

> *"The world may say it's great to be rich, but I am telling you that you will actually see more clearly what is truly important in life if you are poor."*[45]

> *"And the world may say that there is no justice coming for the sad and suffering person, but they will actually find treasures far greater than those of the privileged."*[46]

> *"And blessed are the nerds, for they will one day establish multi-billion-dollar tech companies while the ex-jocks work at Home Depot."*[47]

He also said that "he who loses his life, will find it,"[48] meaning that when we care for others, act selflessly, and practice love we are moving toward our original purpose, our reason for existence. Religion exists because we all wonder why we are here and what our purpose is. Those two fundamental questions haunt us in a way they shouldn't if we are just organic compounds.

During college, my wife Jamie worked at Mother Teresa's Home for the Destitute and Dying in Calcutta. The most ill, terminal cases were brought off the streets, sometimes

---

[45] Matthew 5:3 NPV
[46] Matthew 5:4 NPV
[47] Some people dispute the wording of the particular manuscript in which this saying was found.
[48] Matthew 10:39 NPV

literally from a gutter, to die with dignity and not alone. Nuns and unpaid volunteers like Jamie fed, bathed, and even assisted them with their bodily functions. During one of the days, a woman died in Jamie's arms. Jamie's loving face would have been the last thing that she saw in this world. She didn't die alone.

Ken and Kim were a very young couple from the US. Ken (the friend I traveled to the university with) was from Texas and Kim was from Missouri. They were Christians who traveled to China to teach English in a lesser known city near the border of Guangdong Province and Jiangxi Province. They also visited lepers and took non-religious Chinese college students along with them. The experience was mind-blowing for these Chinese young people. The idea of going out of your way to help lepers was not something that had occurred in the age of Mao or the new China with its moral vacuum. When we would join Ken, Kim, and the Chinese students to visit the lepers it was just as transforming *for them* as it was for the lepers. Suddenly, it felt like there was a little more to life than just making money and being more successful than your neighbor. Those trips tapped into a deep need that those students and all humans have—the need to have a life that has meaning.

Of course, it is not only Christians who do acts of charity. Some of the finest, most moral people I know are atheists and agnostics. I would trust them with my life. Other religions do as well. In my first book, *Passport of Faith: A Christian's Encounter with World Religions* (now a major motion picture on the Hallmark Channel starring John Stamos as Patrick Nachtigall), I wrote about the time I spent at Wat Phranaht in rural, central Thailand. This was a Buddhist monastery that was turned into a clinic in order to take in dying AIDS patients. These were people who were within weeks or days of dying. Rejected by society and a shame to their families, these AIDS patients would otherwise be doomed to dying alone. Buddhist volunteers took care of them, cremated them, and Buddhist priests performed the final rites.

The China Metaphor

In some ways, China is a really great metaphor for where humanity stands at this point in the 21st century. China's origins are mysterious, as are humanity's. Its oldest history is rooted in myth. In time, great religious ideas and philosophies spread and developed tremendous depth. And the Chinese mind produced a great civilization with all sorts of technological advances. China has a long history of understanding that history brings good times and bad times. It is now embracing science and technology to a degree that is unprecedented, and the quality of life has never been higher. It has increasingly abandoned religion and labeled it as not necessary. Yet there is an emptiness that materialism is not filling, and people are literally being reduced to algorithms.

It seems to me that we in the West are also China at this point. Science, technology, and human knowledge have created an impressive world of comfort and luxury. But we also are finding that our new innovations not only come at a cost, but often have very unintended, negative consequences. There is a wisdom and a life affirming nature missing from our societies and it's one that we need to recover.

I had no intention of ever leaving Hong Kong and China. I was heartbroken to my core when we had to move away. But, again, as John Lennon sang, "life is what happens to you when you are busy making other plans." The subsequent ten years would be spent doing many of the same things I was doing in Hong Kong and China, only on a bigger scale in Europe and the Middle East. My job and my writings continued to take me all around the world and I continued to visit mosques, temples, wats, churches, and halls of scientific learning everywhere I went. My dream came true and I found myself bouncing around from continent to continent on airplanes just as I had hoped I would as a child.

I still have a deep love for China and hope my story continues there one day. I have high hopes for China, but it will have to re-learn the lesson that we all will have to learn in our techno-saturated 21st century lives, which is that there is more to life than material success and comfort. If we don't feed the soul, we can never be whole.

My life is no more important or valuable than yours, dear reader. But I do insist that my journey was transcendent and meaningful, not simply a chemical algorithm or the result of too much chocolate milk.

I had a childhood dream. It was a ridiculous dream of feeding rice to starving Chinese people thousands of miles away, even though I was scared to death of eating a piece of rice myself. My insane dream came true when I finally went to China. But in the end, it turned out that the Chinese fed me instead. Funny how that works.

The Beginning: A Conclusion

I have a confession to make. At the beginning of this epic masterpiece when I said I was dead, that was just a literary device. I'm not dead at the time of this writing and I had a glass of chocolate milk this morning. But one day, I will kick the bucket and so will you.

Fear of death has been a universal reason for seeking religious wisdom. Our desire to know where we originated and why we are here also inspires the pursuit of religious answers. But I think we have a capacity to pursue spirituality that goes beyond those intellectually curious and fear-based questions—even if we all have them.

I believe that we act out evidence of an eternal meaning for our lives every day without knowing it. We desire for that perfect vacation or that perfect kiss to last forever. That's evidence that we are hardwired for eternity. Eternity is not an invented concept; it is an actual thing.

We feel an inexpressible love for our children that we can never explain with words or actions. It's a sign that the deepest love we experience is outside the boundaries of being explained by words, concepts, or chemical reactions.

We feel a desire to be touched, seen, known, loved and affirmed all the time. It's not just a sign for the desire to survive, but a sign that we were built for stable, permanent relationships.

We feel a strong need to have our life mean something and to make a difference. That's a sign that our lives are supposed to have meaning.

We feel the need to occasionally go out of our way and make a sacrifice for someone with no expectation of a reward because we instinctively know that human life is valuable and precious.

We even find the need to try to make sense and find a reason for the worst, most painful parts of our lives. That is because some part of you knows that pain and suffering is not supposed to happen.

When my assignment in Hong Kong and China finished, I took another one in Europe and the Middle East. It was a painful move because I had always wanted to permanently live in China. But the lessons China taught me served me well. Along with a wonderful team of fantastic people that my wife and I assembled as well as partners in different countries, we began helping to address needs during the European refugee crisis, work against sex-trafficking, worked alongside young people again, and encouraged churches to reach out and serve the needs of their communities—not just themselves—as my parents had taught me 50 years ago in Costa Rica. I've been able to speak, write, and travel from the mountains of the Andes to the tundra of Siberia. I've been chased by muggers in Kenya, followed by secret police in Cuba, and nearly decapitated by a kangaroo in Australia. All along the way, on six continents and 80 countries, I hope my actions, my speeches, and my writings have made the world a better place. But I know my own limitations and have seen extreme examples of the darkness of this life out of balance: *Koyaanisqatsi* as the Hopi Native Americans called it.

Doing all of that often meant confronting the dark side of humanity and the dark side of myself. And I would not lie to you. It also often meant seeing the dark side of religion and even of the Christian church. Everything, including religion and spirituality, can be corrupted.

We all feel frustrated, angry, hurt, disillusioned, and disgusted by the evil we see and experience in the world. That's a sign that our hearts, minds and spirits know what good is and it wants to live in goodness permanently.

That magic of falling in love, of seeing your small child stretch their little hands up to you, of saving the day with your idea at work, or making the world better when you volunteered are all moments that tug at your spirit, which is more real than the atoms which make up our physical universe. You are real. And you are really important.

But there's also something about the struggle to transcend our limitations, to be forced to engage in our own suffering and the suffering of others, and to love beyond what we thought was our personal capacity which offers us a true experience of ultimate reality. To riff on self-help guru Tony Robbins, "Awaken the Leper Within!"

I promised not to try to convert you, dear reader. Like I said, I am not your priest. And while my faith journey has led me to contemplate, examine and write about atheism, scientific naturalism, agnosticism, and major world religions; my journey will not be your journey—nor should it be. You have your own Irish train to get on without knowing how you will arrive at the final destination. Your own Cliffs of Moher experience awaits you.

Despite the fact that I was an attention-starved child, I never really wanted to write a book about my personal life. I prefer more academic writing or stories of fiction. I also want people to keep their noses out of my business! My guess is that the vast majority of the backlash I will inevitably receive from this book will be personal, painful, and almost entirely from people of my own faith. I'll bet I could write the critical comments from the Christian peanut gallery myself. That will be disappointing, annoying, and unnecessary. But precisely because spirituality deals with our utmost inner-core, it arouses a lot of passion, defensiveness, and misguided anger. After all, I worship a nice guy who offered some helpful spiritual changes to his religion and got stuck on a cross for it. As Chairman Mao once said, "A revolution is not a tea party."

There are many stories from around the world that I did not tell. Perhaps those can end up in the highly anticipated sequel to this book: *Lard Ass Will Travel: A Memoir of Eating Your Way Around the World*. But my sincere hope all along was that this book ended up being about you. That you realized as you read it that every experience that you had whether it was good or bad or even horrifically tragic has meaning and purpose. It's fine to express anger, doubt, and even contempt at the many stupid things that organized religion has done in the name of various gods. But there is a transcendent part of you that must be awoken, not negated.

Obviously, I have made a choice to practice Christianity, although my searching and questioning has been sincere. I don't like to call myself a "Christian" as that term was invented by the Romans and has been rendered nearly meaningless now by people who use and abuse the faith. Neither do I like the more recent term "Christ-follower" because I suck at following Jesus 99.9% of the time. I like to say that I am "Christ-dependent." A little, brown leper who depends on Christ's grace every day. Period.

Wherever your search leads, I hope and pray that the religion or spirituality that you discover is one that is not just a transactional faith rooted in a distant higher power. I hope that it is concretely rooted in **meaning**, **mystery**, **peace**, **love** and **grace**. Look for those words, experiences, and feelings as you go on your journey. If those are absent in your spiritual pilgrimage, I would encourage you to stay on that Irish train a bit longer. I am always available for further processing if you contact me and promise me some chocolate milk.

In my life, there have been times where I have needed to distance myself from religion (with its institutional dysfunctions rooted out of self-preservation) and remind myself that both God and I are in a relationship that no man-made institution or expression can contain in its fullness. For me, the bridge is not my spiritual knowledge or heightened consciousness, but rather grace. We are allowed to connect and are meant to connect with God.

St. Paul wrote:

"Now faith is the assurance of things hoped for, the conviction of things not seen. For by it, the people of old received their commendation. By faith, we understand that the universe was created by the Word of God. So that what is seen was not made out of things that are visible." (Hebrews 11:1-3)

I used to think that the only things that are truly eternal are cockroaches, Keith Richards, and any uneaten McDonald's hamburger patty, but that's not true. You are all eternal too and infinitely more appealing than at least two of those three things (yes, I'm a fan of McDonald's cheeseburgers now).

They say that our bodies are filled with 80% water. Well you are 100% more than your physical body. Be comforted and know that there is hope beyond what we see and that you were made for it. Like a compass that is trying to find true north, even the most hardcore atheist and most committed monk will feel lost on occasion but will also feel a strange magnetic pull toward a desire for hope, love, and ultimate meaning. Go on a spiritual journey and see where it takes you. The farther you travel the more you will find yourself by losing yourself. Organized religion has its place, but it is fundamentally a spiritual voyage. It requires faith, knowledge, hope, and quite possibly, a lot of chocolate milk. Take a chance and get on the train. I still hate vegetables.

END

Contact the Author

To contact the author with questions, comments, or to schedule a speaking engagement, go to getyourworldon.com.